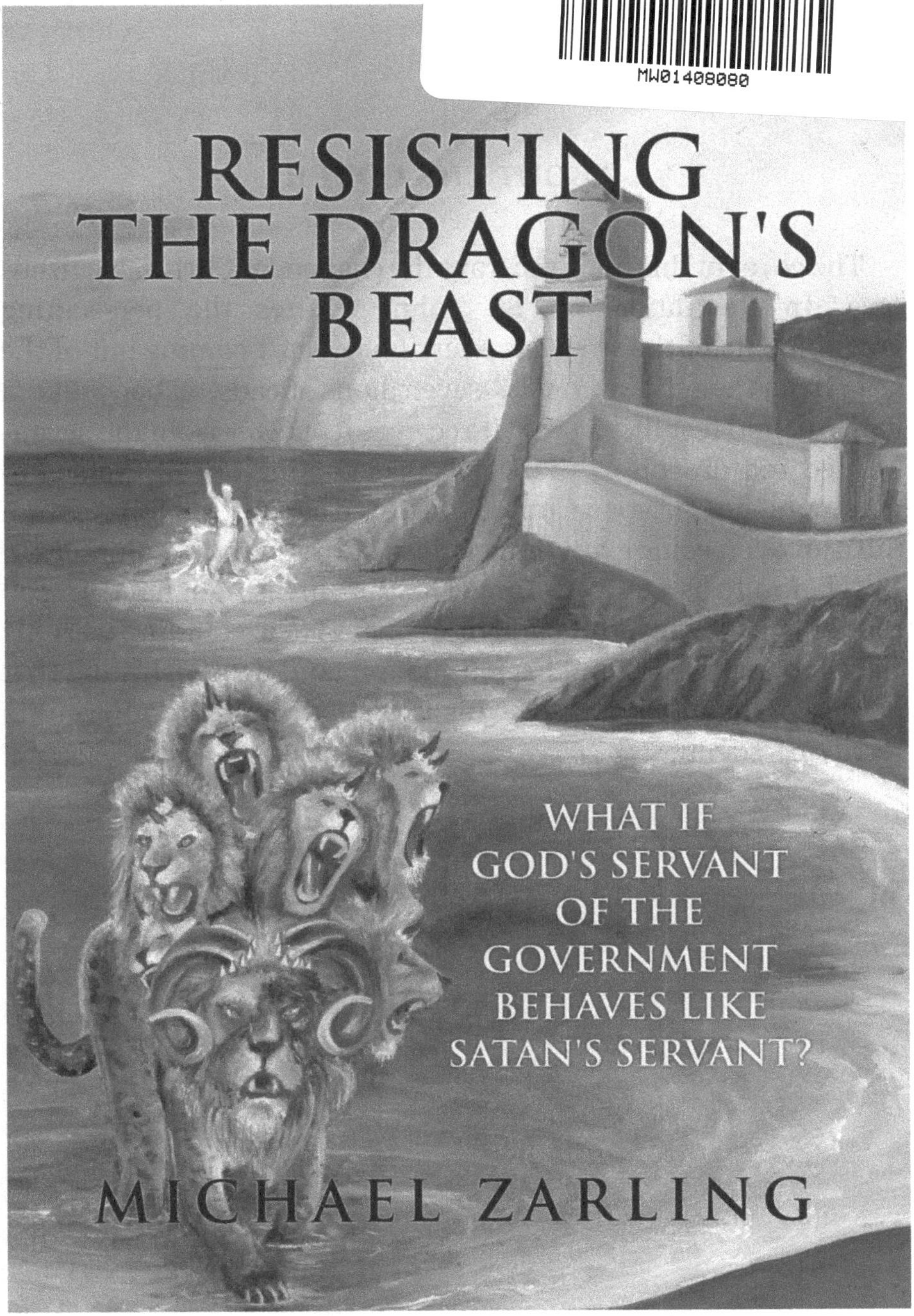
RESISTING
THE DRAGON'S
BEAST
WHAT IF
GOD'S SERVANT
OF THE
GOVERNMENT
BEHAVES LIKE
SATAN'S SERVANT?
MICHAEL ZARLING

ABOUT THE COVER

The cover of this book portrays the challenges Christian citizens face. In Revelation 13, St. John pictures the persecuting governments of the world as a terrifying beast coming out of the sea. It has ten horns on its seven lions' heads, a body like a leopard, and feet like a bear. It receives its power from the seven-headed red dragon of the Devil. It is coming out of the sea to persecute the Christian Church - pictured as a mighty fortress on a hill. But overseeing everything is Jesus Christ, whom John sees in Revelation 10 as a powerful angel holding in his right hand a scroll that only he is powerful enough to open. He is standing with his right foot on the sea and his left foot on land demonstrating that he has ultimate control over his Christian Church and even its terrifying enemies.

Resisting The Dragon's Beast

What if God's Servant of the Government Behaves Like Satan's Servant?

By
Michael Zarling

ATHANATOS
PUBLISHING GROUP

Resisting the Dragon's Beast: What if God's Servant of the Government Behaves Like Satan's Servant?

By **Michael Zarling**

Edited by Peter Hagen

Contact the author at resistingthedragonsbeast@gmail.com

ISBN: 978-1-64594-210-8

Published by Athanatos Publishing Group.
www.athanatos.net

Also available in hard cover: 978-1-64594-058-6
Also available as an ebook: 978-1-64594-211-5

Table of Contents

Introduction

In 2020, the world changed with the invasion of a novel virus. Every person, citizen, government, business, church, etc., had to learn how to navigate through the quickly changing landscape of lockdowns, mandates, and executive orders.

While many churches in our area of southeastern Wisconsin followed our city's and governor's mandates, our congregation left the decision to follow city and state mandates up to individual citizens. We decided that it wasn't the church's business to enforce the government's mandates.

For a time, our church suspended in-person worship. But we continued to have regular small-group gatherings where members could come weekly to receive a brief devotion on God's Word and receive God's Sacrament. When we returned to in-person worship, we followed the guidelines of having families sit in every other pew. We stopped passing the offering plate between the pews. But we didn't mandate that people wear a mask to worship like so many other churches were doing. We didn't even encourage people to wear a mask. Instead, we added a third Sunday worship service where there was no singing and only people wearing a mask would attend.

Though we kept the third mask-only worship service, it didn't take very long for us to return to regular worship for our other two Sunday worship services. We still sang all the verses to all the hymns. We still celebrated the Lord's Supper every Sunday. We offered the people the body of Christ in their hands and the blood of Christ in individual cups and in the chalice. One of our members proudly posted on social media, "This is how gansta' our church is. We have the common cup during Covid." After we had a large funeral where it became necessary to take down the red tape that blocked off every other pew, the tape didn't go back up again. We even went back to passing around the offering plate.

Though our worship looked very normal to our members, it

looked very different from other churches in our area. When a pastor decides to do something a little bit different than other churches in the area ... he then gets tasked with writing a paper about it.

I was asked/tasked with writing a paper for our May 2022 Pastors Conference. You can tell the title of the assignment was written by pastors – it's long and dry: *Tyranny and the Christian: Life, Ministry, and Christian Witness in the Left-Hand Kingdom.* The conference committee explained the theme this way: "We may have thought we had the Scriptural lines of church and state clearly laid our hearts and minds, but the events of 2020 and beyond would say otherwise. In the Holy Christian Church, some circles took to defying restrictions almost immediately while others remained closed for more than a year. Even in our circles, some churches took to resisting the restrictions placed on them more quickly than others. ... There is a growing number in our own circles that are having conversations on when and how to resist things imposed on us as Christians and as individuals. If some of our brothers and sisters are practicing resistance while others think such actions are sinful, we owe it to those in our care to wrestle with these issues for ourselves. What can and can't we say while standing on Scripture — what can and can't we do?"

As I began studying, I found myself writing notes in every notebook in my house or church office; pulling my car to the side of the road to jot down thoughts on post-it notes; highlighting books I purchased to help in my study. The project became much longer than paper-length. It is now book-length.

I also changed the title of my assignment: *Resisting the Dragon's Beast: What If God's Servant of the Government Behaves Like Satan's Servant?* It's still long because it was written by a pastor. But hopefully it is a tad more interesting.

Each of the chapters begins with a famous quote from a TV show or movie. It helps to be geeky to catch all the references. I wrote the book this way because we often take ourselves too seriously. When you read Scripture carefully, you can catch God's divine sarcasm, an inspired writer's humor, and even imagine

Jesus sharing a knowing smile while teaching. I also think that we learn things better when humor is involved.

One of the things I appreciate about going to pastors' study groups and conferences is having time for questions of casuistry. Casuistry are those difficult cases where there is no easy answer. So, we bring the question before fellow brothers in the ministry to get advice on how they might apply God's Word in these difficult situations.

This book is filled with questions of casuistry. A "question of casuistry" is a specific question of Scriptural applications, when there are multiple doctrinal considerations in view.

The problem I've found the past few years is that we no longer take the time nor have the inclination to ask, discuss, or figure out answers to all these questions. We would rather make declarative statements of our position and move on.

It is much better if we can be collaborative as we discuss concepts and bounce ideas off one another in a safe setting. J.R.R. Tolkein and C.S. Lewis joined other authors in the Inklings at Oxford University to read and discuss members' unfinished works. The purpose of the Inklings was to read aloud each other's unfinished works and give advice. One of the members of the Inklings, Warren Lewis recalled, "We were no mutual admiration society: praise for good work was unstinted, but censure for bad work — or even not-so-good work — was often brutally frank."

It would be greatly beneficial to us as brothers and sisters in Christ if we can find the time and place to sit, discuss, correct, reprove, or approve of one another. We can praise good ideas and be brutally frank, as well – all in Christian love. "Iron sharpens iron, and a man sharpens the insight of his friend" (Proverbs 27:17).

Much of what I attempt to do in this book is to read Scripture, then take the time to use our God-given gift of reason to look at various ways to apply that Scripture in difficult circumstances. We may disagree with one another on how to apply Scripture in these situations ... but that's OK. The discussion is oftentimes just as valuable as the application. The goal is always to apply God's

Scriptures in making our Christian decisions.

Together we'll ask all kinds of questions: What does God's Word tell us about resisting government authorities? Is that even a possibility for Christians, or are we to obey all entities unequivocally? What does Scripture say is the difference between submit and obey? What is the difference between resist and rebel? What may be the ramifications of not resisting a tyrannical government? What role does human reason play as we apply Scripture to our current culture? What examples of resistance, non-compliance, and civil disobedience do we find when we examine Scripture, church history, American history, and even current Christianity?

You may not find every answer in what I've written. You may find yourself with more questions after reading each chapter. And that's OK. That's what I'm hoping to do. I want to raise questions of casuistry so we can apply God's Word to difficult situations.

We find it challenging to discuss difficult applications because it is challenging to know and apply Scripture, American laws and history, the words and actions of Lutheran reformers from five centuries ago, as well as current Christian practice. It is arduous to build a consensus on application when there is so much information to know, share, and explain. Hopefully, by studying the pertinent Scriptures, American history and laws, and Lutheran and Christian theologians, we can start building that necessary consensus for a unity of actions.

We must ask these questions of consensus and resistance because we have been entrusted with the Ministry of Christ. We live in a world that thrives on division, jealousy, and one-upmanship; yet even though we live in this world, we have been called out from this world and told to live as strangers here in reverent fear. Let us celebrate a unity that is unlike anything else in our world. Let us celebrate God's love to sinners like us: "See the kind of love the Father has given us that we should be called children of God, and that is what we are" (1 John 3:1)!

As God's blood-bought children, may God bless us with unity as we study and apply his Scriptures together.

Romans 13

In *The Princess Bride*,[1] Sicilian mastermind Vizzini, the giant Fezzik, and the Spaniard swordsman Inigo Montoyo have kidnapped Princess Buttercup. Over and over, Vizzini keeps using the word "inconceivable" to describe his bewilderment: The hero, the Dread Pirate Roberts, is gaining on them through eel-infested waters.

The Dread Pirate Roberts is closing in on the group as he is below them climbing the rope up the Cliffs of Insanity. From the top of the cliff Vizzini cuts the rope. The Dread Pirate Roberts doesn't fall. Instead, he is holding onto the stony face of the Cliffs of Insanity. More than that, he begins climbing the cliff. Once more Vizzini exclaims, "Inconceivable."

Inigo Montoya then challenges Vizzini on his usage of the term. "You keep using that word. I don't think it means what you think it means."

The meaning of "submission"

These past few years we have seen governing authorities govern through mandates and executive orders. They have instituted lockdowns and compelled employees to receive a vaccine. They have enforced masks in public, social distancing in indoor facilities, and required vaccine passports for a variety of events. Whether citizens agree with these changes in public policy or not, we have been told that as Christians we should "submit" to the governing authorities according to Romans 13. In this chapter, we'll take a close look at the word "submit." Like Vizzini who didn't really understand the meaning of "inconceivable," perhaps the meaning of "submit" is also misunderstood.

> St. Paul writes in Romans 13:1-7: "Everyone must submit to the governing authorities. For no authority

---

[1] Consistently ranked in the top 100 movies ... ever!

exists except by God, and the authorities that do exist have been established by God. Therefore the one who rebels against the authority is opposing God's institution, and those who oppose will bring judgment on themselves.

For rulers are not a terror to good conduct, but to evil. Would you like to have no fear of the one in authority? Do what is good, and you will receive praise from him, because he is God's servant for your benefit. But if you do wrong, be afraid, because he does not carry the sword without reason. He is God's servant, a punisher to bring wrath on the wrongdoer. Therefore it is necessary to submit, not only because of wrath, but also because of conscience.

For this reason you also pay taxes, because the authorities are God's ministers, who are employed to do this very thing. Pay what you owe to all of them: taxes to whom taxes are owed, revenue to whom revenue is owed, respect to whom respect is owed, and honor to whom honor is owed.[2]

While it might be a famous blunder to get involved in a land war in Asia - only slightly less well-known is this: To define a word apart from its natural, contextual meaning.

So, what does the word "submit" mean? The Greek verb we translate as "submit" is fairly neutral in the original language, so it is hard to reflect with a single word in English. All our English verbs tend to convey some negative connotations. "The root meaning of the Greek verb means simply 'to rank people or things in order under some specific pattern.'"[3] Scripture lays out a specific pattern for wives to submit to their husbands, children to submit to their parents, slaves to submit to their masters, citizens

---

[2] Scripture references are from *The Holy Bible, Evangelical Heritage Version* TM (EHVTM) copyright © The Wartburg Project. 2019. Used by permission.

[3] Panning, Armin. *The People's Bible: Galatians, Ephesians* (Milwaukee, WI: Northwestern Publishing House, 1997) 202

to submit to their governing authorities, and the Christian Church to submit to Christ.

As we examine what submission means, it is also important to see what it does not mean. Submission is not servitude or slavery. Nor does submit mean "surrender." Submission is yielding to authority. It is willing subjection to another.

Submit is not a synonym for "obey." Otherwise, there would be a lot of unhappy wives if they were called to "obey" their husbands' every word and desire. Submit cannot mean "compelled obedience." Rather, it means humble acceptance, according to the order God has given.

Let's examine how the inspired writers of the epistles use the word "submit" in other applications. Husbands and wives, parents and children, employers and employees are called to submit to one another (Ephesians 5:21). Wives are called to submit to their husbands (Ephesians 5:22). The Church is to submit to Christ (Ephesians 5:24). Slaves are called to submit to their masters (1 Peter 2:18). The sinful nature is to submit to God's law, although it cannot do so (Romans 8:7). The Israelites were to submit to God's righteousness, but they didn't (Romans 10:3). Children are called to submit to their fathers (Hebrews 12:9). Christians are called to submit to their spiritual leaders (Hebrews 13:7). Citizens are called to submit to their governing authorities (Romans 13:1; 1 Peter 2:13). Christians are called to submit to God (James 4:7).

The concept of submission is closely bound to the concept of headship that St. Paul discusses in 1 Corinthians 11. He begins that discussion with the metaphor of a human head and body, "I want you to know that Christ is the head of every man, and man is woman's head, and God is Christ's head" (1 Corinthians 11:3). The head guides and directs what the body does, but never in a selfish way. Rather the head is always seeking the best interest of the body in everything. "To be sure, no one has ever hated his own body, but nourishes and cherishes it, just as Christ does the church" (Ephesians 5:29).

As Paul discusses headship principles, "he never conceives of the man's authority in terms of a harsh subjugation of the woman to his will. The apostle is not granting to men the authority to wield autocratic power, but the responsibility for loving, self-sacrificing service."[4]

The head - whether that is the husband in the home, the pastor in a church, the employer in a business, or the authorities in a government - is not to crush or compel others into submission. Rather, the head is to exercise its headship in loving service to those it leads within the body.

Those within the body - whether that is the wife in the home, the members in a church, the employees in a business, or the citizens in a nation - are to submit to the proper head. Submission is not forced. It is an inward attitude toward ordained order and authority. Jesus Christ submitted to his head. Jesus' head was his heavenly Father and his heavenly Father's will.

The apostles speak a great deal about submission. In every one of these instances, those who are submissive are trusting those with authority to take care of their physical and/or spiritual needs.

Those who have authority over us have received that authority from God himself. Whether that be husbands, parents, pastors, or governing authorities - each is established by God, and accountable to him for their use of authority.

God has placed these authorities over people for their benefit. Husbands care for, love, and support their wives. Parents feed, clothe, teach, and nurture their children. Pastors provide forgiveness, grace, and blessings in sharing God's Word and Sacraments. Governing authorities provide protection, structure, and order to our communities, states, and nation. When God's servants fulfill their vocations in this earthly kingdom, they bring a measure of peace and order. Such peace and order also make it easier for God's servants to live in and share God's heavenly kingdom.

Gladly and willingly entrusting ourselves with an attitude of submission to the authorities God has placed over us is beneficial

---

[4] Lockwood, Gregory J. *Concordia Popular Commentary: 1 Corinthians* (St. Louis, MO: Concordia Publishing House, 2010) 214

to everyone involved. It (usually) brings earthly blessing, avoids earthly punishment, and provides a setting for Christian proclamation.

If that's all there was to Romans 13 - just submit to the governing authorities and move on - then this would be a very short book. In fact, when the topic of resistance to governing authorities has been brought up, people will often say, "Romans 13. Submit." As if that is supposed to end the discussion. Submit and move on. But as a friend of mine wisely put it, "That's the grade school Catechism class answer. What we're discussing with these difficult applications is like a master's degree level class." The Holy Spirit's divinely inspired words deserve a deeper examination. He provides an abundance of nuances as we examine, compare, and apply St. Paul's words in Romans 13.

It is the age-old lie of the devil. He used it with Eve in the Garden. He used it with Jesus in the desert. He appears pious, using godly sounding words: "submit," "honor," "obey." Yet, at the same time discouraging a deeper, thorough study of submitting, honoring, and obeying in various settings and in difficult circumstances.

We need a regular and deeper examination and application of Romans 13 as we may increasingly find ourselves living in a Revelation 13 world.

Who are the governing authorities?

For the rest of this chapter, we'll closely consider what St. Paul wrote in Romans 13. We'll study specific phrases, sentences, and concepts. We'll also compare Paul's words with other inspired words of the apostles. We'll raise some questions and different applications as we go through the verses.

"Everyone must submit to the governing authorities. For no authority exists except by God, and the authorities that do exist have been established by God" (Romans 13:1). Paul's words appear very straightforward. We are to submit to our governing authorities for they have been placed in authority over us by God himself.

As I said in the introduction, my purpose for writing this book is to ask questions. So, who are "the governing authorities"? In Paul's day, the governing authority was the Roman government. It was set up with the emperor, the Senate, and assemblies. In our day, our American system of government is set up with three equal branches – the executive, the legislative and the judicial. Above all these systems is a very unique document entitled *The American Constitution*.

I raise this point because recently we have seen city mayors and state governors announce mandates and the U.S. President announce executive orders. These executive branches have only a limited power to create these mandates and executive orders, and these orders have limited scope to direct the internal affairs of that governmental branch. The founders of America knew what they were doing to prevent a monarchy or dictatorship. They created a balance of power between the three branches so that each branch keeps the others in check.

The power to create laws resides within the legislative branch. Many of us learned that on Saturday mornings watching *I'm Just a Bill* from *Schoolhouse Rock!* [5] A bill is brought to Congress. If Congress passes the bill, then it goes to the President to veto it or sign it into law. It is then the job of the judicial branch to interpret that law.

It is not the job of a president or governor to mandate laws. Nor is it the job of the court system to legislate from the bench. When any of these authorities create legislation – except in very limited ways - they are overstepping the authority that was granted them by virtue of their office.

The only time I ever yelled at my father was when my parents were visiting us at my home in Kentucky. My father became upset at my oldest daughter, who was 2 or 3, for not eating her dinner. So, he yelled at her. Then I got up and yelled at him. I told him, "Dad, you could yell at me about eating my dinner when I was a

---

[5] *I'm Just a Bill* is a 1976 Schoolhouse Rock! segment from my great childhood

kid. But you don't have that authority here. I do." My father had overstepped the authority that was granted him by God. He was taking authority that belonged to me.

When a president creates executive orders intended for the general populace, or a governor makes mandates extended beyond their constitutionally-granted time frame, they are overstepping the authority granted them by God through our U.S. and state constitutions. They are taking authority that belongs to the legislative branch.

If I tell my Catechism students to sit quietly, pull out their Bibles, and work on their lesson, they need to listen to me. I have authority over them by virtue of my office as pastor and their Catechism teacher. If they ignore me and goof around, then they are disobeying me. They aren't respecting my authority. But, if I tell them to come over to my house that evening to shovel the snow off my driveway, are they disobeying me if they don't come? No. I have no authority over them to demand they clear my driveway. I'm actually the one who is wrong by expecting them to do something I have no right to expect from them.

Grammatically, "authorities" in Romans 13:1 is plural. Paul recognized that more than one authority existed, each with a distinct office. As we apply this plural noun to our American form of government, we see that citizens are to submit to various levels of governing authority. But that also means that our governing authorities are to submit to the other various levels of authority.

A city council submits to the mayor. But the mayor also submits to the city council. A police chief or county sheriff submits to a mayor or governor. But there are instances where the police chief and sheriff are over the mayor and governor. A state governor, senators and congresspeople, and state supreme court justices are all on the same levels. They must each submit to the authority of the other branches of government. What is true at the state level is also true at the federal level. The president is not above the senators, congresspeople or supreme court justices. They each submit to the authority of the other levels of government.

In our unique form of American government, all these levels of government must submit to the other levels of government; likewise, the governing authorities also serve as the public servants of the citizens. In America, no government authority is above the law of land. To summarize Thomas Paine, "The law is king. The king is not law."

So, in our unique form of American government, based on the founding documents of our nation, the citizens are actually the authorities who are over the governing authorities. Those who are in positions of government may be considered leaders of the people, but they are first servants of those same people. That fits with how St. Paul describes the authorities as "ministers" or "servants" (Romans 13:6).

Paul continued, "For this reason you also pay taxes, because the authorities are God's ministers, who are employed to do this very thing. Pay what you owe to all of them: taxes to whom taxes are owed, revenue to whom revenue is owed, respect to whom respect is owed, and honor to whom honor is owed" (Romans 13:6, 7). As we apply this to the discussion above, a citizen is required to pay taxes, extend revenue, and give honor to those whom it is owed. But a citizen is not required to pay taxes to whom taxes are not due. Nor is he expected to give revenue or honor to those who are not deserving of it.

Here in America, our governing authorities are given their authority by the people. We do not have a monarchy or a dictatorship that claims power for itself. In America, the citizens give the government authority to govern them. That means that unlike any other government in existence, our American system of government is both given power and has its powers limited by the governed. The Preamble to the U.S. Constitution states: "We the People of the United States, in Order to form a more perfect Union, establish Justice, insure domestic Tranquility, provide for the common defence, promote the general Welfare, and secure the Blessings of Liberty to ourselves and our Posterity, do ordain and establish this Constitution for the United States of America."

One of America's greatest presidents, Abraham Lincoln, stated this eloquently numerous times in speeches. In a speech at Peoria on October 16, 1854, he said, "According to our ancient faith, the just powers of governments are derived from the consent of the governed." In a speech in Kansas in December of 1859, he said, "The people – the people – are the rightful masters of both congresses and courts – not to overthrow the Constitution, but to overthrow the men who pervert it." In a speech on October 19, 1864, he said, "The people's will, constitutionally expressed, is the ultimate law for all." I quote President Lincoln because as both a lawyer and a U.S. President, he knew the application of constitutional powers far better than most of us.

In Romans 13:2, St. Paul writes, "Therefore the one who rebels against the authority is opposing God's institution, and those who oppose will bring judgment on themselves." Various English versions of the Bible will translate the Greek word "rebels," "opposes," "resists," or "stands against."

Disobeying authorities – even civilly – can be disruptive. A community needs order to survive and flourish. If everyone becomes non-compliant about everything, then there is anarchy.

Organizers of civil disobedience have always acknowledged this fact: The First Amendment protects the freedom of peaceful assembly in public space. In that sense, a protest may be inconvenient or disruptive but still "peaceful."

In our American system, may a Christian peacefully disobey?

Before we say that every act of resistance is wrong on a Scriptural basis it is beneficial for us to look at what Lutheran theologians wrote about submitting and obeying governing authorities. The opening words of Article 16 of the Augsburg Confession on Civil Affairs states: "Of Civil Affairs they teach that lawful civil ordinances are good works of God, and that ..."[6]

When the Lutheran confessors write that there are "lawful civil ordinances" that we comply with, they are implying there may be

[6]All quotations from the *Lutheran Confessions* are taken from Concordia: The Lutheran Confessions: A Reader's Edition of the Book of Concord. St. Louis, MO. Concordia Publishing House.

"unlawful civil ordinances" that we do not need to comply with. We are compelled to obey moral, legal laws. That also means we are not compelled to obey immoral or unlawful statements. In chapters 3 and 4, we'll examine how Martin Lutheran and Lutheran theologians reasoned there were times Christian citizens were compelled to resist governing authorities. In later chapters, we'll also investigate the use of human reason, conscience, and morality in determining whether civil ordinances are beneficial or harmful by comparing them to God's Ten Commandments.

God's 4th Commandment states: "Honor your father and mother that it may go well with you and you may enjoy long life on the earth. Martin Luther explains God's commandment this way: "We should fear and love God that we do not dishonor or anger our parents and others in authority, but honor, serve and obey them, and give them love and respect." People have contended that since we are to honor, serve, and obey those in authority, it is therefore wrong to resist or practice civil disobedience.

In his Large Catechism, Luther fills numerous paragraphs talking about the child's role in obeying his parents under the 4th commandment. He then applies the 4th commandment to citizens obeying their government. Toward the end of his discussion, Luther spends time applying the 4th commandment demonstrating that a father has a responsibility over his children. He then applies the 4th commandment demonstrating that the government is the father to its citizens.

> "For [God] does not wish to have in this office and government knaves and tyrants; nor does He assign to them this honor, that is, power and authority to govern, that they should have themselves worshiped; but they should consider that they are under obligations of obedience to God; and that, first of all, they should earnestly and faithfully discharge their office, not only to support and provide for the bodily necessities of their

children, servants, subjects, etc., but, most of all, to train them to the honor and praise of God."[7]

Children and citizens are not to disobey the 4th commandment in their submission to the authority of their parents or government. In the same respect, parents and government are not to disobey the 4th commandment by abusing their authority over their children and citizens.

It is good and right for people to quote the 4th commandment to remind others about obedience to authorities. It is also good and right to quote the 4th commandment back to people reminding them that the authorities also need to obey God's commandment, and to recognize that children belong to the authority of parents before any other authority.

The scriptural basis for governmental authority is found first in the familial authority of the home. In the marriage rite in *Christian Worship: A Lutheran Hymnal* it states that the family provides peace and stability for society. "When God in love created the world, he made man and woman in his own image and bonded them together in marriage. Through this blessed union of husband and wife, God established the family, provided for the physical and spiritual welfare of children, and fostered the peace and stability of society."[8] Because the family unit is so integral to God's design, we dare not cede parental rights to government institutions - except in extreme and rare circumstances.

Perhaps resistance is necessary to hold accountable those with authority. Perhaps it will appear that citizens are breaking the 4th commandment with disobedience to their governing authorities as they are working on keeping the 4th commandment in their responsibility as parents. Perhaps citizens will appear they are breaking the 4th commandment while they are working to keep God's other commandments.

---

[7] Concordia: *The Lutheran Confessions: Luther's Large Catechism, The 4th Commandment*, par. 168

[8] *Christian Worship: A Lutheran Hymnal*. Milwaukee, WI. Northwestern Publishing House, 1993. 141

For example, we've seen local and state governments place restrictions or mandates or lockdowns on businesses. But what if Jim's Gym decides to defy the lockdown and remain open for business? Is Jim breaking the 4th commandment by defying a government order? Or is he keeping the 4th commandment because he knows that's the only way he can provide for his family? Is Jim keeping the 7th, 9th, and 10th commandments where God calls for him to protect his and his employee's property and means of income? If he's not open for business, Jim knows he'll lose everything he's invested in Jim's Gym. When he loses his means of income, he'll also lose his family home and vehicles. He won't be providing for his family as God calls him to do in the 4th commandment. If Jim closes his gym, his employees will be out of work. After losing their means of income, they will lose their property.

So, is Jim breaking the 4th commandment by disobeying the governing authorities as he ignores their lockdown orders? Or is Jim keeping the 4th commandment by disobeying the governing authorities as he ignores their lockdown orders on his privately-owned and legally-operated business? These are the master's degree levels of the Holy Spirit's nuances we need to be discussing, but sadly aren't.

Is Jim wrong in defying lockdowns? Is he breaking the 4th commandment? Or perhaps are the governing authorities wrong for demanding lockdowns? The 7th, 9th, and 10th commandments call for Christians to protect their money, property, house, workers, and family. These commandments also call for Christians to help their neighbors improve and protect their property and means of income. They call for Christians to do all they can to help their neighbors keep their house, workers, and family. So, are governing authorities breaking the 7th, 9th, and 10th commandments by not protecting Jim's income and property and helping him keep it? Are they also breaking these commandments by not allowing Jim to protect and help his employees' keep their property and means of income?

It may appear that African Americans are breaking the 4th

commandment by protesting a police shooting. But in their hearts, they are keeping the 5th commandment about protecting innocent life. It may appear that Latino Americans are breaking the 4th commandment by protesting immigration laws. But in their hearts, they are keeping the 9th commandment of protecting the privileges of their family members coming to America for a better life. It may appear that federal employees are breaking the 4th commandment by resisting a vaccine. But in their hearts, they are keeping the 5th commandment by protecting their bodily autonomy.

And in the way our society is constituted, the citizens have the right and responsibility to publicly advocate for such religious nuances, for the purpose of public debate and shaping of public policy. Our Christian confession is compromised when we thoughtlessly follow a governmental statement without due consideration of the entire circumstance of casuistry. One could plead Jim's plight in the public square on the basis of human reason, as well as recognize the greater Scriptural issues as a basis for civil disobedience.

In a later chapter we'll examine civil disobedience on the basis of human reason, conscience and sincerely held religious beliefs.

Additionally, Jim the citizen might open Jim's Gym for the physical and mental health of his community, and also the livelihood of his employees. Jim the Christian may do so with a clean conscience, choosing the greater good *(not "lesser evil")* of the casuistry foisted upon him.

Jim is a Christian citizen. His sincerely held religious beliefs guide his life. He has a public argument for opening, but uses every private opportunity to frame the issues in the clear light of his proper obedience to his God-given vocations.

We would do well to heed Jesus' words on judging people's hearts and motives. "Stop judging, so that you will not be judged" (Matthew 7:1).

We live in an imperfect world. Earthly laws and divine commandments do not always fit easily alongside each other. That's why it is always beneficial to take the time to discuss, question, and debate. Discover the wonderful nuances of applying God's will in a fallen world that hates God's will.

St. Paul writes in Romans 13:3-5: "For rulers are not a terror to good conduct, but to evil. Would you like to have no fear of the one in authority? Do what is good, and you will receive praise from him, because he is God's servant for your benefit. But if you do wrong, be afraid, because he does not carry the sword without reason. He is God's servant, a punisher to bring wrath on the wrongdoer. Therefore it is necessary to submit, not only because of wrath, but also because of conscience."

The governing authorities are God's servant for our benefit. They are placed in authority over its citizens to protect them from evil. The government should reward responsible behavior not irresponsible behavior. But what if the rulers become a terror to the good? The evildoers are to be afraid of the government's sword. But what if the good people become afraid of the government's sword? What if those in authority misuse or even abuse that God-given authority? What if governing authorities are crushing and coercing citizens into obedience? Are citizens still called to submit to them?

As we look at how Paul has been using the word "submit" in Romans 13, it will be helpful to look at how "submit" is used by other apostles in the inspired epistles.

"Submission" used by the other apostles

In 1 Peter 2 and 3, St. Peter calls for submission of citizens to their government (1 Peter 2:13-17), then slaves to their masters (1 Peter 2:18-25), and finally wives to their husbands (1 Peter 3:1-7). If a husband is abusive to his wife – physically, mentally or sexually - we would advise the wife to seek help and get out of that relationship. If a child is being injured by his parents, or an employee is being harassed by her employer, we would advise them to seek help. For the child, we would call protective services on the parents. For the employee, we would suggest she involve the police.

So, what do we say when a government becomes abusive to its

citizens? Oftentimes, we advise citizens to stay quiet and take it. That's horrific advice to a child, wife, or employee that is in an abusive relationship. Yet, we find that is frequent advice to citizens who are being abused by their tyrannical government. There are times when personal safety or a clear Christian confession necessitate action - peaceable action which the government's founding documents encourage, preserve, and protect.

The writer of Hebrews encourages Christians to submit and obey our spiritual leaders. "Obey your leaders and submit to them, for they are keeping watch over your souls as men who will give an account. Obey them, so that they may do this with joy and not with groaning, for that would be of no benefit to you" (Hebrews 13:17).

Do you ever find yourself disagreeing with your pastor? Perhaps you don't like his choice for the proposed new carpeting in the church. Or you've spoken to him about visiting the homebound members more. Or you've mentioned to him that he should spend less time in the church office and more time with his family.

The Lord of the Church does not demand absolute allegiance to everything your pastor says when he isn't quoting Scripture authoritatively. You may disagree with him on a lot of things. That's good and healthy. You do not owe your pastor unquestioning obedience in all things. We understand that our pastors and other religious leaders are fallible. They make mistakes. That's why we don't follow every idea, ministry expansion or budget item they propose.

Members are to submit to the authority of their pastors. Wives are to submit to the authority of their husbands. Children are to submit to the authority of their parents. Pastors, husbands, and parents are sinful. They are fallible. They make mistakes. It is good to disagree with them when they're wrong. It is healthy to question them when they're making mistakes. It is unhealthy and not beneficial to give these authority figures unquestioning, absolute obedience.

If a husband is lying to his wife, "submit" doesn't mean she has to believe his lies. If a master is creating a false narrative, "submit" doesn't mean the slave has to believe the narrative. And if government officials - along with experts and the media are gaslighting[9], "submit" doesn't mean citizens have to believe the gaslighting.

Those who serve as authorities in the government are sinful. They are fallible. They make mistakes. It is good to disagree with them when they're wrong. It is healthy to question them when they're making mistakes. It is unhealthy and not beneficial to give these authority figures unquestioning, absolute obedience. And in our system of government, such debate is protected and encouraged as the preferred *modus operandi.*[10]

We would encourage the wife to get out of her abusive relationship to save herself and her children. We would encourage and assist a child to get away from his abusers to spare his body and his life. If a pastor is abusive to his flock, we would encourage church authorities to step in to resolve the situation.

It is beneficial for us to look at the clear meaning of Scripture, then use the gift of human reasoning to apply that same Scripture evenly in all cases. As we look at what the Scriptures have to say about submission to authorities, I'm afraid that we are quick to declare that a wife, child, employee, or church member should get out of an abusive relationship, but equally quick to declare that a Christian citizen should stay in the abusive relationship.

There are those who think that as Christians we owe absolute obedience to the government in all things. When we are not allowed to question, doubt or debate – shutting down all discussion and resistance – we make the government into an infallible entity, while shirking our civic responsibility for discourse and neglecting our civic right to peaceably assemble and vocalize our disagreement.

How is absolute, unquestioning obedience any different than

---

[9] Gaslighting is a form of psychological abuse where a person or group causes someone to question their own sanity, memories, or perception of reality. The term "gaslighting" comes from the name of a 1938 play where a husband manipulates his wife into thinking she has a mental illness.

[10] For an example, see Justice Scalia's dissent to *Obergefell.*

worship? In the next chapter we'll examine how St. John records that in the End Times people will be worshiping the beast of the persecuting government (Revelation 13:4). Those who worship the beast follow it with absolute, unquestioning obedience.

In Romans 13, St. Paul addresses Christians in the same way he would address anyone — if you do wrong, you will be punished, because the government has the responsibility and power to do that. In verse 5, Paul writes, "He is God's servant, a punisher to bring wrath on the wrongdoer. Therefore it is necessary to submit, not only because of wrath, but also because of conscience." Paul addresses Christians and gives them another reason to honor the government. What is that? Christians know it pleases God to honor the government. Honoring the government, therefore, does not become something we are compelled to do but something we want to do.

We want to keep our consciences clear before God, so we honor God's representatives. We need to be very careful, study the issues diligently, and talk to other Christians before we decide to resist the governing authorities. We also need to be ready to receive the punishment that may come from resistance. God has given the government the right to punish its citizens. It is our civic duty as citizens to make sure the government is punishing its citizens for evil and not for what's right. This is also our duty as Christians: To speak up for what is right, even when the perpetrator is the government. God calls us to do this in his 8th commandment where Luther explains that Christians are to defend our neighbor's reputation.

Giving to Caesar what only belongs to Caesar

Jesus teaches, "Give to Caesar what is Caesar's, and to God what is God's" (Mark 12:17). That quotation might seem to say that citizens need to obey everything their governments say and do, and any kind of resistance to obedience is wrong.

The background of this Bible verse is that the Pharisees were trying to lay religious traps for Jesus in the temple courtyard during Holy Week. They thought they had found a "no-win situation" for Jesus. They asked him: "Is it lawful to pay a tax to Caesar or not? Should we pay it or not" (Mark 12:14, 15) If Jesus advised them to pay taxes to Caesar, he would upset many Jews who despised Roman rule. If he said to not pay taxes, then the Pharisees would report him to the Roman authorities for going against Roman rule.

The Pharisees' question betrayed a faulty understanding of God's kingdom in connection with the earthly kingdom. They thought God's kingdom stood in opposition to the Romans. What did Jesus teach them? He upheld the right of earthly governments to rule earthly kingdoms. He also upheld that God's kingdom is separate and unique. The enemies we fight as part of God's kingdom are spiritual – sin, death, and Satan. As citizens, we should use our governmentally-guaranteed rights and reasonable human arguments to influence our governing authorities to act morally. But we should also understand that as Christian citizens, living morally within an earthly kingdom is different from the fruits of faith as citizens of God's kingdom.

If we confuse obeying governing authorities with obeying God, then we confuse the two kingdoms. Then we are no better than the Pharisees of old. Keeping civil laws and a government's will is not the same as keeping God's moral laws and his divine will. I think there has been real confusion about that these past few years.

Let's dig deeper into Jesus' words. We need to give to God what is God's. When governing authorities allow for gay marriage and no-fault divorce, they are making a mockery of God's 6th commandment of honoring God's gift of marriage. When public school authorities say that parents have no say in what is being taught to their children, they are making a mockery of God's 4th commandment of honoring the authority of parents over their children. When a government creates laws that promote and subsidize the legalized murder of the unborn, they are making a mockery of God's 5th commandment that protects the life of the unborn. And so on. When governing authorities put themselves over God and in the place of God, they are demanding that we give to Caesar what only belongs to God.

Unquestioning obedience belongs to God, not earthly authorities. This is true according to Scripture as well as the civic documents of the left-hand kingdom.

If we follow the logic of some who say that Romans 13 means we should always submit to the government, and the 4th commandment means we should always obey our governing authorities, and that giving to Caesar means we should give to Caesar whatever he desires, then we should be rooting for the Empire in all the *Star Wars* movies. Then Luke Skywalker, Princess Leia, Han Solo, and the whole Rebel Alliance are the bad guys. Then the Ewoks, the Wookies, and all the other interplanetary species and races that were subjugated and enslaved needed to accept their fate. Then the Rebels are the ones who are resisting, rebelling, and trying to overthrow the emergency authority that was duly granted to Senator Palpatine to become Emperor Palpatine. Then the Emperor, Darth Vader, the Stormtroopers, et al were the good guys.

Conscience, Love, and Submission

St. Paul mentions the conscience at the end of verse Romans 13:5: "Therefore it is necessary to submit, not only because of wrath, but also because of conscience." There is no secular authority who can override your conscience before God. We cannot give to Caesar that which is not Caesar's to possess.

We often end our discussion of submitting to the government with verse 7 of Romans 13. But St. Paul continues to discuss the topic of loving one another in the following verses. In verse 10, Paul writes, "Love does no harm to a neighbor, so love is the fulfillment of the law."

In verse 10, Paul places the words "love" and "harm" close together. Why does he do this? True love will always speak out against sin because it hates sin. Sin will always cause harm to people – physical, mental, emotional, or spiritual harm. Only insincere love will allow sin to go uncontested. In love we speak up and stand up to protect others from the harm of sin.

That may mean we need to speak up and stand up when we feel

the governing authorities are using their power to harm others. We are showing love by not allowing anyone or anything to harm our neighbor. Love is the fulfillment of God's moral law.

Romans 13 teaches Christians to engage in government, society, and culture. It does not teach us to disengage from God's earthly kingdom.

The government is God's servant here on earth. We rightly submit to that servant. We trust that servant is serving for our earthly benefit. We must remember, though, that the government is filled with sinners. They make mistakes. They can be selfish and self-serving. They can watch out for and benefit one group of people while unintentionally – or even intentionally – ignoring and hurting another group of people. That means that the government is fallible. We still submit to the government as God directs. Yet, when Christians are not allowed to question, debate, or even resist, then the government becomes infallible. And the only one who is infallible is God.

Citizens of two kingdoms

As Christians, we are citizens of two kingdoms – God's heavenly kingdom and God's earthly kingdom. We need to remember what the earthly kingdom is for. This secular realm is to limit the outbreak of sin and mischief. It is to create a climate where God's gospel can be preached. As Christians, we live in and benefit from the earthly kingdom as we spread the message of God's heavenly kingdom. As Christians, we dwell simultaneously as citizens in God's right-hand, heavenly kingdom and as citizens in God's left-hand, earthly kingdom.

We do not want to mix these two kingdoms of God's heavenly and earthly kingdoms. Mixing the kingdoms would be confusing their responsibilities or using the tools of one to try and accomplish the goal of the other kingdom. It is not the Church's responsibility to change the world through law, or to legislate morality as though we could create a kingdom here on earth.

Likewise, our American system of government has expressly recognized that the government has no place in restricting the free practice of religion, the peaceable assembly of people, or the freedoms of association, speech, or the press. These five freedoms are reserved to the individual citizens in the First Amendment to the Constitution. And specifically, the founding documents of our government restrict that government from making laws that treat religion favorably or unfavorably.

As Christians, we do not mix the kingdoms. We do not apply the rules or use the tools of the world within the Church; while we recognize and appreciate the role of human reason as servant within the church, we likewise recognize that Christ's Church is only built through his Word and Sacraments.

Even within the Christian Church (where the operating tools are Law and Gospel, where the guiding document is Scripture, and where the spiritual takes priority) we still use wise practices that are in line with human reason – usually for the purpose of good stewardship. For example:

- Meetings utilize Robert's Rules of Order to provide opportunity for discussion by all and to keep meetings focused and short;
- Churches make ministry plans so that the time and effort from the congregation can be used most profitably, and to provide a budgetary estimate for a specific activity;
- Churches set annual budgets prospectively, as an estimate for spending activity that is in line with ministerial activities of the coming year;
- We lock our doors, carry out property maintenance, send newsletters and emails, and make use of social media.

None of these activities is expressly reserved to the Church; while social media (or other media outlets) may provide a platform for Gospel proclamation – they are not tools specific to the Church. The Church makes use of human reason, as well as secular platforms, for the purpose of applying the unique tools that Christ has given for the building of his Church. While the Church makes use of these tools, we do not expect these tools to accomplish what only the Word of God can accomplish.

The reverse is also true. Christians are members of congregations that are registered with the IRS as a 501(c)3 according to IRS tax code. Individual Christians make use of their First Amendment rights nearly every day – and certainly every Sunday. We are Christians by faith and confession, yet we are at the same time citizens of a country with its specific blessings and obligations:

- Donations are recorded and donors receive a statement at year-end for tax purposes.
- Our school cafeterias follow local health regulations.
- The Fire Department comes regularly to our churches and schools to inspect fire extinguishers and exit lights.
- The pastor is registered with the state as an official marrying authority, and couples married within the Church also sign a legal marriage document.

When we talk about the relationship of Christians *(who are at the same time, citizens)* to the God-given authorities above them – let us not be so lazy as to dismiss an argument with the blanket accusation that "We can't do that because that would be mixing the kingdoms." This is a topic that takes careful thought, careful examination of one's own motives, and tenaciously holding on to the Word of God. This is a topic that takes some basic consideration of Constitutional rights, governmental authority, case law (especially a few Supreme Court cases), and applying human reason within the secular sphere.

We carefully study how to live simultaneously in the two kingdoms while knowing from the revealed Word of God that the beast out of the sea will use every opportunity to militate against the Church.

At the same time, we understand and fulfill our responsibilities to the left-hand, earthly kingdom. We understand the obligations laid upon us by the government, and test them back to the Word of God so that we may make a proper Christian confession within a secular society. We also understand the restrictions to governmental authority which the Constitution has reserved (and preserved) to the individual. The faithful and wise Christian will shrewdly manage the freedoms we enjoy in this nation, and strive to keep the governmental authorities accountable to the rules of their own sphere of operation. It is both good citizenship and faithful Christian submission to hold a government to the restrictions placed upon them by our Constitutional system. It is both good government and faithful Christian submission to peaceably discuss, resist, or even protest when that government has overstepped the bounds of its authority.

As Christian citizens we do live in both kingdoms. It is a balance, a paradox, a tension, of how we do this. This topic needs four specific elements in order to carry out clear confession as a Christian citizen in our American system of governance:

1) A clear knowledge of the Word of God, willingness to fully trust that Word, and desire to clearly confess that Word – and a thorough view of Scripture that sees the entirety of Scripture as applicable and a proclamation worth preserving.

2) A basic but clear understanding of Constitutional matters as they apply to individuals and congregations, and an understanding that our decisions on secular matters today will affect the life and confession of generations yet unborn. In our American system, these rights and restrictions are not privileges granted by a government (which may be suspended in the case of emergency) but *absolute* rights that rest with individuals and groups of individuals, restraining the efforts or activities that governmental authorities may exercise.[11]

---

[11] This is unique among nations today. For those living within a Canadian context, the Charter of Rights and Freedoms is similar. However, the *Charter* includes provision for the government to

3) A respect for, submission to, and fear of the authorities over us; Romans 13 and Revelation 13 will both inform the Christian's understanding of our relationship with the government;

4) A willingness to adhere to Constitutionally-protected freedoms, and to support fellow Christians in that activity, even if the individual Christian arrives at a different conclusion as to the timing or activity (and even if a fellow Christian draws the line of peaceable resistance under the First Amendment sooner or differently than we might). Our government respects the application of sincerely-held beliefs.[12] We do not tell our fellow Christian to sit back, cave in, or give up because "It's not that big a deal anyway," and "It doesn't compromise the gospel." Christian love compels us to listen, discuss, understand, and support sincerely held, conscience-bound application of Scriptural truth.

Could Christians – and perhaps especially pastors – wish to

---

suspend particular rights or privileges, encased in the "limitations" and "notwithstanding" clauses. The Charter provides provisional rights, and any particular right is subject to the laws passed by Parliament. Thus, certain elements of Biblical proclamation may be unprotected because they would run afoul of laws regarding hate speech and protected LGBTQ+ status.

In the Canadian system, rights are subject to and restrained by laws. In our American system, the reverse is true: The laws of the land are subject to the individual rights. Let us not forfeit our country's relationship between laws and rights by an unconsidered straw man argument, such as "Mixing the kingdoms" or "Submit means obey." The extended discussion of submission and obedience is considered elsewhere.

[12] Consider especially the majority opinions on *Burwell v. Hobby Lobby Stores* and the subsequent *Little Sisters of the Poor Saints Peter and Paul Home v. Pennsylvania*. The discussion on "sincerely held" is helpful, in that even the government recognizes that faith can be sincerely held and also have applications that develop over time - exactly as the Lutheran Church has always held, that applications may be updated to suit the particular context and to continue providing a clear confession.

dwell only within the one kingdom? Could we be so afraid of mixing the two kingdoms that we separate them so far apart, that we artificially limit our Christian confession within society? Could we separate them so far apart *(as though the Christian were not at the same time both Christian and citizen)* that we live or act as though we artificially step from one kingdom into the next, choosing to say we are acting in whichever kingdom provides the easiest path?

...or could it be that we are not lazy *(in considering specific applications within two kingdoms)* but rather afraid? Have we become so accustomed to a rote, unconsidered citizenship that we are afraid that, somehow, our Christian-citizen stance on a topic would endanger the Church (or its IRS status)?

There are Christians who are adamant that we do not mix the two kingdoms. Yet, many of them also allowed the left-hand kingdom of the government to shut down Christian churches and shutter Christian schools that belong to the right-hand kingdom.

It is easy for pastors to dwell within the heavenly kingdom as they sit in their offices working on sermons, Bible studies, devotions, and more. That is a blessing of the pastoral office. They can dwell for several hours each day in the heavenly kingdom. Then they can walk out of their office door to step into the earthly kingdom.

But the Christians to whom pastors minister are living within the earthly kingdom. They sit in their living room, office space, movie theater, vehicle, etc., as citizens in a very earthly kingdom – yet remaining, AT THE SAME MOMENT, citizens of a very heavenly kingdom. In that sense, the Christian adheres to a higher law, a higher moral and ethical standard, than the unbelieving citizen. But Christians do not step from one kingdom to the next. They dwell in both kingdoms simultaneously. That's not a confusion of the kingdoms. That's the reality – balance, paradox, tension – of the two kingdoms.

During the pandemic, churches and pastors allowed the state to dictate whether hymns would be sung, how communion would be distributed, how many people could worship at one time, how far apart worshipers had to be from each other, and so on. Were those churches and pastors the ones who were confusing the two kingdoms? Were they allowing the left-hand kingdom to dictate what would happen within the right-hand kingdom? Were they putting their submission to their governmental authorities over and above their submission to their divine authority when it came to Word and Sacrament ministries?

Some might say: Why be so passionate about these things? These are in the realm of the earthly kingdom. Yet, when there are lies, those come from the devil. We have the spiritual truth that applies within secular life as well as ecclesiastical life. Even as we understand the distinction of tools, responsibilities, and effects between the two kingdoms – we dare not separate the two kingdoms as though we are merely Christians who happen to be citizens, or citizens who happen to be Christians. We are people whose primary King is Christ, whose primary Kingdom is Heaven, and whose Christian faith is exercised publicly – within the kingdom of the air, where Satan has his little day.

Let us be wise and thoughtful as we consider how we may live and share Christ's heavenly kingdom as we live in Christ's earthly kingdom - where Satan and his two beasts have so much influence.

We pray that governing authorities are thwarted if they attempt to stifle our Christianity. Pray for God to use you and other citizens of this earthly kingdom to move authorities to give Christians free rein to preach Christ crucified in words and share Christian love in actions in our nation and beyond.

We pray for the kind of earthly kingdom where God's heavenly kingdom can be spread. This is what we join in praying for with St. Paul in 1 Timothy 2:1-2: "First of all, then, I urge that petitions, prayers, intercessions, and thanksgivings be made for all people, for kings and all those who are in authority, in order that we might live a quiet and peaceful life in all godliness and dignity."

We join with Paul in praying for our governing authorities. We pray they serve the citizens as God's servants. What benefits does the church derive from good government? When Christians have a good government, that makes it easier to submit to their good rule.

A good government creates peace so that the Church can carry out its God-given responsibilities without hindrance or interference. Then Christians might live "quiet and peaceful lives in all godliness and dignity."

We pray to understand properly and apply accurately God's call to submit. We pray for quiet and peaceful lives of submitting to governing authorities who submit to God's authority.

Revelation 13

In *The Hobbit: The Desolation of Smaug*,[13] Smaug is a large and dangerous dragon who conquers the Dwarf Kingdom of Erebor. He then takes the Lonely Mountain and its vast treasures for himself. 150 years later, a company of thirteen dwarves, led by Thorin Oakenshield, set out to take their home back from the dragon. The dwarves are aided in their quest by the hobbit Bilbo Baggins and the wizard Gandalf the Grey.

Bilbo and the dwarves try to slay the dragon. Smaug is smothered with a deluge of molten gold. He rises out of the gold and flies toward Lake Town to rain down destruction on the village. In mid flight Smaug calls out, "Revenge? Revenge? I will show you revenge! I am fire! I am ... death!"

Smaug is portrayed in *The Hobbit* as being powerful, cunning, ruthless, and destructive. But that's nothing compared to the cunning ruthlessness and the destructive power of the great red dragon St. John sees in the Book of Revelation.

In Revelation 12, St. John receives the first of a series of seven visions. He receives a close-up look at the role of Satan and his earthly allies. Revelation 12 answers the question: What is Satan doing during the time of the New Testament? We learn that Satan and his allies spend their time from Christ's ascension to Christ's glorious return tempting, tormenting, and persecuting Christians.

The seven-headed dragon

Satan is pictured as a huge red seven-headed dragon that goes after the Christian Church on earth, portrayed as a woman giving birth. "There was a huge red dragon that had seven heads and ten horns and seven crowns on his heads. His tail swept away a third of the stars in the sky and threw them to the earth. The dragon stood before the woman, who was about to give birth, so that he could devour the child as soon as it was born" (Revelation 12:3, 4).

---

[13] The *Hobbit* was a great book! The three *Hobbit* movies ... not so much.

The red dragon has seven crowns for his seven heads adorned with ten horns. The number of heads, horns, and crowns, combined with the sweeping power of his tail portray the great power of this dragon. This dragon is easily recognizable as Satan. He is identified by name in chapter 20: "The dragon, the ancient serpent, who is the Devil and Satan ..." (Revelation 20:2). Satan tried to usurp the power of God during his time in heaven. When he was cast out of heaven, "many angels were thrown down with him" (Revelation 12:9). The dragon's attempts to destroy the child of the woman is a picture of all the attempts of Satan to destroy the line of the Savior during the Old Testament. One might recall how Satan influenced King Herod to attempt to kill the King of Jews by murdering all the baby boys in Bethlehem (Matthew 2:16-18).

The woman's child is Jesus. "She gave birth to a son, a male child, who will shepherd all the nations with an iron rod (Revelation 12:5)." King David prophecies in Psalm 2:9 that Jesus will shepherd the nations who follow him and smash those who oppose him. Christ crushed the ancient serpent's head (Genesis 3:15) with his death on the cross and his resurrection from the grave. After defeating Satan, Jesus ascended into heaven. "Her child was snatched up to God and to his throne" (Revelation 12:5).

"Then the woman fled into the wilderness, where she has a place prepared by God in order that she might be fed there for 1,260 days" (Revelation 12:6). The wilderness is this world. The 1,260 days are portrayed elsewhere in Revelation as forty-two months, and times, time, and a half time. These equal 3 ½ years. If God's interaction with the world is pictured as the number 7, then 3 ½ years is the Old Testament period and the other 3 ½ is the period of the New Testament. These 1260 days or 3 ½ years begin with Christ's ascension and end with Christ's return. During that time, the woman is in the wilderness.

Since the dragon missed his chance at the child, he turned his attention back to the woman. But he learned that the woman was protected in the wilderness, so he turned his attention to the children of the woman. "The dragon was angry about what had happened to the woman, and he went away to make war against the rest of her children—those who keep the commandments of God and who hold on to the testimony about Jesus" (Revelation 12:17). Satan cannot defeat the woman of the Christian Church. But he can pick off individual Christians – the woman's children.

The beast out of the sea

The dragon is not alone in his war against Christians. He has two willing allies who assist him on the battlefield. In his next vision, St. John sees these two allies of the dragon:

> "I saw a beast rising out of the sea. He had ten horns with ten crowns on his horns, and seven heads with blasphemous names on his heads. The beast that I saw was like a leopard, and his feet were like those of a bear, and his mouth was like the mouth of a lion. The dragon gave the beast his power, his throne, and great authority. One of his heads seemed to have been fatally wounded, but his fatal wound was healed.
>
> And the whole world that followed the beast was amazed. They worshipped the dragon because he gave authority to the beast. They worshipped the beast, saying, "Who is like the beast, and who can go to war against him?" The beast was also given a mouth that spoke arrogant and blasphemous things. He was given authority to do these things for forty-two months.
>
> The beast opened his mouth to speak blasphemies against God: to blaspheme his name, his dwelling, and those who dwell in heaven. He was also given permission to wage war against the saints and to overcome them, as well as authority over every tribe and people and language and nation. All those who make their home on the earth will worship the beast—those whose names have not been written from the beginning of the world in the Book of Life, which belongs to the Lamb that was slain.
>
> If anyone has an ear, let him hear: If anyone is to be imprisoned, he is going to be imprisoned. If anyone is to

be killed with a sword, he is going to be killed with a sword. Here patient endurance and confidence are needed by the saints" (Revelation 13:1-10).

Revelation 13 begins the second vision. It reveals the beast from the sea. The imagery revealed to St. John is based on Daniel's vision of the four beasts in Daniel 7 that represent four empires: Babylon, Persia, Greece, and Rome. These four beastly empires oppressed God's people between Daniel's time and John's time. In Revelation 13, John sees a beast with seven heads and ten horns rise out of the sea. This beast represents all government power throughout history that opposes and oppresses the Christian Church throughout the New Testament era – 3 ½ years.

Then John sees a second beast arise out of the earth (Revelation 13:11-18). This beast represents the apostate church that tries to imitate Christ, but it is the antichrist and tries to take the place of Christ on earth. It represents all religious power that opposes Christ his Christian Church throughout the New Testament era.

These two beasts are allies of the red seven-headed dragon of the devil. Together, all three wage war against the saints and to try to overcome them (Revelation 13:7).

Like a pet that follows its master around and does its bidding, the beast out of the sea does the bidding of its master, Satan (Revelation 13:1). The beast even looks similar to the dragon with its horns, heads, and crowns (Revelation 12:3). The beast receives its throne, power, and authority from the dragon (Revelation 12:2). Satan gives tyrannical governments their power to persecute Christians.

"The beast opened his mouth to speak blasphemies against God: to blaspheme his name, his dwelling, and those who dwell in heaven" (Revelation 12:6). The beast of the persecuting governments work to abolish God. Then the government becomes the god.

The true God of heaven and earth has given us governing authorities to serve the citizens. Citizens submit to their government when it acts as God's servant (Romans 13:1).

However, we see throughout history that governments can abuse their God-given authority, rebel against their service to God, and become servants of Satan.

The rulers of the world are united against God's rule

The rulers of this sinful world may disagree about a myriad of things ... but they find themselves united on one point – they oppose God's rule. "The kings of the earth take a stand, and the rulers join together against the Lord and against his Anointed One" (Psalms 2:2). God's people must stand up to rulers who stand against the Anointed One and those whom he anoints with the water of Baptism.

We read in the Old Testament of those who opposed God and his people. When they were doing this, they were acting like a servant of Satan, like the dragon's beast out of the sea. Pharaoh enslaved God's people and refused to heed Moses' constant plea of "Let my people go!" King Nebuchadnezzar carried God's people into captivity in Babylon. Shalmaneser king of Assyria exiled Israel to Assyria. God used the actions of these kings and pharaohs to carry out his will for his chosen children. But he did not direct the evil that the kings enacted on God's people. The kings and pharaohs did that as Satan's servants - and God rebuked them for their evil (e.g, Isaiah 13).

Time and time again we read in 1 and 2 Kings where there were evil kings who used the power of their kingdom to oppose God's kingdom. Here are some of the more notorious kings. King Jeroboam created his own worship system in Israel, erecting two golden calves for the people to worship in Bethel (1 Kings 12). King Ahab did more evil in the sight of the Lord than all the kings before him. Together with his Canaanite wife, wicked Queen Jezebel, Ahab instituted the worship of the Canaanite gods Baal and Asherah over Israel (1 Kings 16). Jehu wiped out Ahab's house and put the prophets of Baal to death. Still, he continued to lead the people in worship of Jeroboam's golden calves at Bethel and Dan (2 Kings 10).

It seems like the devil enjoyed using the line of King Herod's to persecute God's kingdom. King Herod tried to wipe out the life of the newborn King (Matthew 2). King Herod Antipas beheaded John the Baptist (Matthew 14). Herod Agrippa I had James put to death with the sword (Acts 12).

Throughout history we've seen various governments persecute Christ and Christ's people. Communist governments in places like Russia and China work diligently to destroy the Christian Church in their nations. Islamic or Buddhist governments refuse to allow Christianity within their borders. Even nations where the gospel has been spread freely for the past few centuries have seen many of those freedoms curtailed or removed in the past few years.

It is common throughout history that the kings of the earth oppose the 2nd petition of the Lord's Prayer where we pray for God's kingdom to come. The kings of the earth attempt to keep the kingdom of heaven from coming.

The authority of governments

Revelation 13 portrays a regime that is given authority from the devil – the dragon. This is the opposite side of the same coin from Romans 13. The government claims for Caesar the things that are God's. The government cannot become an autonomous authority ... otherwise it becomes a god. Nor can an individual become his own autonomous authority ... otherwise he makes himself into a god. (Consider the example of King Nebuchadnezzar in Daniel 4, whom God then humbled). When the Lord is not God, then the government or people will fill the void and become gods unto themselves.

This is why God has called authorities and citizens to serve one another as his servants. When authorities and citizens serve one another, then they are acting as God's servants. When authorities or citizens abuse their authority or act in wrongful disobedience, then they are acting as Satan's servants. Citizens and authorities should desire to give glory to God, not Satan.

Standing up to the bully

If your middle schooler comes home crying about a bully in

school, what advice do you give your child? Eventually you'll encourage your child to stand up to the school bully. Bullies back down when their power is challenged. The devil is a bully. He is the biggest and baddest bully of all. Like any bully, the devil loves to use intimidation, insults and threats to exert his power over us. Like any bully, the devil has a gang that follows him and does his dirty work. The devil is the red dragon. The dragon has recruited the beasts out of the sea and out of the earth. The devil's gang is the persecuting government and the apostate church.

We do not become militant by taking up arms in protest as we see so many people doing on the far left or far right of the political spectrum. But since we are still part of the Church Militant – the Christian Church at war here on earth – we do take up arms. Not physical arms and weapons. But the spiritual weapon of the sword of the Spirit. We use this sword to cut and slash with God's Law pointing out sin and calling to repentance. Sins are cancerous and need to be cut out. Lies are from the devil and need to be fought against. "Then the lawless one will be revealed, whom the Lord Jesus will consume with the breath of his mouth and destroy when he appears in splendor at his coming" (2 Thessalonians 2:8)."We stand up to the bully of the devil and his gang of demons by confronting their lies with the truths of God's Word. We swing the sword of the Spirit (Ephesians 6:7). We go on the offensive with Christ's sword of spiritual warfare.

We also wield this sword like a scalpel. It cuts gently to heal and then the salve of the gospel is applied. We bind up the wounds of the brokenhearted. "For the word of God is living and active, sharper than any double-edged sword. It penetrates even to the point of dividing soul and spirit, joints and marrow, even being able to judge the ideas and thoughts of the heart" (Hebrews 4:12).

The war against Christianity

"[The beast out of the sea] was also given permission to wage war against the saints and to overcome them" (Revelation 13:7). The beast waged war on the saints. We see the attacks most clearly as they pertain to our uniquely Christian values and Christian worldview - our priorities, morals, and ethics.

We see our inner cities being destroyed by drugs, alcohol abuse, crime, homelessness, poverty, race issues, etc. We see women's high school, collegiate, and professional sports being dominated by biological men, while people of conscience are compelled to deny reality by using pronouns detached from either science or common sense. We see public elementary schools, high schools and universities promoting Critical Race Theory, which tries to attain an earthly utopia by retribution and deconstruction. We see the government's promotion and financial support of abortion for the past six decades. We see gender theory promoted from our elementary schools to the top levels of the American government. We've seen the U.S. Supreme Court find a way to allow for homosexual marriage. We've seen the U.S. government approve of no-fault divorce, racial quotas, and financial support to unwed mothers.

The list can go on and on.

While some of these examples might be dismissed as "trying to curb behavior" or "deal with the results of sin" - they create a societal environment where sincere religious belief is discarded as strict, worthless, or hateful. Godly responsibilities and vocations are discarded, and the secular authorities influence and encourage - rather than curb - sin.

The issues on this list are wrong, harmful, and destructive. But if citizens oppose these issues, they can be labeled misogynist, homophobic, transphobic, and racist. They can be prosecuted by the American government.

As Christians, we need to understand that these issues are not political. Unfortunately, we have allowed them to become political issues. Sadly, Christians have stepped back and ceded these issues over to the culture. Politics follows culture. So, then these issues become political issues. And if Christians debate these issues, we are shamed for becoming political.

Politics is downstream from culture, as they say, but culture is always downstream from theology.

These are issues that we as Christians are uniquely equipped to address with theology. We cannot solve the issues, but we can address them with Law and Gospel to get at the root causes. We apply God's 4th commandment and the corresponding Bible verses to building up the homes within our communities. We apply God's 5th commandment and the corresponding Bible verses to life issues. We apply God's 6th commandment and the corresponding Bible verses to issues of sex, gender dysphoria, homosexuality, marriage, and divorce. We apply God's 7th, 9th, and 10th commandments to issues involving taxes, the deficit, and the economy.

We do ourselves, our neighbors, and our nation a disservice when we cede these issues only to the government. Then the issues become political. But they are first moral and theological issues that Christians should be discussing, debating, and deciding.

The dragon and the beasts are working against God's saints on a global, national, and local scale. You can see and feel them at work right now in our world.

But you can also see and feel them at work on a much smaller scale within your home. The grandchild who is addicted to drugs, or alcohol, or pornography. The child who forsakes marriage vows to move away from spouse and children and create a new home with someone else. The couple who used to be so much in love but have grown cold and distant. The teenagers who are trapped in a world of social media and have no concept of communication and physical contact within the real world. The tension that rising food and gas prices exert on the family budget.

What is our reaction when we see all this persecution going on around us? What is our reaction when we feel all this tension within our homes? Let's be honest. Because we are sinners, we usually act negatively. We give up. We curl into the fetal position hoping it will all go away. We don't fight to change things by preaching the gospel. Instead, we turn up the volume on our Netflix and sports shows hoping to drown out whatever is going on around us. We stop talking to God in prayer. We stop worshiping him in church. Because we are no longer filling ourselves up with God's love and mercy in Christ, we are left with only fear, uncertainty, and doubt, which lead to shame and anger. We turn and vomit that fear and anger out on whomever is unfortunate enough to be around us - or we buy the solutions peddled by the world, rather than repent.

If Christians do not step up and step into the culture to share the good news of the true God, then Satan will fill the void with a government that opposes the truths of the Lord God. If Christians do not oppose these lies that are straight out of the pits of hell, then these lies can do great damage to the saints.

Worshiping the beast

People will be tempted to worship the beast of an ungodly government (Revelation 13:4), looking to that earthly institution to provide what only God can provide.

Why do people worship the beast? They reason that if Christ and his Church were not able to defeat the beast, then no one can fight against it. Therefore, the dragon and the beast should be followed. St. John sees that there will be pagan worship of the government. People will clamor to worship the beast out of the sea, led by its high priests promising what only God can accomplish. This happens when citizens are more involved in looking good in the public square than being involved in preaching God in that same public square.

The beast out of the earth makes sure that the people of the earth worship its ally of the beast out of the sea. "He causes the earth and those who make their home on it to worship the first beast" (Revelation 13:12). The antichrist will use its influence and high priests to lead people in worshiping the persecuting governments of the world. This is all an attempt to lead people away from Christ.

We need to use the God-given gift of critical thinking. In Revelation 13 we learn that those without the mark of the beast are not able to buy or sell. "[The beast from the earth] makes all people, small and great, rich and poor, free and slave, receive a mark on their right hands or on their foreheads, in order that no one may buy or sell unless he has the mark" (Revelation 13:16, 17).

Since the beasts out of the sea and earth are seen throughout history, look for these beasts' marks throughout history that limit commerce. I won't speculate what that might be today or in the future. Use your God-given wisdom and critical thinking to apply apocalyptic Scripture to real world events.

Is it possible that the orthodox, true, confessional Christian Church would be complicit in this blasphemy? That is exactly what happens when we lay down the weapons Christ has given us and refuse to fight in this war (Ephesians 6:10-17).

Jesus declared that Satan is the "ruler of this world" (John 12:31). As the ruler of this world, he gives the governing authorities who serve him "permission to wage war against the saints and to overcome them, as well as authority over every tribe and people and language and nation" (Revelation 13:7). This does not have to be a battle where the beast unleashes hell on the saints and turns the earth into its personal killing fields.

St. John specifically describes this as a "war." A "war" is two-sided. The saints put on their spiritual armor and take up arms against the beast and its allies.

> "Put on the full armor of God, so that you can stand against the schemes of the Devil. For our struggle is not against flesh and blood, but against the rulers, against the authorities, against the world rulers of this darkness, against the spiritual forces of evil in the heavenly places. For this reason, take up the full armor of God, so that you will be able to take a stand on the evil day and, after you have done everything, to stand. Stand, then, with the belt of truth buckled around your waist, with the breastplate of righteousness fastened in place, and with the readiness that comes from the gospel of peace tied to your feet like sandals. At all times hold up the shield of faith, with which you will be able to extinguish all the flaming arrows of the Evil One. Also take the helmet of salvation and the sword of the Spirit, which is the word of God" (Ephesians 6:11-17).

God's saints are usually on the defensive. But they don't have to be. They are given the offensive weapon of the sword of the Spirit, which is the Word of God.

We take the spiritual fight to the rulers and authorities of this world. St. Paul uses the same Greek word for "authorities" in both Romans 13:2 and Ephesians 6:12. Whether we are fighting against earthly authorities who serve Satan and his darkness or against the spiritual forces who are the masterminds behind the earthly authorities, it really doesn't matter.

We are in a spiritual war for the souls of God's saints. The point is that the saints don't just lay down and submit to the pounding, persecution, and death. They have means of defending themselves by resisting. They resist the onslaught of the demonic forces by forcefully swinging the sword of the Spirit. They resist the attacks of Satan by a clear confession in word and deed.

What keeps us from bowing down to the beast? By God's grace, our names have been written in the Book of Life. "All those who make their home on the earth will worship the beast—those whose names have not been written from the beginning of the world in the Book of Life, which belongs to the Lamb that was slain" (Revelation 13:8). The Book of Life is God's record of the elected saints who will be saved from this world to enter the world to come (Revelation 20:12-15).

The mark of the beast

The dragon and the two beasts were around in St. John's day in the first century. They have been taunting, tempting and tormenting Christians for the past two millennia. The mark of the beast at the end of Revelation 13 is something that has also been around for the past two millennia. St. John describes the mark of the beast from the land: "He also makes all people, small and great, rich and poor, free and slave, receive a mark on their right hands or on their foreheads, in order that no one may buy or sell unless he has the mark—the name of the beast or the number of his name. Here is wisdom: Let the one who has understanding calculate the number of the beast, because it is the number of a man. His number is 666" (Revelation 13:16-18).

The mark of the beast is whatever people need to do to be tolerated by the alliance of corrupt government and corrupt church. We can see in history where this mark of the beast was the official certificate which stated that the holder had burned incense to the Roman emperor. It was membership in a Communist youth organization as a prerequisite to attending a university. It can be acceptance of abortion as a criterion to run for public office.

There is no reason to fear this mark. For in Revelation 14 we read that God puts his own mark on us. That happened when the pastor made the sign of the cross over our head to our heart at our baptism – marking us as redeemed children of God. So, no matter what earthly marks the dragon and his beasts try to put on people to restrict their commerce, as saints of God, we aren't concerned. Our true commerce is receiving God's grace.

Christ is in control

Reading Revelation 12 and 13 with these visions of a dragon and his beast can be terrifying. That's why we go back to Daniel's vision in Daniel 7. "I kept watching the night visions, and there, in the clouds of heaven, I saw one like a son of man coming. He came to the Ancient of Days, and he was brought before him. To him was given dominion, honor, and a kingdom. All peoples, nations, and languages will worship him. His dominion is an eternal dominion that will not pass away, and his kingdom is one that will not be destroyed" (Daniel 7:13-14).

Daniel sees Jesus as the Son of Man coming on the clouds of heaven into the presence of God the Father as the Ancient of Days. Here we think of Jesus' own words, "You will see the Son of Man sitting at the right hand of power and coming with the clouds of heaven" (Mark 14:62), Though it seems like the world is falling apart around us, we live each day in eager anticipation of seeing Jesus coming in clouds of glory. On the Last Day, Christ will come to take his saints home.

Daniel records that Christ's dominion is an "eternal" dominion that will not pass away, and his kingdom cannot be destroyed.

Don't you love it that God's kingdom is eternal? It is everlasting. It is forever. We are told, "Give thanks to the Lord, for he is good. For his mercy endures forever" (Psalm 136:1). Mercy is God's love and loyalty that never changes. Again, we're told, "Your mercies are new every morning. Great is your faithfulness" (Lamentations 3:22,23). Life is full of changes, many of them not good. Yet God's mercy to us never changes. These mercies are always new. And they are always good.

The control of King Jesus in his kingdom is eternal. It will not pass away. Though other kingdoms rise and fall, his kingdom will never be destroyed.

Though Satan has authority over every tribe, people, language, and nation to make them worship the persecuting governments of the world, Christ has greater authority. "All peoples, nations, and languages will worship him" (Daniel 7:14). "Therefore God also highly exalted him and gave him the name that is above every name, so that at the name of Jesus every knee will bow, in heaven and on earth and under the earth, and every tongue will confess that Jesus Christ is Lord, to the glory of God the Father" (Philippians 2:9-11).

That means that the Son of Man and the Ancient of Days can fulfill St. Paul's words to you in Romans 8:28, "We know that all things work together for the good of those who love God." God worked the terrifying four beasts of Daniel's vision into the good of fulfilling the Messianic prophecy. That means that God will also work the terrifying beasts out of the sea and land in St. John's Revelation into the good of fulfilling the salvation of his saints.

When you see the beasts and dragon of John's vision tempting and tormenting God's saints; when you experience persecution from governments and institutions that oppose your Christianity; when you feel despair and depression in your home; don't give up. Don't curl up. Don't hang your head in defeat. The Son of Man is sitting on his throne at the right of the Ancient of Days. Call out with confidence, "Christ is in control!"

We pray for governing authorities who submit to God's authority, so we may submit to their God-given authority. We pray for the strength to oppose governing authorities when they submit to Satan's authority, so we may not relent, but call them (and those tricked into worshiping them) to repentance.

The government can be the servant of the Lord. It can also be the servant of Satan. Two things can be true at the same time. That's why we need to constantly read, discuss, and apply the Scriptures to make Christian decisions in light of Romans 13 and Revelation 13.

Luther's Warning

In the 1960s television series (also rebooted in 2018) *Lost in Space*,[14] the Robot acts as a surrogate guardian to young Will Robinson as the Robinson family is stranded on a planet. When the youth is unaware of an impending threat, the robot waves his arms around warning, "Danger, Will Robinson! Danger!"

"Danger, Will Robinson! Danger!" is a klaxon call warning of impending danger.

We'll discover in this chapter that Martin Luther's *Warning to My Dear German People* was a klaxon call of impending danger from imperial and papal forces. Luther warns the people with these words:

> "But since I am the 'prophet of the German' *(Justus Jonas and Melancthon had referred to Luther this way for his steadfastness in the face of controversy)* —for this haughty title I will henceforth have to assign to myself, to please and oblige my papists and asses—it is fitting that I, as a faithful teacher, warn my dear Germans against the harm and danger threatening them and impart Christian instruction to them regarding their conduct in the event that the emperor, at the instigation of his devils, the papists, issues a call to arms against the princes and cities on our side. It is not that I worry that His Imperial Majesty will listen to such spiteful people and initiate such an unjust war, but I do not want to neglect my duty. I want to keep my conscience clean unsullied at all events. I would much rather compose a superfluous and unnecessary admonition and warning and impart needless instruction than to neglect my duty and then find, if things go contrary to my expectations, that I am too late and have no other consolation than the words *non putassem*, I

[14] We won't mention the 1998 *Lost in Space* movie. Blech!

> did not intend this. The sages suggest making provision for things even if everything is secure. How much less may we trust any wind and weather, no matter how pleasant it may appear, in these difficult times when the papists' raging provokes God's wrath so terribly! Moreover, in Romans 12 Paul commands those who preside over others to look out for them."[15]

Throughout the 1520s, Martin Luther had consistently argued against active resistance to the Imperial government. He wrote and spoke very strongly against the Peasants' Revolt of 1525. But as the Imperial government threatened to change to become more tyrannical, Luther's views on resistance also began to change.

A seminal date in the history of the Lutheran Church is June 25, 1530. On this date, the Lutheran princes presented their confession of the Lutheran faith to Emperor Charles V at the Diet of Augsburg. This became known as the Augsburg Confession.

The papal theologians then presented their refutation of the Lutheran confession. Negotiations between the Roman Catholics and the Lutheran were to take place. The Lutherans refused to negotiate. Charles declared a recess and ordered the Lutheran princes to restore Catholic practices in their lands. If they refused to do so, they would suffer the consequences in six months.

In late 1530, it seemed as if Emperor Charles V was looking to turn his attention from the Turks to his south to his own princes. There was rising concern that the pope and the emperor would ally themselves against the Lutheran princes. The princes decided that if an attack by the emperor would come, they would resist. They looked to their theologians and lawyers for scriptural and legal support.

In October of 1530, the Lutheran theologians were summoned to Torgau to discuss with the princes' legal scholars the right of

---

[15] Pelikan, Jaroslav J., H. C. Oswald, and H. T. Lehmann, eds. "*A Warning to My Dear German People.*" Luther's Works, American Edition, vol. 47. Martin H. Bertram, trans. Philadelphia: Fortress Press, 1971. 3-55.

resistance to Emperor Charles V. There the Lutheran confession of the Torgau Declaration was written. In the Declaration, the princes' lawyers made a strong case for resistance based on the Constitution of the Holy Roman Empire. The emperor was not entitled to absolute obedience by the princes or their subjects. This was because the emperor was not a monarch appointed by family heirs. Rather, political power was shared between the emperor and his princes because these princes served as the electors of the emperor to his lofty position. The princes had the responsibility to not only choose who the emperor should be, but also to hold the emperor responsible to his imperial office.

Legal and theological reasons to resist the Emperor

Two questions were being asked of the Lutheran lawyers and theologians at Torgau:

1. Is it permissible for Christians resist authority?
2. Can Christians resist the authority preemptively, before the government strikes at the Christians?

The answer to both questions was affirmative, legally (under Imperial law) and theologically (according to Scripture).

The lawyers went back to Imperial law. The law declared that the emperor was not an absolute ruler. He was elected to his position by German princes. That's why they had the name of Electors. The emperor's authority was granted him by lower magistrates. His power was balanced by the power of the electors. There were seven electors who elected the emperor. These electors then had the power to choose whom they desired as their Holy Roman Emperor. The electors also had the power to correct, or even depose, if necessary.

The lawyers claimed interposition. Interposition is where an upper official is trampling over the constitutional rights of the people, so a lower official has a duty to step in to protect the citizens. Luther himself was protected by an act of interposition from an imperial edict on his life following the Diet of Worms in

1521. Frederick the Wise, Luther's prince, staged a kidnapping of Luther and hid him safely away in Wartburg Castle. The emperor had declared Luther an outlaw and demanded that anyone who found Luther could kill him without fear of punishment. Instead, Frederick defied the emperor and rescued Luther from the emperor's edict.

This is an example of interposition by a lower magistrate intervening when a higher magistrate was wrong. This teaching of interposition by lower magistrates is explained more fully in *The Magdeburg Confession* that we'll examine in the next chapter.

We have seen examples of interposition in the United States with police officers refusing their mayor's orders, sheriffs refusing to enforce their governor's mandates, and governors going through their state legislators to protect their states from the president's executive orders.

What the 16th century lawyers discovered in their Imperial law is very similar to our American Constitution. The U.S. President or a state's governor are not absolute rulers. They are elected to their positions by the people. Their authority is granted to them by the people.

Governing authorities follow the rules of their government

The Lutheran theologians went back to Romans 13. They saw that St. Paul's inspired words do not say to submit to a ruler. It says to submit to the governing authorities that have been established by God. These authorities who govern need to follow the rules of their own government. Otherwise, they are the ones who are wrong and disobedient.

If Emperor Charles were the absolute monarch, then the electors may have had no legal or scriptural basis for resistance. However, since the emperor was not an absolute monarch, but received his authority to govern from the governed – the electors – then the emperor also had to obey his electors. He could not act unilaterally. He had to follow the rule of law himself.

It is very much the same in the United States. A U.S. President is not an absolute monarch. He cannot make unilateral decisions, and only has limited powers for creating executive orders. Rather, there is a balance among the three branches of government. A governor cannot make unilateral decisions, and only has limited powers for making statewide mandates on her own. Mayors, governors, or presidents in the United States must follow the rule of law. They, too, must follow Romans 13 and submit to the other authorities that govern them.

Applying Romans 13 to either 16th century Germany or 21st century America means that we submit ourselves to the various layers of the governing authorities. Emperor Charles V had to submit to the governing authorities who had elected him to that position. U.S. presidents, governors, mayors, sheriffs, etc., must also submit to their citizens who elect them to those positions of authority.

The Torgau Declaration

Under the constitution of the Holy Roman Empire, the Lutheran theologians agreed that the princes had a legal right to resistance. Their theological position was summarized in the Torgau Declaration, issued in late October 1530. It was written by Luther, Melanchthon and other theologians. It stated:

> "We are in receipt of a memorandum from which we learn that the doctors of law have come to an agreement on the question: In what situations may one resist the government? Since this possibility has now been established by these doctors and experts in the law, and since we certainly are in the kind of situation in which, as they show, resistance to the government is permissible, and since, further, we have always taught that one should acknowledge civil laws, submit to them, and respect their authority, inasmuch as the Gospel does not militate against civil laws, we cannot invalidate from Scripture the right of men to defend themselves even against the emperor in person, or anyone acting in his name. And now that the

> situation everywhere has become so dangerous that events may daily make it necessary for men to take immediate measure to protect themselves, not only on the basis of civil law but on the grounds of duty and distress of conscience, it is fitting for them to arm themselves and to be prepared to defend themselves against the use of force; and such may easily occur, to judge by the present pattern and course of events. For in previously teaching that resistance to governmental authorities is altogether forbidden, we were unaware that this right has been granted by the government's own laws which we have diligently taught are to be obeyed at all times."[16]

Luther repeated the constitutional argument that the emperor was not a monarch who ruled alone. The emperor ruled together with the Electors. Luther wrote: "These times are not the times of the martyrs, when Diocletian reigned alone and tyrannized Christians. This is a different empire, the emperor rules together with the seven electors. Without the seven the emperor has no authority ... this empire is no longer a monarchy, where one alone rules (as with the Turks). If this was like Diocletian's empire, then we would have to readily submit to him and suffer."[17]

We can then make the comparison to American constitutional law which allows for resistance to tyranny. It states in the second paragraph of one of our nation's founding documents, the Declaration of Independence:

> "Governments are instituted among Men, deriving their just powers from the consent of the governed, --That whenever any Form of Government becomes destructive of these ends, it is the Right of the People to alter or to abolish

---

[16] W.D.J. Cargill Thompson, *"Luther and the Right of Resistance to the Emperor," in Church, Society, and Politics*, ed. Derek Baker; Oxford: Basil Blackwell for The Ecclesiastical History Society, 1975

[17] Whitford, David Mark. *Tyranny and Resistance: The Magdeburg Confession and the Lutheran Tradition*. St. Louis: Concordia Publishing House, 2001.

> it, and to institute new Government, laying its foundation on such principles and organizing its powers in such form, as to them shall seem most likely to effect their Safety and Happiness. Prudence, indeed, will dictate that Governments long established should not be changed for light and transient causes; and accordingly all experience hath shewn, that mankind are more disposed to suffer, while evils are sufferable, than to right themselves by abolishing the forms to which they are accustomed. But when a long train of abuses and usurpations, pursuing invariably the same Object evinces a design to reduce them under absolute Despotism, it is their right, it is their duty, to throw off such Government, and to provide new Guards for their future security."

These same thoughts - liberty, justice, domestic tranquility, and a governance by the people - are echoed in the Preamble to our Constitution. And what is written in our American Constitution seems to be quite similar to what was written in the Constitution of the Holy Roman Empire 500 years ago.

Lutheran princes created a military alliance called the Smalcaldic League within the Holy Roman Empire during the 16th century. They joined together to protect themselves from the Turks (Muslims). But they also formed to protect themselves from the Pope and the Emperor who appeared to be allying themselves together against the Lutherans.

Luther's treatise on resistance

In October of 1530, Philip of Hesse, asked Martin Luther specifically to write a treatise regarding the idea of resistance. Luther published this treatise in April of 1531 which he titled, *A Warning to My Dear German People*. Luther was always very careful and hesitant in what he wrote about political resistance. And rightly so. Still, he set a defiant tone in his *Warning*.

Luther had spoken against the Peasants' Revolt of 1525. Now he says that if war is coming that is brought on by the emperor's forces, he won't speak out against those who rise up in opposition.

> "It is not fitting for me, a preacher, vested with the spiritual office, to wage war or to counsel war or incite it, but rather to dissuade from war and to direct to peace, as I have done until now with all diligence. All the world must bear witness to this. However, our enemies do not want to have peace, but war. If war should come now, I will surely hold my pen in check and keep silent and not intervene as I did in the last uprising."[18]

People quoted Matthew 22:21 to Luther of giving Caesar what belongs to Caesar. He replied, "A Christian knows very well what he is to do— namely, to render to God the things that are God's and to Caesar the things that are Caesar's [Matthew 22:21], but not to render to the bloodhounds the things that are not theirs."[19]

Luther stated that resistance is not rebellion

Roman theologians tried equating resistance with rebellion, which would then be sinful. Luther condemned that equation. Instead, Luther equated resistance with self-defense - a reasonable, proportionate action in response to unprovoked attack.. Luther writes, "Furthermore, if war breaks out – which God forbid – I will not reprove those who defend themselves against the murderous and bloodthirsty papists, nor let anyone else rebuke them as being seditious."[20]

As a pastor, Luther wanted to protect the delicate consciences of those within his spiritual care. He states there is an allowance for resistance under the law and therefore legal. He also condemns the notion that resistance equals rebellion. It is in fact, self-defense. People were charging that the Lutherans who resisted were sinning in their rebellion. Luther retorted,

---

[18] Luther, Martin. *A Warning to My Dear German People.*
[19] Ibid.
[20] Ibid.

> "We must not let everything be considered rebellious which the bloodhounds designate as such. For in that way they want to silence the lips and tie the hands of the entire world, so that no one may either reprove them with preaching or defend himself with his fist, while they keep their mouth open and their hands free. Thus, they want to frighten and ensnare all the world with the name "insurrection," and at the same time comfort and reassure themselves. No, dear fellow, we must submit to you a different interpretation and definition of that term. To act contrary to law is not rebellion; otherwise, every violation of the law would be rebellion. No, he is an insurrectionist who refuses to submit to government and law, who attacks and fights against them, and attempts to overthrow them with a view to making himself ruler and establishing the law, as Münzer did; that is the true definition of a rebel. Aliud est invasor, aliud transgressor. ("An invader is one thing; a transgressor is another.") In accordance with this definition, self-defense against the bloodhounds cannot be rebellious."[21]

If resistance to the state is always sinful, then the Christian will eventually support tyrannical rule while disregarding their God-given responsibility to act as salt to a world without savor.

Luther was unwilling to give a governing authority carte blanche authority. In fact, in this instance, Luther says that God has strictly forbidden obedience to the emperor if he were to attack. He even goes so far to say that if a citizen sides with the emperor, then he is being disobedient to God.

> "This is my sincere advice: If the emperor should issue a call to arms against us on behalf of the pope or because of our teaching, as the papists at present horribly gloat and boast—though I do not yet expect this of the emperor—no one should lend himself to it or obey the emperor in this

[21] Ibid.

event. All may rest assured that God has strictly forbidden compliance with such a command of the emperor. Whoever does obey him can be certain that he is disobedient to God and will lose both body and soul eternally in the war. For in this case the emperor would not only act in contravention of God and divine law but also in violation of his own imperial law, vow, duty, seal, and edicts. And lest you imagine that this is just my own idea or that such advice is dictated by my fancy, I shall submit clear and strong reasons and arguments to convince you that this is not my own counsel, but God's earnest, manifold, and stringent command. Before his anger you surely ought to be terrified and, in the end, must be terrified."[22]

Luther and the other theologians reached out to the emperor and the papists. But they refused to listen. The Lutherans, for their part, refused to be conformed to the theology of the papists.

What ought we to do today if discussion hasn't worked? Direct action must be taken. Conformity is out of the question. The answer that is left is non-conformity.

Luther was resistant to resist

As Luther saw his church under attack, he saw the greater need for resistance. Yet, as you read Luther, he is hesitant – resistant – to resist. For Luther, this was a last resort.

> "Let this suffice for the time being as an apology for the emperor. Now we want to issue a warning, giving reasons why everyone should rightly beware and fear to obey the emperor in such an instance and to wage war against our side. I repeat what I said earlier, that I do not wish to advise or incite anyone to engage in war. My ardent wish and plea is that peace be preserved and that neither side start a war or give cause for it. For I do not want my conscience burdened, nor do I want to be known before God or the

[22] Ibid.

world as having counseled or desired anyone to wage war or to offer resistance except those who are enjoined and authorized to do so (Romans 13). But wherever the devil has so completely possessed the papists that they cannot and will not keep or tolerate peace, or where they absolutely want to wage war or provoke it, that will rest upon their conscience. There is nothing I can do about it, since my remonstrances are ignored and futile."[23]

Luther wrote that the Lutherans were the ones who were at peace. They were spreading a message of peace. They wished to live in peace. So, if that peace was broken, it wasn't because of the Lutherans. "We cannot be blamed or accused either before God or before the world of fomenting war or insurrection."[24]

But what happens when governing authorities will not allow us to live in peace? Then they are the aggressors.

We pray for God's justice

If governing authorities attack Christians, we pray for God's justice and rejoice as God's people prayed for and rejoiced at God's justice along the bank of the Red Sea. We join with the psalmists who prayed for God's justice upon the kings and nations that conspire against him and his people. "Why do the nations rage? Why do the peoples grumble in vain? The kings of the earth take a stand, and the rulers join together against the Lord and against his Anointed One" (Psalm 2:1, 2).

Peter and John prayed with the saints after their release from prison (Acts 4:24-28). They state clearly in their prayers that kings, rulers, and nations conspire against the Lord. By his sovereign power, the Lord of all uses their feeble attempts to his benefit. God's will restrains the tyranny and evil that rulers inflict on God's people. The nations who act as God's servants are often his unwilling servants.

---

[23] Ibid.

[24] Ibid.

We desire for the governing authorities to fulfill the words of Psalm 148 and join the rest of creation in praising the Lord. "Kings of the earth and all peoples, officials and all judges on earth, young men and also young women, old people with young people. Let them praise the name of the Lord, for his name alone is exalted. His splendor is above the earth and the heavens" (Psalm 148:11-13).

When we are opposed and terrorized by kings and rulers, God may rescue us as he rescued Lot in Sodom or spared Jerusalem from the Assyrians (Genesis 14). Even if we are not spared, we do not compromise our confession (Daniel 3:18) and we rejoice that we are counted worthy to suffer for the name of Christ (Acts 5:41). We know we will be taken to safety under the Lord's altar (Revelation 6). We also know that the kings and rulers who opposed Christ and his saints were cast into the abyss of hell (Revelation 20). "Thus, we shall go to our death together, they to Hell in the name of all devils, I to Heaven in the name of God."[25]

We know that when we are called to fight in this war between light and darkness, Christ and Christian soldiers against the dragon and his beasts, we will be victorious. We are fighting alongside the Lord. That means the enemies of the gospel are fighting against the Almighty Lord of heaven and earth. They will not and cannot win.

> "For he who fights and contends against the Gospel necessarily fights simultaneously against God, against Jesus Christ, against the Holy Spirit, against the precious blood of Christ, against his death, against God's Word, against all the articles of faith, against all the sacraments, against all the doctrines which are given, confirmed, and preserved by the Gospel, for example, the doctrine regarding government, regarding worldly peace, worldly estates, in brief, against all angels and saints, against Heaven and Earth and all creatures. For he who fights against God must fight against all that is of God or that has to do with God."

---

[25] Ibid.

The Magdeburg Confession

The 1980s cartoon, *G.I. Joe*[26] ended each of its cartoons with the PSA, "Now you know. And knowing is half the battle." The episodes ended with a group of kids unintentionally doing something dangerous – like running into traffic. One of the G.I. Joes would gather the group of kids around him and explain the dangerous situation. Then the kids would gleefully shout, "Now we know!"

Then one of the Joes would reply, "And knowing is half the battle."

Good, strong Christian people have called resisting governing authorities as "not being Christian." They think like this because they don't know what Martin Luther and other Lutheran Reformers have written about the practice of resistance...and knowing is half the battle.

In the 1530s, the Lutheran princes formed the Smalcaldic League and requested both legal and theological answers to resisting the emperor if he used imperial force against them. But the emperor did not attack.

During Luther's time, the emperor was kept busy by the French to the west and the Turks to the east. But by 1546, the situations on both fronts were abated. The emperor could now turn his attention to the Lutherans in Germany.

Martin Luther died on February 18, 1546. On June 7, 1546, the emperor signed a treaty with the pope for an alliance. The pope pledged financial support and 12,000 troops to the cause of assisting the emperor in extinguishing Lutheran teaching in Germany. The two beasts were allying themselves against the Church. It was an example of what St. John had seen in Revelation 13.

On May 15, 1548, Charles V issued his infamous Augsburg Interim at the Diet of Augsburg. For the sake of peace, the

---

[26] A half-hour Saturday morning cartoon based on the toyline from Hasbro.

Augsburg Interim allowed Lutherans to hold onto some of their teachings, but also ordered them to readopt traditional Roman Catholic teachings and practices, including the seven sacraments. This was the emperor's attempt to smash the Protestant Reformation.

Lutheran local magistrates were divided. Some chose to conform to the emperor's decree by force. Others chose resistance. The walled and fortified city of Magdeburg took a stand and resisted the emperor's might.

In 1550, the state governed by the emperor was bullying the Church. It had put itself over the Church. In these ways, the government was doubly a persecutor of God. First, it had broken its own constitutional law. Second, it was trying to break apart the Lutheran Church.

Together, the emperor and the pope brought the sword down upon the Lutherans. The Lutherans were badly outnumbered. The Catholic princes of the Holy Roman Empire, led by the Holy Roman Emperor Charles V, decisively defeated the Lutheran Smalcaldic League of the Lutheran princes. Philip of Hesse and John Frederick were leading the Lutheran princes. They were arrested and kept in prison for years. Other Lutheran cities (like Wittenberg) soon fell, as well.

The city of Magdeburg

The pastors of Magdeburg issued their Confession and Defense of the Pastors and Other Ministers of the Church of Magdeburg on April 13, 1550.

Five months after issuing their Confession, Charles V's forces marched on Magdeburg. The people of Magdeburg burned everything outside the city walls and closed the city gates. The siege of Magdeburg had begun. It lasted 400 days.

The Magdeburg Confession gives us a guide to the Christian middle ground between anarchy and absolute obedience to absolute power by the government. And as with all matters of practical doctrinal application, the specific and contextual details are of utmost importance.

The Magdeburg Confession was written for a specific reason at a specific time. It was one town's confession during one historical episode that lasted one year. That's why it was never adopted as a church-wide confession. The Augsburg Confession and Apology of the Augsburg Confession were broader, church-wide statements. They were written to create a clear confession of the Christian faith, while at the same time refuting certain false doctrines. The Smalcald Articles were drafted as a similar, broad confession. Although the larger meeting to discuss the articles didn't happen as expected, the document was still used that way.

The Formula of Concord was written specifically to address intra-Lutheran and Lutheran-Reformed debates. Lutherans in Germany signed the Formula of Concord because these were the theological debates that were happening in Germany.[27] Though the Magdeburg Confession is technically not in the Lutheran Confessions, that does not make this a second-rate confession. The Formula of Concord Article X gives credence and reasoning for the pastors in the city of Magdeburg in writing the Magdeburg Confession.

> "We believe, teach, and confess that in time of persecution, when a plain [and steadfast] confession is required of us, we should not yield to the enemies in regard to such adiaphora, as the apostle has written Gal. 5:1: Stand fast, therefore, in the liberty wherewith Christ hath made us free, and be not entangled again in the yoke of bondage. Also 2 Cor. 6:14: Be ye not unequally yoked together with unbelievers, etc. For what concord hath light with darkness? Also Gal. 2:5: To whom we gave place, no, not for an hour, that the truth of the Gospel might remain with you. For in such a case it is no longer a question

---

[27] It's interesting that the Scandinavian Lutherans didn't use the Formula of Concord as part of their confessions simply because they weren't having those kinds of theological debates among the Lutherans in Scandinavia. It isn't that they disagreed with the Formula of Concord. It was merely that the Augsburg Confession was sufficient for them.

> concerning adiaphora, but concerning the truth of the Gospel, concerning [preserving] Christian liberty, and concerning sanctioning open idolatry, as also concerning the prevention of offense to the weak in the faith [how care should be taken lest idolatry be openly sanctioned and the weak in faith be offended]; in which we have nothing to concede, but should plainly confess and suffer on that account what God sends, and what He allows the enemies of His Word to inflict upon us."[28]

Speaking as a Lutheran, if we Lutherans subscribe to the reasoning of Article X of the Formula of Concord, we also subscribe to the reasoning of the Magdeburg Confession. We accept the principles in both confessions not because they are Lutheran ... but because they are scriptural. The ultimate question about subscription to the Magdeburg Confession is not about who did or did not officially subscribe, but is it theological – does it agree with Scripture? Since the Magdeburg Confession appeals to Scripture and the writings of Martin Luther that explain and apply Scripture, we therefore subscribe to the Magdeburg Confession.

The pastors' reasons for writing their confession

It is important to know who some of the pastors in Magdeburg were who then signed the Magdeburg Confession. They were no theological slouches. Matthias Flacius Illyricus was a young follower of Martin Luther. He made his way to Magdeburg where another close friend of Luther's, Nikolaus von Amsdorf was head of the Magdeburg churches. Nikolaus von Amsdorf was one of Luther's closest friends. He is the first signer of the Magdeburg Confession. Magdeburg "attracted men such as Amsdorf, Gallus (who already had a reputation for fierce rhetoric and a willingness to resist), Erasmus Alberus (a harsh critic of the Interim), and Flacius (perhaps the most vehement opponent of the Interim).[29]

---

[28] *Formula of Concord*, Article X, par. 4

[29] *Tyranny and Resistance: The Magdeburg Confession and the Lutheran Tradition*, p. 65

The Magdeburg Confession connects itself to Luther's *Warning* in the introduction. The signers saw the Magdeburg Confession more of a continuation of Luther's works than an original work from their hands.

The reason for pastors writing the Magdeburg Confession: "They did not simply write to edify their readers but to reassure the convinced, to persuade the unsure, and to convince the opposed."[30]

The pastors divided the Magdeburg Confession into the three parts. Part one contains Articles of Christian Doctrine. Part two is Concerning Resistance. And part three is The Exhortation.

In the Introduction to the Magdeburg Confession, the pastors quote three Bible verses. There is meaning behind the choosing of each of them.

> **Psalm 119:46**: "I spoke of your testimonies in the sight of kings and was not put to shame." This verse provides the rationale for the pastor's writing. Like Pastor Nathan who spoke God's testimony before King David, so the pastors must speak God's testimony before the emperor.

> **Romans 13:3**: "Rulers are not a terror for good works, but for evil." The pastors assert that the emperor is the aggressor and the pastor's resistance is defensive in nature. The pastors allege that the emperor and his allies – not the citizens of Magdeburg – are the ones disturbing the peace by their persecution. The citizens are upright and moral. They have done nothing wrong. They should be left alone. The pastors assert that the emperor had turned the sword on the good, when it was meant to punish the evil. The emperor should use the sword against the real evildoers. By terrorizing the Lutheran citizens of Germany, the ruler had forsaken his God-given authority

[30] Ibid. p. 67-68

to rule. His unprovoked, offensive attack against Magdeburg demonstrated his misuse of the sword and, thus, his illegitimate claim to proper, God-ordained authority to rule.

Acts 9:4: "Saul, Saul, why are you persecuting me? It is hard for you to kick against the goad." In this verse, Jesus rebukes Saul of Tarsus for persecuting his Church - even when granted a measure of civil authority. With this verse, the pastors are comparing the emperor to Saul as a persecutor of the true Church of Christ. All persecutors are subject to God's judgment, and a civic pretense is never sufficient justification for persecuting Jesus.

These three Bible verses set the tone for the pastors' arguments in their confession. In their confession, the Magdeburg pastors, (like Martin Luther before them) consistently followed the fundamental position that authority ought to be obeyed. Yet, obedience is never to be a blind obedience. It has limits. They were figuring out the balance of Romans 13 and Revelation 13.

In their arguments, the pastors of Magdeburg declare the idea of unlimited obeisance to the State as "an invention of the devil." They rightly assert that all authority is delegated from God. Therefore, if the one in authority makes commands contrary to the Law or Word of God, those subject to his authority have both a right not to obey and a duty to actively resist. The pastors state, "Divine laws necessarily trump human ones."[31]

The pastors set out to clearly define in the first part that they are adhering to the pure doctrine of the ancient Church. The pastors summarized the doctrine of the Church founded on the prophetic and apostolic scriptures, as expressed in the articles of the Augsburg Confession. By the kindness of God, this pure and uncorrupted doctrine continued to be taught within their churches.

---

[31] *The Magdeburg Confession: Thirteenth of April 1550 AD.* Matthew Colvin, trans. North Charleston, SC: CreateSpace, 2012. p. xi

With this repetition of the Augsburg Confession, the pastors create the setting for the doctrine of resistance.

> "Therefore we now have written this confession with our name and the name of our churches. The names of all men who are still openly pious and have not yet bowed their knees to Baal, who are with us in spirit, and whose prayers and groans are, we doubt not, joined with us. We have done this, first, so that we may render a witness of the truth to Christ who is now hanging on the cross; and so that we may present the necessary worship which he now urgently demands from all men; second, so that we may strengthen our brothers in Christ, wherever they are, by our opinion and example; and finally, so that we may free ourselves as well from suspicion of novelty or faction in true doctrine or true worship."[32]

Obedience is not blind, nor is authority absolute

Before moving on to the second part, the pastors make it clear in *vii.: Of Politics and Economy and the Power of Each* that they were not endorsing general resistance. They stated repeatedly that subjects "must be obedient to their authorities."[33] They liken citizens honoring their governing authorities to children honoring their parents and servants honoring their masters, for the governing authorities are God's servants. But when those servants no longer serve God, then they are serving the devil.

> "In these matters, just as subjects necessarily owe obedience to their magistrates; and children and the rest of the family, to their parents and masters, on account of God; so on the other hand, when magistrates and parents themselves lead their charges away from true piety and uprightness, obedience is not owed to them from the word

[32] Ibid. p. 46

[33] This obedience, though, is not blind. Nor is the authority absolute. Only God has absolute authority.

> of God. Also, when they professedly persecute piety and uprightness, they remove themselves from the honor of magistrate and parents before God and their own consciences, and instead of being an ordinance before God they become and ordinance of the Devil, which can and ought to be resisted by His order for the sake of one's calling."[34]

Nikolaus von Amsdorf, the first signer of the Magdeburg Confession, noted that "the distinguishing mark of an officer in Satan's kingdom" is persecuting the Church.[35]

As we go through the argument of the pastors for resistance to the emperor, we see them state and restate their position at various times in differing ways. "The appeal to the emperor has an almost revolving pattern of arguments. The pastors explore a topic, move on, return to it from a different side, move on, and so forth. Although the appeal may seem redundant, the authors are attempting to build an airtight case for the defensive nature of their resistance."[36]

The pastors call for allegiance to both God and Caesar. But when Caesar exceeds his powers, then he is attempting to exert the powers of Christ. This is not a doctrine of revolution, nor that of rebellion. It is a doctrine of resistance. It is resistance when the governing authorities are not following their own laws or God's laws:

> "We command [the whole Church], by the word of Christ, to render unto God the things that are God's and to Caesar, though he be different in religion, the things that are Caesar's. They render these duties of double obedience and conduct themselves without rancor, when both sides keep themselves within the limits of their duty prescribed by God and by the laws. Again, when there is a departure

[34] Ibid. p. 42

[35] Ibid. footnote, p. 59

[36] *Tyranny and Resistance: The Magdeburg Confession and the Lutheran Tradition*, p. 80

on either side from these limits, then horrible sins and severe unrest cannot but arise. In this way now, you, Charles Caesar, are exceeding the limits of your dominion and you are extending it into the dominion of Christ."[37]

Like Luther before them, the pastors are careful with a call to resistance. They are laying out the legitimate legal and scriptural reasons for resistance. But they know that sinful people will abuse this doctrine of resistance. "For this very reason, we know that the greatest theologians before us were especially cautious, hesitant, and careful in setting forth this opinion, since it was not yet necessary nor beneficial for every curious inquirer to know it."[38]

The three arguments for resistance

In the second part of the Magdeburg Confession, the pastors lay out their three arguments for resistance, centered on the theological idea of the "lesser magistrate doctrine." This doctrinal concept teaches that when a superior authority makes immoral or unjust laws or decrees, the lesser magistrate or lesser authority has a God-given right and duty to resist those immoral or unjust laws or decrees.[39]

The first argument for resistance is based on Martin Luther's distinction of the two kingdoms – God's kingdom and the earthly kingdom. In God's kingdom, those called to be in authority proclaim the Word of God and administer his Sacraments. In the earthly kingdom, those called to be in authority limit evil and punish the wicked. As Christians and citizens there is a balance as we dwell within both kingdoms.

But when the magistrate or governing authority becomes

---

37 *The Magdeburg Confession*, p. 52-53

38 Ibid. p. 53

39 The "lesser magistrate" doctrine is also operant as a legal principle within our own society and its layers of government - most visibly at a local or county level. County clerks have refused to carry out official duties that conflicted with conscience, or county sheriffs have refused to comply with state-level guidelines that would infringe upon individual freedom.

tyrannical and forsakes his proper, God-given role, then the lesser magistrates are called by God to limit the superior magistrate's evil and promote good. "The Magistrate is an ordinance of God for honor to good works, and a terror to evil works (Rom. 13). Therefore when he begins to be a terror to good works and honor to evil, there is no longer in him, because he does thus, the ordinance of God, but the ordinance of the devil. But he who resists, it is necessary that he resist in his own station, as a matter of his calling."[40]

The pastors at Magdeburg understood from history that sinful humans, entrusted with governmental power, will use that power for reasons or purposes that are not in the best interest of the citizens under their care. This had happened numerous times under Charles V. When the governing authorities acted as God's servants, they deserved submission as citizens give to Caesar what is Caesar's. However, when the governing authorities abused that authority and claimed for Caesar what rightfully belonged to God, then they no longer deserved submission. The Magdeburg pastors asserted two points: When governing authorities claimed authority beyond their God-given responsibility, they did not deserve their citizens' obedience and forfeited the citizens' submission when the citizens were submitting to the greater good of God's will.

The pastors begin the second argument:

> "When Christ commands, with an affirmative and by clear inference that the things which are Caesar's are to be rendered unto Caesar, and the things which are God's to be rendered unto God, we rightly infer from the affirmative a negative, likewise by clear inference, just as negative commandments, as in the Decalogue, always include an affirmative sentence by direct inference. And so by the force of this precept, the things which are God's are not to be rendered unto Caesar, just as the Apostles hand down this rule and precept, "We must obey God rather than men." And by refusing obedience to superiors in

---

40 *The Magdeburg Confession*, p. 57

> those things which are contrary to God, they do not violate the majesty of their superiors, nor can they be judged obstinate or rebellious, as Daniel says, "I have committed no crime against you, O King." [41]

In the third argument, the pastors assert that God does not support evil tyrants. If so, that would make God an instituter of evil.

> "If God wanted superior magistrates (who have become tyrants) to be inviolable because of his ordinance and commandment, how many impious and absurd things would follow from this? Chiefly it would follow that God, by his own ordinance and command, is strengthening, nay, honoring and abetting evil works, and is hindering, nay, destroying good works." [42] [43]

The four levels of injustice

The Magdeburg Confession then lays out four levels of injustice.

First is the "not excessively atrocious injustice." "First, then, as all men do, so especially magistrates by their natural weakness have their own vices and sins, by which, either knowingly or wantonly, they sometimes do injuries, not excessively atrocious, but remediable." [44]

---

[41] Ibid. p. 63

[42] Ibid. p. 67

[43] One might wonder how the final sentence of this paragraph would relate to the doctrine of concurrence, which says that God provides ability but not culpability for the moral or ethical import of that action. When considering this third argument, we especially remember the specific setting of this confession: The Magdeburg pastors were choosing to resist an evil government act, in service of God's higher law; and they were doing so in a setting where they were able to influence the government, which bore both sword and culpability. The argument here is that resistance is permitted, lest God-given authority be abused by the tyrant with no correction from the Christians under their care.

[44] *The Magdeburg Confession,* p. 58

1) **The first level: A governing authority makes mistakes.** They may be mistakes of a sinful nature, weakness, trying to do good but it doesn't work out, etc. The recognition is that no authority is going to be perfect. So, we bear patiently. We turn the other cheek. We learn perseverance during suffering. Lower magistrates may warn the higher authorities about this if they so choose. The confession gives direction that the people must patiently bear these injustices. This is not the time to rise in complaint. The first injustice is thus making allowances for bad policy.

2) **The second level: The lawless tyrant.** "The second level is that of atrocious and notorious injuries."[45] This is not merely an oversight or an imperfection. This is not an accident or something not quite working out right. There seems to be a purposeful neglect of duty, a willful disregard for the constitution, or a systemic twisting of the rule of law – and at the expense of the governed. As the governing authorities increase their forceful disregard for proper governing, the Magdeburg Confession increases the force the lower magistrates then place on the higher authorities.

According to conscience, the lower magistrate may decide how much to concede or how much to interpose. Various magistrates at different places or different times may decide differently whether to concede or interpose. They are contemplating action as individual magistrates and collectively as a group. But the Magdeburg Confession is still calling upon the citizens to grin and bear it. To turn the other cheek. To be patient and endure. The pastors allude that a Christian may resist in defense of others, but they encourage Christians to endure suffering if it affects them personally. "We will hope that in this circumstance Christian magistrates are prepared to suffer even injuries of this sort, and to leave vengeance to God, when the injury affects individual men, or

[45] Ibid. p. 58

a few men; and when the injury is able to be tolerated without sin."[46]

The citizens are trusting and conversing with the lower magistrates to intercede on their behalf with the higher authorities. The citizens may call upon the magistrates to bring about change. But it isn't yet to the level for the citizens to enact that change.

3) **The third level: The coercive tyrant.** The mandates of the governing authorities have become increasingly and consistently tyrannical. This is a difference of degree with level two. Innocent toleration is no longer possible. At this point, the lower magistrates can no longer decide between concession and interposing. It is now their duty to interpose for the good of the citizens they themselves are governing. They must defend the rights and freedoms of their citizens with diplomacy and even arms, if necessary. Here "an inferior magistrate is so forced to certain sin, that he is not able to suffer it without sin if defense is omitted."[47] The pastors are saying that the lower magistrates are sinning if they are not interposing on behalf of their citizens.

The citizens again humbly submit to the lower magistrates. But the lower magistrate is called to action. He may resist in two ways. First, he can practice civil disobedience for himself and those whom he governs by simply refusing to obey the command. Or the lower magistrate may raise the sword against the higher magistrate in defense of his people. But before the second option, the pastors advise the lower magistrate consult the fourth level of tyranny.

4) **The fourth level: the persecutor of God.** This is when the governing authorities are no longer mere tyrants, either by accident or purpose. They are now persecutors of God.

---

[46] Ibid. p. 59
[47] Ibid. p. 59

> Not just a persecutor of the people, but a persecutor of God himself. "It is when tyrants begin to be so mad that they may persecute with guile and arms ... and that they persecute God, the author of right in persons, not by any sudden and momentary fury, but with a deliberate and persistent attempt to destroy good works for all posterity."[48] The Magdeburg Confession calls this person a Beerwolf, a werewolf, an antichrist, "holding office in the kingdom of the Devil."[49]

Here the pastors are setting up a dichotomy between servants of God and servants of the devil. "The pastors were able to interpret and apply Paul's command to be subject to authority by demonstrating that the tyrant who opposes God is an ordinance of the devil. Such a tyrant, therefore, fails to be a part of God's ordering of creation and, instead, is in league with chaos. By failing this test, the tyrant ceases to be a legitimate ruler, and, therefore, can be resisted."[50]

This fourth level of injustice is when the governing authority has shut down the proclamation of the gospel. The pastors in Magdeburg concluded that the emperor had reached this fourth level. This is because the emperor was forcing them to be Roman Catholic – to denounce the biblical definition of justification by faith, the Sacraments, etc.

The persecutor of the church is when the governing authority dictates what the church can and cannot do. It becomes a church unto itself, asserting authority in spiritual matters to the detriment of orthodox belief. They have reached the level of the beast out of the sea. Level four is when the protector of God's people becomes the persecutor of those same people.

Where are we on these levels?

---

[48] Ibid. p. 59

[49] Ibid. p. 59

[50] *Tyranny and Resistance: The Magdeburg Confession and the Lutheran Tradition*, p. 84

The questions that the pastors in Magdeburg asked are the same questions Christian citizens today must ask: Where are we on these levels? Is the government in any way trying to prevent the salvation of mankind? Is the government – whether unknowingly or purposefully – in any way restricting Christians from fulfilling the first two petitions of the Lord's Prayer of hallowing God's name and allowing his kingdom to come on earth? Are governing authorities substituting a righteousness of following their rules, ordinances, and mandates over coming together as the Christian Church for receiving Christ's righteousness?

When governing authorities prevent the speaking and teaching of God's Word, then they become what Luther called a Beerwolf. In a 1539 debate, Luther compared the pope and the emperor to a monster of German folklore, the Beerwolf, or werewolf. The beast nullifies the Word of God. The servant of the devil tells Christians they cannot worship the way Scripture instructs them to worship. The beast out of the sea abolishes the laws of God and establishes the laws of men.

Then the governing authorities are no longer servants of God (Romans 13). They are now servants of Satan (Revelation 13).

What can we learn from the Magdeburg Confession?

This confession lays the groundwork for a middle ground between absolute obedience and unbridled anarchy – a Scriptural, historical precedent for maintaining Biblical balance during changing worldly circumstances.

The pastors realized that their responsibility was not to make political change, but to preach the gospel. This emphasis is borne out in the Confession, as their civic response to unjust persecution by the government.

Our responsibility is the same. As we'll see in the next chapter, sometimes we need to resist, practice civil disobedience, and stand up to injustice so that we can continue to share the gospel freely.

The sword resides with the governing authorities. That means that Christians do not use the physical sword to go on the offensive to rebel against tyrannical authorities. However, Christians do have the sword of the Spirit. We use that spiritual sword to go against Satan as he coerces governing authorities to misuse their physical swords.

The Magdeburg Confession asserts that we may resist when the governing authorities go against divine and natural law. This argument is rooted in *Luther's Warning* as we saw in the previous chapter. This argument is also rooted in the examples throughout biblical and secular history of Christians resisting tyrannical governments in a sanctified way.

The results of Magdeburg resisting the Emperor

What was the result of the city of Magdeburg standing strong against the tyranny of the emperor? Magdeburg was besieged for over a year. The citizens withstood this siege for 400 days. The Lutheran prince Maurice (who had previously been a traitor and sided with the emperor) reverted and allied himself once more with the German princes. He declared himself the Liberator. After freeing Magdeburg from the emperor's siege, Maurice then turned his armies south toward Augsburg where he drove out the imperial forces. Magdeburg and other Lutheran cities were freed from the emperor and the pope.

What is the result of the writing of the Magdeburg Confession? "The Magdeburg Confession is an important historical work because the men of Magdeburg were the first in the history of mankind to set forth in a doctrinal format what only later came to be known as the doctrine of the lesser magistrate."[51] "The Magdeburg Confession is one of the most important documents of the Reformation on political theology; and it played a key and positive role in the development of resistance theory."[52]

Now we know about the Magdeburg Confession. And knowing is half the battle.

The pastors conclude the Magdeburg Confession by quoting Psalm 93. Whether they are tyrants, antichrists, Beerwolfs or

---

[51] *The Magdeburg Confession*, p. viii

[52] *Tyranny and Resistance: The Magdeburg Confession and the Lutheran Tradition,* p. 61

beasts out of the sea and the earth – all allying themselves with the red dragon of the devil – the Lord on high is still mighty.

> The Lord reigns. He is clothed in majesty.
> The Lord is clothed-he wears strength like a belt.
> Yes, the world stands firm. It will not be moved.
> Your throne was established long ago.
> You are from eternity.
> The waves have lifted up, O Lord,
> the waves have lifted up their voice.
> The waves roar loudly.
> Mightier than the thundering of the great waters,
> mightier than the breakers of the sea,
> the Lord on high is mighty.
> Your testimonies stand very firm.
> Holiness beautifies your house for endless days,
> O Lord (Psalm 93:1-5).

Resistance

In *Star Trek: The Next Generation*, the crew of the USS Enterprise repeatedly face the Borg. The Borg are cyborgs intent on assimilating the biological creatures of the universe into their collective. The standard message used by the Borg when they encounter an alien race they intend to assimilate is, "Resistance is futile."[53]

In one episode, the Borg capture Starfleet Captain Jean Luc Picard and assimilate him, giving him the name Locutus of Borg. He responds to the crew of the Enterprise, "I am Locutus of Borg. Resistance is futile. Your life as it has been, is over. From this time forward, you will service us."

But is resistance futile? What is resistance?

What is resistance?

Resistance is not about revolution or rebellion. Resistance is objection. It is defiance. It is non-compliance. It can be civil disobedience.

Resistance can be as simple as refusing to participate in something. It is non-conformity. It is saying "No" when told to say "Yes."

Resistance is standing up when we are told to kneel. It's kneeling when we are told to move along. It's staying when we are told to leave. It's speaking up when we are told to be silent.

Resistance is shouting the truth until it's heard. It's standing firm when being pushed. It's insisting on freedoms when they are being removed. It's insisting that authorities follow moral laws when they are being ignored. It's not following immoral laws when they are being instituted by authorities.

Resistance is promoting courtesy, morality, and freedoms when we see incivility, immorality, and tyranny promoted. Resistance is

---

[53] The Borg first appeared in episode 16 of season 2 of *Star Trek: The Next Generation.*

speaking clearly in our confession of talk, and acting accordingly in our confession of walk.

Resistance is letting Christ's light shine as the darkness looms. It's appealing to logic and truth as we see emotions and lies emerging. It's standing up for those who can't stand for themselves, speaking up for those who have been silenced, and defending the defenseless.

In civil disobedience, you are making a stand for a moral cause. Optics and narrative are very important. You need to retain the moral high ground. It is a better vantage point, anyhow. Do not become belligerent. You need to have a lot of discipline. You cannot appear to be the aggressor. You have to oppose the beast ... while not becoming the beast yourself.

Resistance is often dismissed as rebellion because people misunderstand Paul's words about submission in Romans 13. Civil disobedience makes people uneasy because it has the word "disobedience" in it and that seems to go against the Fourth Commandment. Non-conformity makes people nervous because they assume we need to conform with everything the governing authorities dictate.

In the last two chapters we've examined what Martin Luther and other pastors of the Lutheran Reformation taught about resistance. In this chapter, we'll examine sacred and secular histories of God's people resisting governing authorities.

Resistance may take various forms, depending on the specific details of the crisis at hand.

Sometimes resistance is **direct defiance** to an immoral edict or ungodly order or a tyrannical ruler.

At other times, resistance involves **indirect defiance**.

Sometimes, resistance is **just saying "No"** when an authority figure oversteps the confines of their God-given authority.

Biblical examples of resistance

The Hebrew midwives directly defied the murderous edict of the Egyptian Pharaoh who demanded that they kill the newborn boys while they sat on the delivery stool (Exodus 1). The midwives refused to kill the baby boys born to the Hebrew slaves. They did not owe their cooperation to the evil orders of Pharaoh. Their disobedience to Pharaoh was obedience to God, and God blessed their defiance. "So God treated the midwives well. The people also increased in number and became very numerous. Because the midwives feared God, he gave them families" (Exodus 1:20, 21).

The parents of Moses hid their infant son for three months (Exodus 2). They disobeyed Pharaoh's evil order of putting their baby boy to death. The inspired writer commends them for their faith in their disobedience by including them in the Hall of Faith saying, "they were not afraid of the king's order" (Hebrews 11:23).

Jehu took up arms against wicked King Ahab and his house. The pastors of Magdeburg write of Jehu, "And though he did this by a special calling of God, and also did certain unique things, nonetheless God wanted to illustrate by this example the general calling of pious magistrates, by which they ought to resist their superiors who persecute the true worship and the true Church."[54]

Asa removed his mother from office and abolished her idols (1 Kings 15). The pastors of the Magdeburg Confession noted this comparison, saying that it "brings no small degree of light and weight to this debate."[55]

Mordecai refused to bow down and kneel to Haman after King Xerxes had promoted Haman and placed him over all the other officials (Esther 3). Queen Esther initially told her cousin Mordecai that she could not go in to see her husband the king (Esther 4). Even though Mordecai had overheard the terrible news of the king's decree to destroy the Jews, Esther was afraid of defying the law of entering the king's courts unannounced because it would mean death to her. Finally, Esther changed her mind and said to Mordecai, "I will go to the king, contrary to the law. And then, if I perish, I perish" (Esther 4:16)!

Shadrak, Meshak, and Abednego defied King Nebuchadnezzar and refused to fall down before his ninety-foot golden statue

54 *The Magdeburg Confession*, p. 71
55 Ibid, p. 71

(Daniel 3). Everyone else had bowed down. These three men stood out by standing up.

Daniel's habit was to pray three times daily to the Lord in his open window that faced Jerusalem. The government officials took advantage of Daniel's diligence by urging King Darius to establish a decree that prohibited anyone to pray to any god for thirty days except the king (Daniel 6). Daniel could have easily kept praying by closing the shades to the window or going to an upper room to pray. But Daniel daringly defied the king's decree. By divine inspiration he recorded his actions, "Now, when Daniel learned that the document had been signed, he went to his house. It had windows on its upper story that opened toward Jerusalem. Three times each day he would get on his knees and pray and offer praise before his God. He continued to do that, just as he had been doing before this" (Daniel 6:10).

The Magi had been instructed by King Herod to find the newborn king of the Jews and report his whereabouts to the king (Matthew 2). The Magi defied this direct order from a king "since they had been warned in a dream not to return to Herod, they went back to their own country by another route" (Matthew 2:12).

Jesus obeyed and respected his religious and political leaders. But he also resisted them when they tried exercising authority over him they didn't have. When Jesus was accused by the chief priests and elders, he didn't say anything to them (Matthew 27:12). Jesus didn't answer one word of Governor Pilate's questions (Matthew 27:14). Jesus refused to answer King Herod's questions or perform any miracles for him (Luke 23:8-12).

Peter and John were arrested and put in prison for "proclaiming the resurrection from the dead in connection with Jesus" (Acts 4:2). After they were released, Peter and John were commanded not "to speak or teach at all in the name of Jesus" (Acts 4:18). But Peter and John answered them, "Decide whether it is right in the sight of God to listen to you rather than to God. For we cannot stop speaking about what we have seen and heard" (Acts 4:19, 20). The apostles were willing to go to jail rather than close the new Christian Church.

The apostles were again arrested for continually disobeying the authorities because they refused to stop preaching and healing in the name of Jesus (Acts 5). The apostles were accused of defying the strict orders they had been given. Peter and the other apostles replied, "We must obey God rather than man" (Acts 5:29). They put God's first table of the Law of obeying their heavenly authority above the second table of the Law of obeying their earthly authorities.

God's people obey the Lord's commands, even if earthly authorities forbid it. God's people abstain from what the Lord forbids, even if earthly authorities command it.

Acts 5:29 is a call to oppose no mere human authority but human authority that is opposed to God. Human authority that is aligned with the powers and principalities in the heavenly realms. It is the beastly human authority that has sided with the seven-headed dragon. To disobey then becomes an obligation, even when that disobedience is more indirect – as a natural result of obeying God's law, rather than the direct disobedience of an unjust government edict. "We must disobey."

Paul and Silas were imprisoned for disturbing certain people in Philippi (Acts 16). Preaching God's Word with conviction will always be disturbing to the allies of Satan. We see often in the book of Acts how the apostles defied earthly authorities and kept proclaiming salvation through Jesus in the face of opposition. It would have been much more peaceful for everyone involved if they would have been less bold in their delivery of God's message. But God's message demands clarity and boldness. That will very likely mean disturbing the peace – but this disturbance is a consequence of the message, properly divided and rightly declared.

When Paul was in custody, Governor Festus wanted to transfer Paul's trial to Jerusalem (Acts 25). Paul resisted the governor and refused a trial in Jerusalem. Instead, he appealed to a superior magistrate: "I appeal to Caesar!"

And sometimes resistance isn't directly disobeying an edict or law; sometimes resistance isn't the natural result of confessing the faith; sometimes resistance is just saying "No" to someone in authority.

Naboth refused to sell his family vineyard to King Ahab (1 Kings 21). The king did not declare eminent domain to take the land by law; he made a fair offer to purchase or trade for Naboth's vineyard. But Naboth didn't want to part with his ancestral lands. So he said "No" to the king.

Daniel decided he would not defile himself by eating the king's special food or drink (Daniel 1). He said "No" to the king's diet and consumed only vegetables and water.

Jesus reacted with bemusement to his mother Mary's hint to do something for the wedding couple who had run out of wine in Cana. He said, "Woman, what does that have to do with you and me? My time has not come yet" (John 2:4). Jesus' answer was a little cryptic, but it certainly carried a sense of "No." Jesus was respectful, yet he made it clear: Even though Mary was his mother, she could not direct his ministry. That was not her right. That right belongs only to his heavenly Father. Jesus was not breaking the 4th Commandment by disobeying his mother, because Mary could not exercise authority that did not belong to her.

I'm confident there are more examples in sacred history, but these give some background of God's people who have found it necessary at various times to resist those in authority over them.

St. Paul warns us against rebelling against governing authorities. "Therefore the one who rebels against the authority is opposing God's institution, and those who oppose will bring judgment on themselves" (Romans 13:2). Rebellion is trying to overturn the authorities God has established. That's quite different from resistance. Resistance is holding the governing authorities accountable to the laws of the nation that govern them. It is also holding them accountable to the God who gave them their ruling authority.

The government's main responsibilities are to protect its citizens and protect its citizens' civil rights. But when the government goes beyond its boundaries, it is now breaking the laws that govern the government. Sometimes intentional civil disobedience against one branch of government may be the only way to appeal to another branch of government.

Examples of resistance in secular history

Let's examine a few examples in secular history of citizens resisting – but not rebelling against – their governing authorities.

In the Magdeburg Confession, the pastors listed a few examples from secular history. They mention how the Maccabees resisted King Antiochus when he desired to make a single common religion of all the nations in his empire (1 Maccabees 2). The Magdeburg Confession uses two other examples from secular history. "Emperor Constantine took up arms for the defense of Christians against Licinius his co-emperor." And "emperor Trajan ... when he appointed a Master of the Horse for himself, he handed a sword to him saying, "Use this sword against my enemies, if I give righteous commands; but if I give unrighteous commands, use it against me."[56]

American colonists were outraged with the British government's Tea Act of 1773, which was designed to help the struggling East India Company by giving it essentially a monopoly on selling tea in the American colonies. Colonists protested the Tea Act by dumping tea bricks from ships into the Boston harbor. This act of protest led to the colonists boycotting British tea as a beverage. This famous act of civil disobedience eventually led to the American colonies seeking their freedom from British tyranny through the American Revolution.

Perhaps the largest act of nonviolent civil disobedience in history was the Salt March of 1930. It was led by Mahatma Gandhi in India, which was then under British rule. Britain's Salt Act of 1882 prohibited Indian citizens from collecting or selling sea salt, which was a staple of their diet. Instead, Indian citizens were forced to purchase salt from their British rulers who not only had a monopoly on the manufacture and sale of salt, but also charged exorbitant taxes on the salt.

After 170 years of Parliamentary discussion and opposition to

[56] *The Magdeburg Confession*, p. 72

the Indian salt tax (in all its various forms), and 40 years of his own public opposition in writing – Gandhi did not promote open rebellion. Rather, he led a peaceful march to the sea where the Indian people wouldn't have to purchase salt from the British East India Company.

Mahatma Gandhi used the Salt Act to unify Indian citizens to work toward independence from British rule. Gandhi led the 241-mile Salt March from his ashram, or religious retreat, near Ahmedabad to the Arabian Sea coast. Gandhi and his supporters meant to defy the British Salt Act by making salt from seawater.

As Gandhi marched west, he addressed large crowds all along the way. Each day more Indian citizens joined in the march toward the Arabian Sea. Gandhi and over 50,000 of his followers were arrested – but this non-violent act of civil disobedience was an important milestone leading to India being granted its independence in 1947.

One of the most famous examples of American civil disobedience began on December 1, 1955. Rosa Parks, an African American woman, boarded a bus in Montgomery, Alabama. African Americans were designated to sit in the back of the bus. Rosa sat in the front. When the bus started to fill up with white passengers, the bus driver asked Parks to move to the back of the bus. She refused. Her resistance began one of the largest changes of society in American history.

Parks's resistance didn't end there. She then helped organize and plan the Montgomery Bus Boycott. African American leaders across Montgomery followed Parks's lead and began to support the cause of protesting. For the next year, from December 5, 1955 to December 20, 1956, approximately 40,000 African Americans refused to travel on Montgomery buses. Instead, they walked, carpooled, or took taxis. The protests eventually led to the integration of the bus system, both in hiring Black bus drivers and instituting a first-come first-seated policy for passengers.

Five African-American women sued the city of Montgomery in the U.S. District Court. They were suing to have segregation laws declared illegal. In fact, in December of 1956, the U.S. Supreme

Court did declare the segregation laws in Alabama to be unconstitutional. These acts of civil disobedience led to Martin Luther King, Jr. and the civil rights movement that changed much of the American landscape for African American citizens.

One of my favorite examples of civil disobedience was the Rosenstrasse (Rose Street) protest in Berlin. In the 1940s, the Gestapo were arresting and deporting Jews from Germany. Some of the last Jews to be deported were those in "mixed-marriages" – Jewish men married to German women.

On February 27, 1943, the Gestapo began a massive action to arrest and deport the last of the remaining Jews from Berlin to labor camps or Auschwitz. Jewish men married to German women were arrested and taken to a welfare office located on Rosenstrasse in central Berlin.

When family members – especially the German wives – heard the news of the arrests, they rushed to Rosenstrasse. The small group grew to a predominantly-female crowd of 6,000+ protestors. The Nazis demanded they disperse, threatening them with gunfire. But the protestors remained yelling, chanting, and sometimes just standing silently in solidarity. News of the demonstration spread quickly through Germany and even to the international press.

The Nazis feared more protests throughout the country and were afraid of international attention that might hinder their cause.. German propaganda minister Joseph Goebbels ordered the release of the prisoners at Rosenstrasse on March 6, 1943. Goebbels even returned a group of 35 previously-deported Jewish men who were married to German women.

The German women stood strong in the face of grave danger to save the lives of their husbands. They sent a strong message of public dissent to Nazi authorities. It shows what good can be achieved when people stand up in the face of great evil.

Adolf Hitler was a bully and an evil tyrant. There were numerous assassination attempts on Hitler's life, none of them successful. But these German women stood up to the bully of Nazi Germany and he backed down.

That also begs the question: What would have happened if German people had spoken up and stood up sooner when they saw their Jewish neighbors being rounded up and deported? What would have happened if the Garrison Church of Potsdam, and other Lutheran churches in Germany, had resisted the Nazi zeitgeist? How many millions would have survived if the baptized Germans had collectively, peacefully resisted the ungodly tyranny of Chancellor Hitler? After all, "baptized Germans" made up 95% of the German population.

I am the pastor of a church in the Wisconsin Evangelical Lutheran Synod (WELS). We've examined how Martin Luther and other Lutheran pastors resisted the government in the 16th century. We have seen examples of peaceful resistance from the past century. I'll share one example of resistance by Lutherans to an overreach of governing authorities.

The Bennett Law was a controversial state law passed in Wisconsin in 1889. The Bennett Law, passed by a Republican state legislature, required the use of English to teach subjects in all public and private elementary and high schools. It was meant to strike at the German language used predominantly in Catholic and Lutheran parochial schools. The Bennett Law also stated that students could only attend schools within their own school districts. This caused a problem for parochial schools which often drew students from several districts. The Bennett Law also did not recognize the Christian calendar used by Catholics and Lutherans. This would make the celebration of sacred holy days during the week nearly impossible.

The Bennett Law would have hampered WELS parochial schools and could have closed many of the church-run schools. Wisconsin Synod Lutherans strongly resisted the Bennett Law. Lutherans campaigned against the Republicans and for the Democrats. The Wisconsin Synod even created a committee to study the Bennett Law and its effects on WELS churches and schools. The committee listed twelve reasons stating why the Bennett Law was hostile to their schools. The Synod then published a statement: "We are ever willing to pay our taxes for the support of the public schools. ... But we insist upon enjoying the privilege of founding private schools with our own means of regulating and governing them, without external interference, according to our conviction."[57]

In February 1890, nineteen Wisconsin and Lutheran Church Missouri Synod (LC-MS) congregations in Milwaukee passed a joint resolution which denounced the Bennett Law and pledged to support only those candidates who promised its repeal. The Wisconsin Synod publication, the *Gemeindeblatt*, urged pastors to "watch their local papers so that they may continue to fight the enemy publicly where necessary." The synod committee volunteered to help such pastors wherever they needed it.[58]

The next election was an overwhelming defeat for the Republicans with some Wisconsin Synod towns voting as high as 96.8% Democrat. The Republicans were buried by what Democratic Party members termed "the Lutheran landslide."[59] The resistance to the Bennett Law was felt swiftly. The law was repealed. Republicans lost the governorship and the legislature, handing huge wins to the Democrat party.

This is an example where Lutherans did not only passively resist. They actively resisted the Bennett Law. They actively and publicly campaigned – not only as individual Christians – but as pastors, churches, a church body, and with other member synods of the Synodical Conference against a law they felt was harmful to their ministry.

Do times of civil disobedience only become acceptable after we have looked at them through the lens of history and approved of them? Is civil disobedience only proper when our favorite cable news program tells us that we ought to be upset? Or, is it possible that we also put our emotions and preconceived notions on pause, that we might wisely consider – even approve – similar acts of civil

---

57 Gurgel, Stephen Scott. "The War to End All Germans: Wisconsin Synod Lutherans and the First World War." M.A. thesis, University of Wisconsin-Milwaukee, 2012. p. 1

58 Ibid. p. 2

59 Ibid. p. 1

disobedience, out of love for Lord and neighbor?

America protects and encourages resistance

It is vital to know that in America, resistance is not only accepted, but also encouraged. It is encouraged by our nation's founding fathers and in our nation's founding documents. Resistance is protected and promoted as the grassroots manner by which social change is either stymied or effected, as (e.g.) Justice Scalia noted in his *Obergefell* dissent:

> Until the courts put a stop to it, public debate over same-sex marriage displayed American democracy at its best. Individuals on both sides of the issue passionately, but respectfully, attempted to persuade their fellow citizens to accept their views. Americans considered the arguments and put the question to a vote.[60]

John Knox was a Scottish minister, theologian, and writer. He was a leader in Scotland's Reformation. He was also the founder of the Presbyterian Church of Scotland. In 1564, Knox wrote about resistance, "To resist tyranny is not to resist God, nor yet his ordinance."

Knox's quotation is echoed by two of America's greatest founding fathers. Both Benjamin Franklin and Thomas Jefferson embraced this motto: "Rebellion against tyrants is obedience to God." Franklin thought so highly of this motto that he desired this phrase to be around America's Great Seal, with the seal picturing the Exodus where the people confronted a tyrant to gain their freedom. Jefferson liked the phrase so much he used it on his own personal seal.

As stated previously, there is a difference between resistance and rebellion. Resistance is allowed – especially in America. In that regard, Rev. John Knox likely had a better understanding of the Christian citizen's responsibilities than the atheist Franklin or humanist Jefferson.

---

60 *Obergefell v. Hodges,* accessed at Supremecourt.gov/opinions

God calls for us to submit to his governing authorities. Here in the United States of America, we submit to governing authorities who were wise enough to put checks and balances in place to restrain the powers of the government. One of those checks on the government is the call for resistance.

The difference between rebellion and resistance

There is a difference between rebellion and resistance. There are countless examples of resistance throughout history. Cubans marching in the streets to protest their communist Cuban government, citizens of Australia protesting lockdowns, while citizens of France publicly burn vaccine passports as a show of solidarity with those who refuse Covid vaccination. In Alberta, Canada, unvaccinated people cannot eat inside restaurants – so both vaccinated and unvaccinated people bring picnic lunches and blankets to picnic in the streets, protesting the restaurants' enforcement of the Alberta government's discriminatory laws. Dutch, Italian, and other European farmers protest against restrictive green policies. Front line workers in hospitals, fire departments, police departments, and more, are demonstrating against mandatory vaccine policies for their workplaces. Parents and students are speaking out at school board meetings protesting the teaching of critical race theory, Marxism, gender theory, and mandating of masks in the classroom.

The citizens are not rebelling. They are not trying to overthrow the government. That would be wrong and sinful. They are protesting and resisting the government for the purpose of changing it. If it is out of love for their family and the welfare of their nation, as Christian citizens, they can have proper sanctified motivation. They aren't sinning.

We hold parents accountable if they aren't following God's will. We hold companies accountable if they are doing something dangerous. We hold pastors accountable if they commit a public sin that could disqualify them from the ministry.

We must also hold governing authorities accountable. We can go to the polls. We can write letters. We can make our voices heard. But what if those things aren't working? It is easy for letters and phone calls to be ignored. It is convenient to drown out voices with other interest groups who have louder voices and larger coffers.

Then the only thing left to citizens may be to simply say "no."

Disbelieving compliance – that is, outward compliance while inwardly unconvinced – takes the lid off the pressure cooker of change. Civil disobedience, on the other hand, compels the authorities to expose their tyranny to the masses. We need to hold them accountable.

Yes, there is risk involved. Too often we find ourselves risk averse. But imagine what happens if everyone remains quiet, keeps their heads down and toes an amoral line. The blessings of freedom are lost when citizens don't provoke public debate. Even more importantly, the proclamation of the gospel is hindered when Christians neglect their duty to shrewdly consider how their confession in deed can best support their confession of word.

Christian citizens must continually ask themselves whether the laws, mandates or orders that are being given to follow are, in themselves, legal laws, mandates, or orders. It is much easier to adopt our quietism and obey the governing authorities. If the laws, mandates or orders are later found to be unconstitutional, unlawful, and illegal, does that mean those who encouraged and enforced those laws and mandates are complicit in promoting what is illegal and unlawful?

When citizens are quiet and don't challenge laws or mandates or orders they consider to be immoral or unlawful, then we do a disservice: A disservice to ourselves, disservice to our fellow citizens, and a disservice to our governing authorities because we are not holding them accountable.

What about Romans 13? The Magdeburg Confession, modern secular history, and Christian history demonstrate that Christian quietism is a disservice to our God. He wants his governing authorities to properly submit to the other governing authorities within our American system of law.

What to do?

When we feel injustices in our own lives and see injustices in the lives of others, what do we do?

- Become bitter and silent?
- Mumble to ourselves?
- Grumble to our family?
- Complain to anyone who will listen?
- Comfort ourselves with our favorite talking head?

And what, then, of the 8th commandment where God commands, "You shall not give false testimony against your neighbor." Martin Luther explains the commandment this way: "We should fear and love God that we do not tell lies about our neighbor, betray him, or give him a bad name, but defend him, speak well of him, and take his words and actions in the kindest possible way." Shall we be too timid to defend our neighbor ... too timid to speak well (where possible) of those who oppose us ... too timid to exercise Christian resistance, after measured investigation and brotherly discussion?

Wouldn't it be better if when we felt and saw these injustices we exposed them, spoke out about them, and worked to curb and correct them? Or at the very least – bring injustice to light? Sometimes the only way to do that is through civil disobedience.

"Acquitting a guilty person and convicting an innocent person – both of these are disgusting to the Lord" (Proverbs 17:15). We are called upon to oppose evil. We cannot avert our eyes and turn our backs on that evil because it is being performed by government officials. When we see evil and harm being perpetrated upon citizens by a government, we dare never excuse that evil and harm as right and godly. God finds these evils as repulsive and disgusting to his eyes. Therefore, they should be disgusting and repulsive before our eyes. To say nothing is to do nothing. Silent acquiescence is still acquiescence. Dietrich Bonhoeffer summarized it well: "Silence in the face of evil is itself evil: God will not hold us guiltless. Not to speak is to speak. Not to act is to act." St. Paul also stated, "Love does not delight in evil but rejoices with the truth" (1 Corinthians 13:6).

America belongs to the citizens – not to the government. Therefore, all citizens have the right to protect what they have earned by hard work and been given by God's grace. As Christians, we also have the right to protect our neighbors' possessions and personal freedoms as granted to them in God's 7th, 9th, and 10th commandments.

As citizens, we need to be vigilant of governing authorities transferring more power to themselves. Authority and power are two different things. A government or politician may have the authority to do something, but not the power to do something. They may also have the power to do something, but they haven't been given the proper authority to do that thing.

The more power governing authorities claim for themselves, the more dangerous the threat that they become the beast out of the sea. Just as governing authorities are a curb to keep its citizens from sinning and allying themselves with the devil, so also citizens are a curb to the governing authorities to keep them from allying themselves with the devil.

All wrongdoing is sin. Our vocation as Christians is to call out sin and to call to repentance. That doesn't stop when someone becomes a government authority. We stand up for what is good, right, and true. We need to be willing to call our neighbors to repentance and exhort them to behave themselves. That call to repentance doesn't cease once our neighbor is elected as a government official. We still need to tell them to behave themselves. We teach them not to abuse the trust and respect the citizens are entrusting to them.

American citizens are to hold their governing authorities accountable. When citizens remain silent and absent, then they are not doing their jobs. They are avoiding their vocation as citizens.

Our American government has restrictions on what it can and cannot do. When citizens resist, they are often reminding the government of its own self-imposed restrictions. The government may have the power to do something or withhold something. That does not mean they have the constitutional authority to do so.

The First Amendment states: "Congress shall make no law respecting an establishment of religion, or prohibiting the free exercise thereof; or abridging the freedom of speech, or of the press; or the right of the people peaceably to assemble, and to petition the Government for a redress of grievances."

The First Amendment grants freedom of speech, freedom of assembly, freedom of the press, freedom of association, and freedom of religion. This allows American citizens the great privilege and right to worship and speak freely. We take these rights and freedoms extremely seriously.

Yet, in 2020 we saw state and local governments call for the closure of churches during the Covid-19 pandemic. Most churches willingly complied. However, there were churches that defied government's orders and remained open. Those churches were vilified in the press and, in some cases, levied huge fines by their governments. A Lutheran church in West Bend, WI had its worship service stopped by the local police department.

The cases of those churches who were fined were brought before the state and federal Supreme Courts. The U.S. Supreme Court ruled in favor of the churches. The local and state governments needed to allow churches to remain open. That is their guaranteed First Amendment rights.

Personally, if governing authorities tell churches to go virtual again, I will resist. Understand, I'm not speaking for my congregation or my church body. Personally, I will not shut down church services again. Church leaders – synod-wide or individual congregations – can decide differently. But for myself, from now on, as long as I am called to be a pastor of a church, I will be there for worship services. Or I'll have worship services in my house or in my yard, much like the early Christians did with their house churches. I desire to say with the apostles, "Decide whether it is right in the sight of God to listen to you rather than to God. For we cannot stop speaking about what we have seen and heard" (Acts 4:19, 20). The apostles were willing to go to jail rather than close the new Christian Church. Personally, I will not allow the government to deem the Christian Church "non-essential" during the next emergency. I hope and pray that as Christians in America we do not return to a time where the Church so willingly accepts the judgments of authorities who deem her ministries as "not essential" and can be closed for a time.

During times of persecution, some will flee and others will stay. Some will fight and others will hide. We cannot judge others' sanctified actions and decisions. Christians will do what is best for them and their families - all to the glory of God. Who are we to judge another's sanctification (Matthew 7:1)? I can only speak for my words and actions.

Tyranny doesn't always start with tyrannical terror. Tyranny is often a difference of degree – but not of kind. Tyranny happens when one authority goes beyond its ordained limits to impose its will, often transgressing moral, ethical, and Scriptural guidelines.

Churches that succumb to tyranny won't die with a bang. They'll atrophy with a whimper.

The civic duty to hold the government accountable

The government has certain business to do. As citizens, we have put people in place to carry out that business. So as citizens, we then need to be willing and able to tell the government, "Mind your own business."

As American citizens we are allowed to resist our government. If we must submit to our government without question, then we would have no recourse when the state is prosecuting us. But we can appeal a traffic ticket. We can mount a defense if we are falsely accused by a state-appointed prosecutor. That's in line with the 8th Commandment. We can appeal to the Fifth Amendment if the government attempts to take our property by eminent domain. That's also in line with the 10th commandment. In all these ways we are submitting to the governing authorities, while at the same time holding those same authorities accountable for being wrong – in our opinion – and resisting them.

Citizens actively resist all the time. If taxes are too high in a city or state, citizens move to a city or state with lower taxes. If a town requires people to wear a mask to eat in that city's restaurants, people may freely drive to the next town over to eat lunch. If a local government requires people to show a vaccine passport to attend a concert in their city, people may gladly stay home and play board games with their family while listening to that same band on the music app on their phone. If a public-school board is teaching CRT in their classrooms, parents may sign petitions to recall the school board members, speak at school board meetings, and ultimately pull their children out of that school.

Citizens often use every legal means possible to file for exemptions, protest, even hold the government accountable to their own laws by hiring a lawyer. All these are acts of civil disobedience and resistance that are wonderfully permitted - and protected - by the American Constitution.

Yet for the past two years, American citizens have been denounced for questioning, debating, doubting, or resisting our local, state, and national governing authorities. The exact opposite is true. It is our Christian and civic duty to hold our governing leaders accountable. We do them a disservice when we don't know our U.S. Constitution or State Constitution and fail to hold our governing authorities to the laws that govern them.

The Wisconsin Governor Tony Evers enacted emergency authority to mandate masks across the state. He had the executive authority to enact such extraordinary emergency powers. But he only had that authority for 60 days. Still, Governor Evers kept extending his emergency authority.

I was asked numerous times by various people why I wasn't following Governor Ever's mask mandate. I told them that the emergency mandate was unconstitutional. They invariably replied that we should follow it until the Wisconsin Supreme Court decides whether it's constitutional or unconstitutional. I shared the same example with them every time. I said, "If a guy breaks into my house, he isn't a robber when he's put on trial and convicted. He's a robber the moment he breaks into my house. The governor isn't unconstitutional when the court finds his mandate unconstitutional. It's unconstitutional on day 61."

Wisconsin Supreme Court Judge Hagedorn said exactly that when he delivered the majority opinion when the case against the governor's mandate was brought to trial.

> "Over the last year, a dangerous new virus has spread throughout the world, disrupted our economy, and taken far too many lives. In response, Governor Tony Evers declared multiple states of emergency under Wis. No. 2020AP1718-OA 2 Stat. § 323.10 (2019-20),1 triggering a statutory grant of extraordinary powers to the governor and the Department of Health Services (DHS) to combat the emergent threat. The question in this case is not whether the Governor acted wisely; it is whether he acted lawfully. We conclude he did not.
>
> "Wisconsin Stat. § 323.10 specifies that no state of emergency may last longer than 60 days unless it "is extended by joint resolution of the legislature," and that the legislature may cut short a state of emergency by joint resolution. The statute contemplates that the power to end and to refuse to extend a state of emergency resides with the legislature even when the underlying occurrence creating the emergency remains a threat. Pursuant to this straightforward statutory language, the governor may not deploy his emergency powers by issuing new states of emergency for the same statutory occurrence." [61]

Judge Hagedorn noted that Evers had unconstitutionally – and therefore unlawfully, and thus illegally – expanded the governor's executive powers over the pandemic. The legislature has the authority to grant or shorten the governor's emergency authority. But the governor has no authority to do so on his own.

It is our civic duty to know the laws that govern our city, state, and nation. It is our civic duty to hold our governing authorities accountable when they are breaking the laws that are over them. It

---

[61] Supreme Court of Wisconsin. Case No. 2020AP1718-OA

is also our civic duty to not comply with illegal, unlawful, and unconstitutional laws, mandates, or edicts.

When a citizen does something illegal and unlawful, he is prosecuted. What will happen to our governing officials - a mayor, a governor, a president - who enforced mandates that were deemed by the courts to be unconstitutional, and therefore illegal and unlawful? How complicit are any of us if we in any way enforced or encouraged an illegal and unlawful mandate?

And as pastors, how might we have dissuaded public debate from our people because of a simplistic and cursory understanding of Romans 13 – to say nothing of ignorance about the doctrine and historic practice of resistance?

Who will stand up to the beast?

The United States of America was built upon the foundation of being able to criticize one's leaders and hold them accountable. That does not nor cannot happen in countries ruled by communists or dictators. Together we can learn from our mistakes and make better decisions moving forward – but not unless we have honest reflections upon our leader's actions or inactions.

We cannot wait for unbelievers to stand up to the government. They are the ones who are prophesied to worship the government. "All those who make their home on the earth will worship the beast—those whose names have not been written from the beginning of the world in the Book of Life, which belongs to the Lamb that was slain" (Revelation 13:8).

Blind obedience is a windfall to government oppression. It allows for even greater oppression. Christians may complain when a government becomes oppressive. But if they loudly complain, without quietly resisting, the government has freedom to do whatever it pleases. When there's no pushback from the populace, the government will continue to push its anti-Christian influence. It's been done throughout the history of governments and will continue to be done until Christ comes again. That's the nature of the Revelation 13 beast, who even *(as seen in German history)* makes use of a simplistic Romans 13 door.

America is unique. The governed allow the government to govern them. The government is by the people and for the people. American citizens were given liberties under the U.S. Constitution. When the government opposes the people and begins to strip away those liberties, it is doing a disservice to the people it was created to serve. And we Christians are commanded to love our neighbor, to support them when they are suffering, and to be willing to lay down our lives for them, if necessary.

What happens if we see the government becoming oppressive and we do nothing? If we hide in our homes, binging on Netflix and Doritos, are we really following Christ's command to lay down our lives for our neighbor?

In America we are obedient to the protection of liberty; nor are we subservient to the government that restricts liberty. We submit to the governing authorities when they submit to God's authority. We resist the governing authorities when they are submitting to Satan's authority.

Nowhere does the Bible obligate Christians to simply comply with evil. Otherwise, Rahab would have been obligated to expose the spies rather than tell her government, "They went that way," when in fact they went the other way (Joshua 2). Her faith combined with action was rewarded with the special privilege of being called a "hero of faith" in the Book of Hebrews (Hebrews 11:31) and of being listed in the genealogy of Jesus (Matthew 1:5).

It is said often today that pastors should not speak about issues involving the government for fear of becoming too political. Martin Luther disagreed. He said that pastors should have something to say to the government: "Pastors should serve as the club that lays next to the dog." The dog in this analogy is the government. Pastors have the responsibility and voice to say something to the people who are citizens of a government, just as they have the responsibility and voice to say something to the people who make up the government.

We have created a false dichotomy of the separation of church and state in America. There is no separation of church and state in Scripture. St. Paul spoke to King Agrippa. Joseph advised Pharaoh.

Daniel advised King Nebuchadnezzar and King Darius. Moses confronted Egypt's Pharaoh. Elijah confronted King Ahab. The prophets Jeremiah and Isaiah confronted their kings. Nathan called King David to repentance. John the Baptist called out King Herod's infidelity. Pastors have a right and a duty to advise and call out government officials, exercising law and gospel proclamation. That's not being political. That's being scriptural.

One of my favorite sayings is, "We need a little courage now, or we'll need a lot of courage later." If our courage is lacking today, then how much courage will our children need?

Resistance is not futile

Some last thoughts on encouraging or limiting resistance, and understanding that resistance is not futile.

When citizens are resisting, Christians (and others) should examine governing authorities to make sure that the laws and mandates are not overstepping constitutional authority; moreover, what is being imposed ought not be immoral or illogical. We want to give our brothers and sisters in Christ the benefit of the doubt, be careful to judge their actions and motives, and always keep the 8th commandment of taking their words and actions in the kindest possible way.

A true difficulty with resistance is our sinful nature. It will always want more. It will always push back. It doesn't like being told what to do. So, if you are considering resisting, you need to examine why you're resisting. Is it your sinful nature that wants to resist to protect what you enjoy, wanting to find an excuse and stick it to those on the other side? Or is it your sanctified spirit that moves your resistance, to protect what you and others have been granted by God?

It is in our nature to have a self-serving attitude. As we look at resistance, we cannot resist to serve ourselves. Yet, is our resistance based on our service and protection of others?

The danger of resisting needs to be debated alongside the danger of not resisting. We need to curb our sinful nature. But by resisting we may also help governing authorities to curb their sinful natures (as they are clamoring for more power) by saying "No" to them. When we consider the nature of resistance, it cannot be about what is best for me. That's looking for a position of our own power, much the way James and John did in asking for position on Jesus' left and right in his kingdom (Mark 10). Rather, when we consider resistance, we must consider what is best for our family, our community, our morals, and our Christian faith.

Resistance is not about what I want or don't want to do as an individual. It is about protecting the rights of others. It is about advancing God's Kingdom with the proclamation of his gospel.

Doing what is best for me is idolatry. It is the way of the world. It is the path to destruction. But allowing governing authorities to have absolute power can lead them to idolatry. It can lead them to become the beast out of the sea that demands worship by its followers.

What happens so often when governing authorities seize power is that they become tyrannical and brutal. That's what happened to Jafar in *Aladdin*. At the end of the movie, the king's vizier, Jafar uses his third wish. He receives phenomenal, cosmic power at his command. He seizes control of the cosmos and declares himself ruler of the universe. Thankfully, this doesn't last long. Aladdin points out that the power of a genie comes with a price as he traps Jafar into a black genie's lamp, "Phenomenal, cosmic powers ... itty bitty living space." It is in the sinful nature of governing authorities to use their power to become powerful in this world. They need to remember that they are serving God, whose powers are greater than phenomenal and cosmic. God has the right to punish them for abusing the power he allowed them to have.

We must not be looking to wear crowns or sit on thrones. Resisting is not about power, glory, exalting or exulting. It is rather about restraining power, protecting God's glory, and having the freedom to exalt and exult Christ.

We resist knowing full well this resistance may result in weakness and humility, suffering and affliction.

This is always a difficult dichotomy. Martin Luther echoes Jesus in Mark 10 when he taught, "A Christian is a perfectly free lord of all, subject to none." But he also taught, "A Christian is a perfectly dutiful servant of all, subject to all."

May God bless us with the wisdom and sanctified spirit to submit to our governing authorities when they are submitting to the Lord as his established servants. May God also bless us with the wisdom and sanctified spirit to resist our governing authorities when they are submitting to the dragon as the beast out of the sea. May God use his governing authorities to curb our sinful nature. May God use us to curb the sinful nature of governing authorities.

Above all, may God grant us a spirit of peace and brotherly love, that we may wrestle with these difficult topics for the purpose of gospel proclamation today – and the freedom to proclaim that gospel tomorrow.

Spiritual warfare

"Winter is coming" is the motto of the House of Stark, in the HBO series *Game of Thrones*. [62] The Starks are the lords of the North. Their motto literally means what it says – winter is coming. The land of Westeros where the Starks rule can have very long periods of summer and winter that can switch suddenly.

As their family motto, "Winter is coming" means for the Starks that they need to be constantly vigilant. As rulers of the North, they need to be prepared for anything to happen – the Lanisters, dragons, or White Walkers. Something could happen ... and eventually will.

According to the Emmy winning novelist and scriptwriter of *Game of Thrones*, George R.R. Martin, "'Winter is coming" also expresses the sentiment that there are always dark periods in each of our lives, and even if things are good now – "summer," we must always be ready for a dark period where events turn against us – "winter.'"

Winter is coming for us as Christians in America. For decades we have enjoyed religious freedom and relative peace to share the gospel of Jesus Christ. But it appears as if the "summer" of easily and freely sharing that gospel is quickly coming to an end. The warfare of winter is coming. It's already here.

Heaven's war brought to earth

The war began in heaven. St. John writes: "There was war in heaven. Michael and his angels fought against the dragon, and the dragon and his angels fought back. But he was not strong enough, and they lost their place in heaven. The great dragon was hurled down-- that ancient serpent called the devil, or Satan, who leads the whole world astray. He was hurled to the earth, and his angels with him" (Revelation 12:7-9).

---

[62] Game of Thrones is a big-budget fantasy series depicting brutal battles, graphic violence, sexuality and foul language. Other than that, it's a good series ... except for the ending.

The Lord kicked Satan out of heaven. God called upon St. Michael and his fellow angels to be his enforcers. The devil became a trespasser on God's property, and the holy angels were the military force who made sure he left. Satan is pictured as a dragon, the ancient serpent (Genesis 3:1). The dragon and his angelic allies did not want to go quietly. It became necessary to boot them out by force. So there was war in heaven, a titanic struggle between the hosts of heaven and the hosts of hell. Jesus witnessed their demise: "I saw Satan fall like lightning from heaven" (Luke 10:18).

The great news for us is that St. Michael and his angelic army are more powerful than Satan and his angelic allies. The bad news for us is that that spiritual war in the heavenly realms has been brought to earth. "He was hurled to the earth, and his angels with him. ... Woe to the earth and the sea, because the devil has gone down to you! He is filled with fury, because he knows that his time is short" (Revelation 12:9, 12).

Satan is filled with furious rage against God. He knows he has a limited time before Judgment Day ends all his wicked activity forever. So he is busy, attacking ferociously like a dragon. We see Satan attacking us in our nation in various means and ways - and many of these ways are visible, tangible transgressions of the natural knowledge of God. Satan certainly attacks the revealed Word of God (and our confidence in it!), but in this war ... he doesn't have to.

Satan's attacks take on various forms, such as:

- Coaxing the tearing apart God's design of marriage between a man and a woman with laws permitting homosexual marriage;
- Goading our government to subsidize the legalized murder of unborn children in the wombs of their mothers;
- Urging on atheists and unbelievers to verbally abuse Christians.

No doubt you could name more ways that the great Dragon incites the world to attack Christians and Christian belief. But these external, obvious attacks aren't his only tactic. Satan snickers as citizens segregate themselves into various groups and classes based on their skin color or vaccine status. He screams with delight as universities, corporations, and government entities celebrate modern gnosticism – transgender ideology – while at the same time castigating anyone who speaks out against body mutilation. He snorts with glee as Christians willingly close the doors of their churches. After all, he's been trying to do this for centuries!

Satan may have been kicked out of heaven, but he is alive and well here on earth, in our nation, in our lives, always pursuing the offspring of the Church. Satan's end game – whether it is a full-frontal attack, or slight irritations, or appearing as an angel of light – is the same. His single, solitary goal is to distract the citizens of this world from Jesus Christ and the salvation he won in the world to come.

Satan is a furious dragon who works to steal you and your children away from the Good Shepherd. He wants to devour you like a lion consuming his prey. His ploys may send a shiver down your back to terrify you or up your leg to seduce you.

There is an ongoing war in our society. It is a culture war for the hearts and minds – and souls – of our young people. We are in a war against those who want to destroy the Christian faith, those who are acting in allegiance with the father of lies.

If you pay attention to certain media outlets, you will hear pundits claiming that Christians are the aggressors in this culture war. But this portrayal is absurd. Every influential platform in our culture belongs to those who oppose a Christian worldview – the media, big business, academia, Hollywood, and more. This should not be a surprise, since Christ's Church has been called out of darkness, living IN this world yet not OF it. But, dear friend: The culture around us has never been neutral. It is not neutral, nor will it ever be neutral. The culture does the bidding of Satan, as he carries out his warfare against the Bride of Christ.

Christians are certainly not the aggressors in this culture war ... to our great shame. We should be the aggressors. When Jesus said that the gates of hell cannot stand against his Church – that is a clear statement of fact, a declaration of spiritual reality. It is a call for Christians to be confident in the clear Word of God, and to apply this Word in our lives even as we declare its truth to a culture that purposely ignores it. For far too long, Christians have fought a defensive war. And we've fought it poorly. We've been lackadaisical, indifferent, apathetic – even pathetic – in this war. We've laid down our weapons, silenced our mouths, and shut our Bibles.

Going on the offensive

We need to go on the offensive again. Not with the physical weapons of modern warfare, but with the ancient and time-tested weapon of the gospel:

> Finally, be strong in the Lord and in his mighty power. Put on the full armor of God, so that you can stand against the schemes of the Devil. For our struggle is not against flesh and blood, but against the rulers, against the authorities, against the world rulers of this darkness, against the spiritual forces of evil in the heavenly places. For this reason, take up the full armor of God, so that you will be able to take a stand on the evil day and, after you have done everything, to stand. Stand, then, with the belt of truth buckled around your waist, with the breastplate of righteousness fastened in place, and with the readiness that comes from the gospel of peace tied to your feet like sandals. At all times hold up the shield of faith, with which you will be able to extinguish all the flaming arrows of the Evil One. Also take the helmet of salvation and the sword of the Spirit, which is the word of God (Ephesians 6:10-17).

Christians are called to speak up in the public square and on social media platforms about good and godly things. We received this directive from St. Paul: "Finally, brothers, whatever is true, whatever is honorable, whatever is right, whatever is pure, whatever is lovely, whatever is commendable, if anything is excellent, and if anything is praiseworthy, think about these things. The things that you learned, received, heard, and saw in me: Keep doing these things. And the God of peace will be with you" (Philippians 4:8,9). We think about these things to protect them – and speak about these things to project them.

The devil is the ruler of this world (John 12:31). But we must go on the offensive to break Satan's stranglehold on our culture. Jesus wants to use his Word to bring freedom for those enslaved in sin, and hope for those deluded by temptation. It is not our goal to change the culture, but to preach Jesus Christ and him crucified into the culture.

The culture soothes the troubled minds of young ladies that they can find acceptance – or at least tolerance – by becoming transgender. The culture shouts that having compassion for women who are single and pregnant means allowing them to terminate their pregnancy. The culture screams that anyone who is not vaccinated and boosted is an uncaring person and should be segregated from society. The culture screeches that there is systemic racism in our nation, laws, and corporations, and the way to solve that is by teaching anti-racism in schools, universities, businesses, and institutions.

These are cultural issues. Sexual vices are claiming our children through Tik Tok videos. Abortion is claiming our young people through emotion over logic. Segregation is claiming people over their fear of a virus. Racism is claiming disciples under the guise of anti-racism.

These are all cultural issues. But Christians have allowed them to be hijacked and portrayed as simple political issues. These issues, first and foremost, belong in the area of the family, the home, and the church. These issues have no quick and simple answers because they deal with sin, self, and the body. Lately, Christians have remained silent on these issues because we have allowed them to drift into the area of politics – and perhaps Christians wrongly believe that they ought not comment on politics. Perhaps Christian churches believe that such "political" issues would divide a congregation, or somehow endanger the tax status of their 501(c)3.

Perhaps Christians and Christian churches believe these ideas about so-called "political" topics. And to our shame ... perhaps Christians hide behind such shallow excuses, and then parrot these shallow excuses as they assuage their consciences. Christians will sound very pious as they claim they are only preaching the gospel. Jesus and his apostles preached the gospel. But they also taught how to live the gospel in the real world. Read any of St. Paul's epistles and see how he confronted the culture head-on with the gospel. What he preached and taught was not political, it was theological. He applied theological answers to cultural questions.

It is time for us to claim these cultural issues and bring them back into the theology of the Christian Church.

These cultural issues frustrate, dishearten, and anger us. The voices that promote the evil and wickedness in our culture are legion and loud. They are waging a war on our infants, our children, our college students, our young adults, single people, parents, and senior citizens. The war is against every structure God designed for society, structures that even the nonreligious can recognize as beneficial. The devil and his demonic horde are whispering into the ears of our nation ... and they appear to be winning. Winter is sweeping over our land.

Yet, God has promised that St. Michael and his angelic army are fighting for us in the spiritual realms. All the plans of the Evil One will ultimately fail. The Word of Christ still drives out demons, and his Church will prevail against the gates of hell. And even as the demons try to destroy God's work, they will ultimately serve the will of God. God will use their antagonism to provide new opportunities for Christian witness and new blessings to his Church. Demonic shrieks, screams, and shouts cannot drown out our prayers. "The Lord is far away from the wicked, but he hears the prayer of the righteous" (Proverbs 15:29).

Pray for deliverance

We pray a difficult but timely prayer. We join with King David who wrote the words of Psalm 140. There David prayed to the Lord for deliverance from his enemies. He also prayed to the Lord with confidence that God would bring his justice upon those same enemies. David's words are strong, menacing, and powerful. We pray for God to bring the judgment on his enemies that the enemies desire for us. These are not easy words for us to pray ... but this is a battle for the souls of our children and the hearts of our nation. This is a battle the devil has every intention of winning. He will not back down. Neither can we. So we join with David in praying:

> "Keep me safe, Lord, from the evil man. Protect me from the violent man, who plans evil in his heart. Every day they gather for battle. They sharpen their tongues like a snake. The poison of vipers is under their lips. Keep me safe, Lord, from the hands of the wicked. Protect me from the violent man, who plans to trip my feet. The proud have hidden a snare for me, and ropes. They have spread out a net along my route. They have set traps for me. I say to the Lord, "You are my God." Hear, O Lord, the sound of my cry for mercy. O Lord, my Lord, the strength of my salvation, you cover my head on the day for weapons. Do not grant, O Lord, the desires of the wicked. Do not let their scheme succeed, when they rise up. May the trouble caused by their lips fall on the heads of those who surround me. Let burning coals fall on them. Cause them to fall into the fire, or into pits from which they will never rise. Do not let the slanderer be established in the land. As for the man of violence- may evil hunt him and beat him down. I know that the Lord will provide justice for the oppressed judgment for the poor. Surely the righteous will give thanks to your name. The upright will live in your presence" (Psalm 140).

Hopefully you are praying the Lord's Prayer regularly. In the Third Petition of the Lord's Prayer we pray, "Thy will be done on earth as it is in heaven." Luther taught in his explanation of the Third Petition, "God's will is done when he breaks and defeats every evil plan and purpose of the devil, the world and our sinful flesh, which try to prevent us from keeping God's name holy and letting his kingdom come."

When we pray for God's will to be done, we are equally praying that the devil's will be broken. This hurts the devil. It causes a breach in his kingdom. Therefore, he chafes and rages as a fierce enemy with all his power and might." [63]

In his Large Catechism, Martin Luther warns us: "If we would be Christians, therefore, we must surely expect and count on having the devil with all his angels and the world as our enemies [Matthew 25:41; Revelation 12:9]. They will bring every possible misfortune and grief upon us. For where God's Word is preached, accepted, or believed and produces fruit, there the holy cross cannot be missing [Acts 14:22]. And let no one think that he shall have peace [Matthew 10:34]." [64]

That's exactly what Jesus predicted: "Do you think that I came to bring peace on the earth? No, I tell you, but rather division. Yes, from now on there will be five divided in one household: three against two, and two against three. They will be divided: father against son, and son against father; mother against daughter, and daughter against mother; mother-in-law against her daughter-in-law, and daughter-in-law against her mother-in-law" (Luke 12:51-53).

What is Jesus talking about here? Didn't the Christmas angels announce that Jesus was born to bring "peace on earth" (Luke 2:14). Yes, they did! But Jesus has come to bring peace between sinful humanity and a holy God. He brings the peace of salvation in the place of destruction in hell. He brings the peace of the resurrection instead of the sorrow and finality of death. He brings

[63] *Large Catechism, Part III, The Lord's Prayer*, par. 62
[64] Ibid. par. 62

the peace of forgiveness for sins, baptismal waters that wash away guilt, and eternal joy in the midst of earthly sadness.

Jesus is the Prince of Peace – but by his standards, not the world's. And when people reject the peace he offers and grants, they will receive his judgment in its place.

The Prince of Peace calls us to war. The Prince of Peace calls us to go into battle against the Ruler of this world, and he calls us to participate in bringing his Word of peace to those trapped under demonic delusion.

Jesus is the Prince of Peace, but he and his teachings are divisive. They always have been! Let us not whimsically wish for a past that never was, when our nation was a "Christian nation." God's chosen people rejected his prophets and persecuted the apostles. They crucified the Christ because they hated Christ and his absolute, unchanging claims.

After all, Jesus is the Absolute Truth (John 14:6). People cannot handle the absolute truth of Christ. In a world filled with false ideas about "relative truth," Jesus boldly states that we must be for him or against him. "Whoever is not with me is against me, and whoever does not gather with me scatters" (Luke 11:23).

There is no love or compassion apart from the truth. "Do not just pretend to love others. Hate what is evil. Cling to what is good" (Romans 12:9).

Since we are for Jesus and his truth, that means we need to be ready for the war in our culture against Jesus and his truth.

The violence against Christians will not prevail

The ways of the devil are always violent and destructive. While John the Baptist was in prison, the people were asking Jesus about John. The ESV translates Jesus' response this way: "From the days of John the Baptist until now the kingdom of heaven has suffered violence, and the violent take it by force" (Matthew 11:12). Early Christians suffered violence for being citizens of the kingdom of heaven. "Others experienced mocking and lashes, in addition to chains and imprisonment. They were stoned; they were sawed in two; they were tempted; they were killed with the sword; they went around in sheepskins and goatskins, needy, afflicted, and mistreated" (Hebrews 11:36-37).

Throughout the history of the Christian Church, Christians have been held captive as prisoners, had bounties on their heads, been bludgeoned, beheaded, burned at the stake, fed to the lions, crucified, and any of numerous creatively macabre ways to be killed. In every age, the kingdom of heaven is threatened by the allies of hell and suffers violence against it. We should expect nothing else.

The ways of the devil remain violent and destructive. The Christian Church, with her proclamation of a crucified Christ, continues to appear weak and wimpy in comparison.

Christ and his apostles tell us to expect this violence against us. Jesus promised, "Then they will hand you over to be persecuted, and they will put you to death. You will be hated by all nations because of my name" (Matthew 24:9). St. Paul wrote to the Thessalonian Christians to let them know that Timothy was sent to them to prepare them for suffering, "We sent him to strengthen and encourage you in your faith, so that no one will be shaken by these trials, for you know well that we are destined for this. In fact, even when we were with you, we told you ahead of time that we were going to suffer" (1 Thessalonians 3:2-4). St. Paul told the Philippians that by God's grace they were given both the gift of faith in Christ and also the gift of suffering in Christ's name: "For it has been graciously granted to you on behalf of Christ, not only to believe in him, but also to suffer for him" (Philippians 1:29).

This violence against Christians and the Christian Church will continue to come. But the violence will not prevail. The dragon and his demonic horde have already gone down in defeat. But like a lion caught in a trap, the roaring lion of the devil is unwilling to surrender. He continues to thrash, claw, roar, bite, and maul. Satan and his allies will do whatever they can as they "wage war against the saints to overcome them" (Revelation 13:7).

In the face of threats of violence, we proclaim the eternal gospel to those who live on the earth, to every nation, tribe, language, and people (Revelation 14:6). We stand upon the solid rock of Jesus

Christ. We will not simply endure; we will prevail against the forces of Satan. The baptized saints of God are not being sent into a fairy tale world where everything is rainbows and unicorns. They are being sent to war against the dragon and his destructive beasts. Yet these baptized saints are equipped as soldiers of the cross. Do not fear anything you are about to suffer! You have received and believed Christ's promise that when you are faithful unto death, he will give you the crown of life" (Revelation 2:10).

The EHV translates Jesus' words differently than the ESV: "From the days of John the Baptist until now, the kingdom of heaven has been advancing forcefully and forceful people are seizing it" (Matthew 11:12). With this translation, it is the kingdom of heaven that is advancing forcefully against Satan's kingdom.

The way for us to win the war for our children's souls and the hearts of the people is by using the same weapons we've always been given – God's Word and Sacraments. These weapons seem like weakness in the face of the enemies' onslaught. Yet the Lord promises, "He is the one who gives strength to the weak, and he increases the strength of those who lack power" (Isaiah 40:29). We join with St. Paul as we rejoice in our weaknesses so that we can rely on the strengths of our Almighty God: "I will be glad to boast all the more in my weaknesses, so that the power of Christ may shelter me. That is why I delight in weaknesses, in insults, in hardships, in persecutions, in difficulties, for the sake of Christ. For whenever I am weak, then am I strong" (2 Corinthians 12:9-10).

We listen to the Word so that we can then share that Word with those who have closed their ears and hearts to the Lord. We remember that we have been made heirs of heaven through our Baptism so we can invite those claimed by the devil to be baptized and dispossessed of the devil. We rejoice in the forgiveness of our sins so we can encourage others to find acceptance in Christ instead of searching for acceptance in the world. We celebrate the unity we receive when we commune together at the Lord's Table as we invite others to set aside their petty differences about skin color, political party affiliation, or anything else the devil uses to divide us into little tribes.

With these humble means of Word and Sacrament, we are advancing forcefully into our neighborhoods, into our culture, and against the devil's domain.

We trust as the violence comes upon us - just as God called his chosen people out of Egypt - so he will deliver us from spiritual oppression and destruction. He will enable the citizens of his kingdom to conquer all things, and – yes – to endure all things for the sake of his name.

Yet we can be sure that just as God called his Son out of Egypt, he will call us out of Egypt, too, and deliver us from all forms of spiritual oppression and captivity. He will enable the members of his kingdom to advance forcefully against Satan's forces.

Winter is coming. We need to be prepared for the war. The way to be prepared is not by laying down our weapons and being silent. The way to be prepared is by taking up the weapons Christ has given us and being watchmen on the wall warning when we see the Enemy's forces on the horizon.

Christian Quietism

In the opening of the classic *Looney Tunes* [65] cartoon *Rabbit Fire*, Elmer Fudd sees rabbit tracks. He looks at the audience and says, "Shh! Be vewy, vewy quiet! I'm hunting wabbits!"

As Christians, I think we have adopted a lifestyle of being vewy, vewy quiet. I call it the spirit of "quietism." We quietly go about our lives hoping that people don't notice us too much. We also don't want to notice very much, either. We like being left alone. We like a live-and-let-live type of lifestyle. We allow the culture to go where it wants, as long as it doesn't impact us too much.

We need to stand up and speak up. We need to take St. Paul's words to heart that if we are going to be sincere in our love, then we will "hate what is evil and cling to what is good" (Romans 12:9). This means we cannot be timid in the town square when we speak out against homosexuality, transgenderism, critical race theory, wokeness, abortion, euthanasia or whatever is influencing our culture.

We speak up with Christian truth to bring spiritual freedom for those trapped in darkness ... and we do so, recognizing that the person promoting sin may be just as much a victim of demonic deception. If we are to counteract our quietism, we must recognize the broader cultural warfare while also knowing whether to gently empathize or strongly rebuke.

The devil's lies fill the silence

With our spirit of quietism, we may think that if we leave our culture alone it will leave us and our children alone. But it doesn't work like that. It is naïve to think that the Church will be left alone to do what it does. We need to assess our culture – where it is attacking us – and devise a game plan, both defensive and offensive.

---

65 *Looney Tunes* is one of the greatest cartoons of all time. Turn off the drivel that passes as entertainment today and let your children watch *Looney Tunes* instead.

When Christians remain quiet, the lies of the devil fill the silence.

Christians interact with the culture every day in many ways – workplace, school, university, media, social media, Hollywood, etc. You interact with culture every time you step out your door, every time you turn on the television, every time you doomscroll your phone. It is naïve to believe that one hour once a week is enough for Christians to counteract the influence that 16 hours every day in the culture has on them. To counteract the influence of our culture on us and our children – and to also have an influence on our culture – we Christians need to engage our game plan.

The devil's attack on the third use of the Law

What is that game plan? We faithfully proclaim Law and Gospel. In our Lutheran heritage we speak of the three uses of the Law: 1. Mirror; 2. Curb; 3. Guide. We apply the first use of the Law as a mirror to show us our sins. Then we apply the Gospel to show the Savior who forgives all our sins. We apply the second use of the Law as a curb to keep us away from other sins. But we can miss applying the third use of the Law, which is to use the Law as a guide.

But it is this precise area of the third use of the Law – how we live as Christians in the world - where the attacks from Satan come in our culture. We need to know and we need to tell others how to live as Christian spouses, Christian parents, Christian children, Christian employers and employees, and Christian students. We need to continually catechize our congregations so Christians may know how to apply Scriptural truths in everyday life.

Oftentimes pastors will not talk about homosexuality, transgenderism, CRT, wokeness, abortion (and other topics), because these issues seem political. They are political issues only because we have allowed them to become political. They are first theological issues. Then they are moral and ethical issues. Then they become cultural issues. Finally, they become political issues.

When pastors and churches divorce themselves from these theological and moral issues, the only other places to discuss them is in the cultural and political arenas.

Because Christians have absented themselves from the discussion, the world fills the void.

If we feel that Christians have lost ground in this culture war, we should ask ourselves if it's our own fault. Have we remained silent, retreated into our quietism, and absented ourselves from the culture?

Real-life issues

Consider these questions currently being asked within our culture:

- What are we to do with life in the womb?
- How are we to feel if there is an attraction to someone of the same sex?
- What are we do if we feel there is a different gender trapped within the body?
- Is there racism that is systemic within the workplace?
- What do we do with our parents when they become elderly?
- Who makes the decisions about the end of life?
- At what point do we submit or resist governing authorities?
- Who has authority and responsibility to decide what (and when) the children in our schools are taught particular topics, or exposed to certain ideas?

All of these are real-life issues. These are issues Christians wrestle with in their personal lives. These are issues non-Christians are grappling with in their lives. Yet, when was the last time you heard these subjects discussed in a Bible study? Or in a sermon? Or ... ever in the church?

These topics need to be discussed theologically. Otherwise, people become practical atheists as portrayed in Psalm 14 and Psalm 53 where the fool says in his heart there is no God. When we do not bring God and his Word into the discussion for these real-world issues, are we making ourselves into fools?

Each generation of Christians needs to study, discuss, debate, and apply Scripture to these real-life issues. If one generation fails in this calling, the failure multiplies and metastasizes for subsequent generations.

As Christians, we are often content to merely "hold the line" in a culture war. But is holding the line enough?

The enemy is constantly waging war against us. He is never content with merely holding the line. The only acceptable outcome for the devil is the total destruction of the Christian Church on earth.

Passion for expanding Christ's kingdom

Fellow Christians, where is our passion? Where is our fervor? Where is our intensity? The only acceptable outcome for us in the war between Christ's kingdom and Satan's kingdom is the expansion of the Christian Church throughout all of humanity. The passion of another infant's head dripping wet with the water of Baptism. The fervor of a youth who has clung to Jesus in her confirmation vows. The intensity of a young adult who has kept his bed pure for marriage. The joy of Christians gathered at the Table, and rejoicing together through tears at another Christian funeral. We need to be celebrating every precious soul that Christ wins away from the devil. We cannot be quiet about these celebrations.

God has given us so much in his kingdom. In this kingdom we need to preserve and prosper. Defend to extend. We cannot be content to merely hold the line. Preaching Christ's Kingdom is never about holding the line. It is always about moving the line further and further into the devil's territory.

A bit of wisdom from one of the great academic minds of our times - Albus Dumbledore: "Dark times lie ahead of us and there will be a time when we must choose between what is easy and what is right." [66]

It is easy to remain quiet and absent ourselves from the culture. But we should not be surprised then when the culture claims our children, schools, corporations, media, entertainment, social

---

[66] Rowling, J.K. *Harry Potter and the Goblet of Fire.*

media, government, and even our churches. It is much more difficult to choose to do what is right. Professor Dumbledore, the head of Hogwarts is right.

I put it this way when I speak to people about coming out of our quiet cocoons and engaging the culture in the public arena: We either need a little courage now ... or we will need a lot of courage later.

"On July 17, 180 A.D., twelve inhabitants of Carthage, North Africa, were executed for being Christians. There were seven men and five women. Their names were Speratus, Nartzalus, Cintinus (Cittinus), Veturius, Felix, Aquilinus, Laetantius, Januaria, Generosa, Vestia, Donata, and Secunda. Speratus was their spokesman. He claimed for himself and his companions that they had lived quiet and moral lives—paying their taxes and doing no wrong to their neighbors. But when called upon to swear by the name of the emperor, he replied, 'We do not recognize the empire of this world. We serve the God whom no one has seen.' The Christians were offered a delay of thirty days to reconsider their decision, which they all refused. They were put to death by the sword." [67]

These twelve Christians were martyred for their faith. They were not the first martyrs, nor are they the last. Throughout the history of the world, Christians have been put to death for their faith in Christ.

Confessing Christ requires courage. The writer to the Hebrews recounts the courage of Christians as they endured imprisonment, torture, and even horrific deaths.

> "By faith they conquered kingdoms, carried out justice, obtained things that were promised, shut the mouths of lions, quenched the power of fire, escaped the edges of the sword, were made powerful after being weak, became mighty in battle, and caused foreign armies to flee. Women received back their dead by resurrection. And

---

[67] *wels.net devotion 9/23/2021*

> others who were tortured did not accept their release, so that they may take part in a better resurrection. Still others experienced mocking and lashes, in addition to chains and imprisonment. They were stoned; they were sawed in two; they were tempted; they were killed with the sword; they went around in sheepskins and goatskins, needy, afflicted, and mistreated. The world was not worthy of them as they wandered in deserts and mountains and caves and holes in the ground" (Hebrews 11:33-38).

Christians will be persecuted for their faith. There may be skepticism and mockery, the loss of wages and property, the loss of status and employment. There may be imprisonment and cruelty. There may be death.

Still, we are called to be aggressive with the gospel. Be Elijah. Be John the Baptist. Be Martin Luther. Too often we are passive and meek with the gospel. We have made the Spirit's fiery gospel tepid. No wonder people are turned off by it. Jesus spits us out of his mouth when we are lukewarm (Revelation 3:15). We want to be like the cool kids of Hebrews 11 that were willing to become martyrs for their faith. We want to be fiery like the prophets and apostles. They weren't milquetoast, as my college dean used to say.

God's Word is offensive. It should be offending sinful sensibilities. It is aggressive. It doesn't want us to remain allies of Satan. This is a war!

At the end of his epistle, the holy writer asks for Christians to converse with those in prison and risk the same fate. "Remember those in prison, as if you were fellow prisoners, and those who are mistreated, as if you yourselves were also suffering bodily" (Hebrews 13:3). Perhaps as American Christians we aren't being put in prison by governing authorities because we are so tepid and meek in our gospel presentation. We are going along to get along. We tend to look down on anyone who is being aggressive with the gospel or drawing too much attention.

Jesus said to his disciples, "If anyone wants to follow me, let him deny himself, take up his cross, and follow me" (Matthew 16:24). These strong words of Jesus impact us because as 21st century American Christians we have become soft. We don't like being threatened, booed, canceled, etc. We enjoy our quietism of staying by ourselves, keeping our heads down, and not stirring up trouble. Jesus says that trouble is coming simply because of our connection to him. It sounds harsh – but we are in harsh times: If we don't want persecution, then we should go join the other side.

But if we're going to be on Jesus' side, then we'd better strap on our gospel armor and get ready for battle (Ephesians 6:10-17). It's time to go on the offensive with the sword of the Spirit!

John the Baptist was not too timid to preach a strong message of repentance (Matthew 3:2). If John were preaching today, he certainly would be canceled by our culture. He may even be asked to tone it down by other Christians, pastors, and church leaders. But God's work is done when people turn to God in repentance and have faith in Jesus for the forgiveness of sins. That's how God's kingdom comes in this world.

We need to be aggressive like John and preach boldly by being both defensive and offensive with the kingdom of God. We defensively resist the devil and the devil's beasts of the persecuting government and the apostate church. We offensively go into the killing fields of this world with the message of John the Baptist preaching repentance and forgiveness of sins.

Suffering for the name of Jesus

Jesus teaches, "A disciple is not above his teacher, nor is a servant above his master. It is enough for the disciple to be like his teacher and the servant like his master. If the master of the house was called Beelzebul, how much more the members of his household" (Matthew 24:24,25)! Being connected to the name of Jesus can mean hardships and hazards.

As Jesus sends out his apostles, he warns them that he will be called "Beelzebul," the prince of demons. He would be beaten, flogged and finally crucified. Life was not always fun and easy for Jesus.

The same was true for Jesus' apostles. Church history tells us that all of them suffered a martyr's death, except John. Yet even John was exiled to a prison island. Life was not always fun and easy for the apostles of Jesus. If life was not easy for Jesus the Master Teacher, it wouldn't always be easy for his student-servants.

As citizens of Christ's kingdom, the dragon, his beasts, and their allies will cause us to be hated, persecuted, mocked, intimidated, humiliated, slandered, misrepresented, fined by the governing authorities for hate speech, censored in the name of tolerance, imprisoned, or even suffer death. People will hate us because we bear the name of Christ. They will ridicule us for believing in Jesus alone as the way to salvation. They will berate us because we believe what the Bible says about morality. They will cancel us because we believe in the sanctity of marriage. They will lampoon us because we believe in the value of life in the womb and on the death bed.

As the Lord Jesus showed Paul how much he must suffer in Christ's name (Acts 9:16), so we know we are called to suffer for having Christ's name put on us in our Baptism. Sadly, many Christians and churches are tempted to compromise God's Word, forsake Christ's name, and bow before the altars of tolerance and acceptance. We, too, will be tempted to exchange praising Christ for accepting the fleeting praise of people.

We covet the praise of our friends, so we quiet our confession of Christ. We desire peace within our family, so we remain quiet about the Prince of Peace. We would rather encounter the culture than being counter-cultural through Christ. We find it easier to keep our mouths shut, keep our faith to ourselves, and privately live as Christians away from the public eye than let everyone hear and see what we really believe.

After all, no one likes conflict. Conflict brings suffering and anguish. And no one likes suffering and anguish. The truth is, we'll go to great lengths to avoid it! So, what do we do? We'll keep quiet, keep our heads down, and mind our own business.

We are sinners who desire a life of ease rather than service. We so often want to just sit in church rather than be the Church. But that's why Jesus went to the cross, to pay the damning curse for such sinful thoughts and such sinful inactivity.

We must each ask ourselves, "Whom do I respect and fear more? My friends, family, government, and culture who can make life miserable for me? Or the almighty and eternal God who can damn me to an eternity in hell?"

Fellow witnesses, hear the Savior and take to heart his Word when he says, "Do not fear those who kill the body but cannot kill the soul. Rather, fear the one who is able to destroy both soul and body in hell" (Matthew 10:28). Repent of your timidity! Repent and fear God – not with a cowering fear that drives you away from God – but with a holy fear, the kind of fear that bows before the Lord your God. Do not be ashamed to bear the life-giving name of Jesus before this dying world. Do not hide your light under a bushel. No! Do not let the words of Christ that sanctified your ears and heart stop there. Allow them to sanctify your mouth so you may announce with Isaiah, "Here I am! Send me" (Isaiah 6:8)!

Do not fear angry atheists, malicious mobs, censoring social media, or fervent family and friends. St. Paul encourages, "God did not give us a timid spirit, but a spirit of power and love and sound judgment. So do not be ashamed of the testimony about our Lord" (2 Timothy 1:7, 8).

Fellow saints who witness despite persecution, God treasures you as his own. Through Christ's cross and the open grave, God has proven that you are worth more than a smattering of sparrows. You are worth – though not deserving of – the blood of his Son. Therefore, you are no longer your own, for you have been purchased with the blood of Jesus. His life, death, and resurrection applied to you in your Baptism has sealed you for the day of Judgment and preserves you from the fires of hell.

Not only does the Lord treasure you, but he also treasures all those who are lost. Christ died for the sins of all, and he earnestly and seriously wants all people to be saved. So, as you live out your life as a baptized child of God, bring the presence of the Triune God to all those around you.

Be proud that at your Baptism God placed his name on you and gave you the name of Christian at the baptismal font. That name includes all God's blessings, power, and promises – for you! As you walk out the doors of your church to engage the culture, trust Christ's name. Bow at that name. Cherish that name. Live in that name. Boldly proclaim that name. Do not fear the threats of the world. Fear God! Trust God! Love God! He will not abandon you. He will not let one hair on your head be harmed apart from his will.

Witness despite persecution. Don't fear the cross! Confess the cross! Bring God's presence upon others as you bring them the name that is above every name, so that on the Last Day they can join you "so that at the name of Jesus every knee will bow, in heaven and on earth and under the earth, and every tongue will confess that Jesus Christ is Lord, to the glory of God the Father" (Philippians 2:10, 11). Change the culture by preaching Christ into the culture – by talking about Jesus with the individuals whom Christ brings into your life.

Fellow Christian, you can't change the world while remaining comfortable. You cannot expect the culture to change as you sit in your basement watching Hulu and eating Hot Pockets. You need to be up and active. You must be willing to sacrifice. You need to counteract your quietism by standing, speaking up, and speaking out. Solomon counteracts Christian quietism when he wisely writes: "Speak up for those who cannot speak for themselves" (Proverbs 31:8).

The Gift of Reason

In the beginning of *Braveheart*,[68] young William Wallace wants to join the Scottish clans in fighting the British. Malcolm Wallace says to his son, William, "I know you can fight. But it's our wits that make us men."

God has given us our wits, our human reason. He has also given us a conscience, our awareness of our relationship with God. In this chapter we'll look at why so many Christians used their gifts of reason and conscience specifically with their resistance to masks, mandates, lockdowns, the Covid-19 vaccine, vaccine passports, and similar governmental influences on everyday life.

In his book, *The Narrow Lutheran Middle*, the now-sainted Daniel Deutschlander describes reason this way: "Reason, to be sure, is one of the greatest gifts that God has given to us. It is second after the gospel in Word and sacraments with its faith-creating message of salvation by grace through faith in Christ and his work for our salvation. God wants us to use the precious gift of reason in our daily lives." [69]

God-given wits

We are to use our God-given wits. We are to use the gift of reason God has instilled in each of us. But these past few years it seems as if we have been told to shut off our brains. We have been told to stop thinking for ourselves and "follow the science" and "trust the experts." While such advice may have application in specific, unique, and personal situations (as when talking with your cardiologist or your auto mechanic), no expert has the specific credentials or authority to promote blanket statements over personalized advice and choices.

---

[68] An epic red-blooded battle epic filled with love, patriotism and treachery.

[69] Deutschlander, Daniel W. *The Narrow Lutheran Middle: Following the Scriptural Road*. Milwaukee: Northwestern Publishing House, 2011. p. 4

In short, something is broken when we are told to disregard our wits in favor of someone else's will.

What happens when we don't use our wits, when we stop using the gift of reason? "Without the use of reason, life descends into a swamp of disorder, then into a sea of chaos, and finally into certain misery. How many people do you know who, as the saying goes, 'never use their heads'? They have no grasp of the concept of cause and effect, no ability to see any further than the moment. Abandoning the use of reason, their attention spans are fixed on the fleeting and their lives are devoted only to the moment. They have the attention span of a gerbil!"[70]

That seems to be an apt description of what we've allowed ourselves to experience these past few years. Government authorities, school officials, employers, citizens, and so many more did not have the ability to see beyond the moment ... or they purposely chose to ignore what was beyond the moment. Using our wits - our God-given reason - isn't something that happens passively. The gift of reason is given for the purpose of exercising it actively through thorough thoughtfulness – not simply settling for the path of least resistance.

I have been asked many times, "Why are you drawing a line at wearing a mask?" I'm confident countless other Christians who resisted wearing a mask were asked similar questions. The answer I gave to those questions was that I was using the gift of reason. I can't speak for other Christians, but I'm guessing they gave similar answers to their questioners. Together, we were using common sense.

It's been said that Covid-19 was a novel virus – something that had never been seen before. It was new. It may have been produced in a lab, or accidentally released after some research and experimentation; no matter its origins, the virus confounded and confused cultures around the world. We understand that experts are fallible and make mistakes.

To keep from being infected with Covid, many local and state

---

[70] Ibid. p. 5

governments, businesses, restaurants, airlines, and others, mandated the wearing of face masks. These public and government institutions were following the guidance of the Center for Disease Control (CDC), Dr. Anthony Fauci, scientists, and medical experts. They gave the advice that any type of face covering was acceptable. It could be an N95 mask, a surgical mask, a gaiter, or a homemade cloth mask. We were advised they would all be effective.

Common sense questions to Covid

Common sense told us to question the assertions by these experts. Industrial masks have ratings for the percentage of molecules they filter for the wearer. Even OSHA will say that an N95 and a P100 mask have very different uses, functions, and applications. Common sense told us that equating an N95 to a cloth facial covering is nonsensical. A cloth facial covering doesn't have a tested, verifiable standard that proves it is effective against microscopic viral particles.

All the science, the experts, and the peer-reviewed studies prior to 2020 said that regular surgical masks or cloth masks could not prevent an airborne virus from infecting individuals. In the early days of the pandemic, Dr. Anthony Fauci, director of the National Institute of Allergy and Infectious Diseases, advised the public not to bother with masks.

On February 5, 2020, Fauci wrote in an email to Sylvia Burwell, President Obama's health and human services secretary: "Masks are really for infected people to prevent them from spreading infection to people who are not infected rather than protecting uninfected people from acquiring infection. The typical mask you buy in the drug store is not really effective in keeping out virus, which is small enough to pass through material. It might, however, provide some slight benefit in keep out gross droplets if someone coughs or sneezes on you."[71]

Very quickly, Dr. Fauci reversed course. Then the public was

[71] Newsweek.com (6/2/2021)

directed to also reverse course and ignore all the science that had come before and start donning masks. Follow the experts – but when? And which experts, especially when the various levels of government promulgate different advisories and orders?

Dear Christian, let us not lose our wits or leave our reason unexercised. Do not disregard your wits in favor of someone else's will.

It seemed that if the American public waited long enough, the earlier statements of Dr. Fauci, the CDC, medical experts, government authorities, and others would always be contradicted by later statements from Dr. Fauci, the CDC, medical experts, government authorities, and others. All these conflicting statements confused the common sense of the American public, as well as provided new opportunities for division within the community at large.

People opposed masks early on in 2020. They argued that regular masks like surgical, cloth or neck gaiters could not keep out an airborne virus. They said that masks are ineffective because people are touching them all the time. Masks are meant to be worn for a short time and thrown away, but people wear the same dirty masks all the time. Children were compelled to wear the same dirty masks for 6-8 hours a day in school, some even wearing them for recess and sports.

Those who opposed masks maintained that children need to be able to see the faces of their teachers and their students. They have been dehumanized as they wouldn't be able to see the facial expressions of people. Children were taught they were potential virus-spreaders. Children saw that human interaction was dangerous, while adults stayed far away – seeing children as dirty. Little kids were made to feel guilty if they weren't always wearing the mask properly, even though the experts also said that the virus proved of little risk to children. Those who opposed masks stated that separation and isolation from other students would be harmful to the psyche and mental health of students. Natural immunity was being ignored; all that mattered was wearing a mask.

But when parents and other concerned individuals made these objections public, they were quickly labeled as false information on Facebook. They had their accounts suspended on Twitter. They were told by other Christians to submit to the governing authorities and obey the 4th Commandment, or that Christians are loving people and wearing a mask is the loving thing to do (thereby also implying that the discussion was over, and reason had no freedom to exercise itself in dialogue).

Two years after being told to "follow the science" and wear cloth masks, we heard from Noah Haber, an interdisciplinary scientist and a co-author of a systematic review of Covid-19 mitigation policies. He called the research done by the CDC "so unreliable that it probably should not have been entered into the public discourse." [72]

For two years of having to wear a cloth mask to enter schools, businesses, restaurants, airports, and more, we learned from the CNN Health Correspondent: "Cloth masks are not appropriate for this pandemic. It was not appropriate for omicron. It was not appropriate for delta, alpha, or any of the previous variants either because we're dealing with something that's airborne. Don't wear a cloth mask. Cloth masks are little more than facial decorations. There's no place for them in light of omicron."[73]

Follow the experts or exercise your reason? In January of 2022, the CDC conceded that cloth masks were not effective at stopping the transmission of an airborne virus.[74] And this is exactly what those who resisted wearing masks had been saying for two years. Yet they were told to shut off their reason and follow the experts. Two years later the experts are agreeing with what was common sense two years prior.

It defied common sense that masks were necessary while entering a restaurant, but then were no longer necessary when the patrons sat down to eat in that restaurant. It seemed like Covid

[72] Theatlantic.com (12/16/2021)
[73] Msn.com (12/21/2021)
[74] Nytimes.com (1/14/2021)

lost its potency while people ate. Then the potency increased again as the patrons paid their bill, putting on their masks for the 30-foot walk to exit the restaurant.

It defied common sense that Covid is so deadly that people needed to wear masks wherever they went ... unless they were drinking beer at a bar or eating at a restaurant or nibbling cookies on an airplane. Then suddenly Covid was ineffective.

Those who resisted wearing masks also stated that the masks would become filthy and full of germs. We witnessed young children constantly touching and playing with their masks, grade school students coughing and sneezing into their masks, and high school athletes playing sports while wearing masks. We all know that elementary and high schools are Petri dishes of germs. So, it makes sense that these masks were also filled with germs.

To have scientific proof of the germs on masks, a group of concerned parents in Gainesville, FL sent their children's used face masks to a lab at the University of Florida. The lab detected eleven "dangerous pathogens" on the kids' masks: streptococcus pneumoniae (pneumonia); mycobacterium tuberculosis; neisseria meningitidis; acanthamoeba polyphaga; acinetobacter baumannii; escherichia coli; borrelia burgdorferi; corynebacterium diphtheriae; legionella pneumophila; staphylococcus pyogenes serotype M3; staphylococcus aureus.[75]

If you're like me, you probably can't pronounce most of those. But they sound both scary and serious. And yet, parents are told to ignore these germs to protect from a virus. These germs can have devastating and deadly effects on children – but we ought to ignore them and wear an ineffective mask for a virus that has virtually a zero percent chance of serious illness or death for these same children.

For two years, there were many citizens who were saying that a piece of fabric over your face couldn't do anything to stop an airborne virus. There was even a Cambridge University study that claimed that wearing pantyhose over an N95 mask made it more

---

[75] Theblaze.com (6/16/2021)

secure and thus more effective. [76] But then in January 2022, The Wall Street Journal published an article entitled *Why Cloth Masks Might Not Be Enough As Omicron Spreads.*[77] Fox News, CNN, The New York Times, and other media outlets all shared similar headlines at the same time. Two years prior this same statement was deemed dangerous misinformation. That was until the legacy media gave its permission to allow common sense to once again enter the conversation.

Common sense led to admissions of harming our children

Common sense and moral judgment said that Americans were harming our children with these ineffective attempts to contain a virus. Right before Christmas 2021, a CNN host allowed us to admit that perhaps the best way to deal with this virus is for everyone to get the virus.[78] *(Similar statements were made nearly two years previously on the Joe Rogan Experience, when Joe interviewed Michael Osterholm).*[79] Common sense people were saying all along we needed herd immunity. When I was a child, I remember my parents taking me over to a classmate's home that had chicken pox. Seriously, there used to be chicken pox parties decades ago. Our parents were creating herd immunity.

Maybe we needed Covid parties. We needed to develop a herd immunity to Covid.

The CNN host finally admitted that our children were suffering. He said we should stop online school. He didn't go so far as to encourage taking off the masks or stopping the Covid testing. But he acted as if he had an epiphany that this was damaging to our children – something parents with common sense had been saying and even shouting at school board meetings for two years.

In January of 2022, Jaclyn Theek, a speech therapist in Florida said that her clinic had seen a 364% increase in referrals of babies

---

[76] journals.plos.org (2/2/2022)
[77] wsj.com (1/10/2022)
[78] Brian Stelter on CNN (12/19/2021)
[79] Joe Rogan Experience #1439

and toddlers since the beginning of the pandemic. [80] The therapist said that masks were "most definitely" a factor in the speech impediment of these young children.

Children learn speech by observing the mouths of adults. But they couldn't see lips moving or words being formed because their teachers, daycare workers, parents, and all other adults were wearing masks.

Other similar studies on the speech impediments of young children show that we're seeing a large increase of children who are demonstrating what looks like Autism. [81] The children are not making any attempts at forming words and are not communicating with their family. These are otherwise perfectly healthy children who demonstrate the signs of Autism. The statistics point out that these speech impediments began being observed in young children at the same time young children were no longer able to observe the faces of the adults who cared for them.

Follow the experts? Or exercise human reason?

After two full years of pandemic response, in 2022 America's mental health crisis was at an all-time high. 71% of parents said that the pandemic had taken a toll on their child's mental health.[82] There were 38% more mental health cases in emergency rooms. There were 54% more suicide attempts in the third quarter of 2021 compared to 2020 according to the Children's Hospital Association.[83] Christian Family Solutions reported a nearly-exponential increase in requests for counseling. Experts claimed that the pandemic caused a pandemic of mental health problems – but that's not true. This virus, by God's grace, never posed a significant threat to healthy children. It is the response to the virus that caused this abuse to our children.

Of course, children were going to be mentally affected by the adults' response to the pandemic. Children look to adults for how to respond, and for how to mitigate and manage their own

---

[80] wpbf.com (11/9/2021)

[81] Ibid.

[82] Apa.org (1/1/2022)

[83] Latimes.com (12/7/2021)

emotions. Children didn't know what their friends' faces looked like anymore. Children felt guilty as if they were sinning by not wearing a mask. Children were taught they were like contagious lepers. They became fearful as if they were potential death carriers – "Wear a mask so you don't kill grandma!" They were fed a constant diet of fear and paranoia, and were compelled to wear a constant reminder of their own culpability and mortality. They were trained to believe that God's wonderful air was toxic and their body's amazing immune system was automatically compromised.

How could children not be mentally scarred by all this? How could parents acquiesce to such abuse, rather than exercising their reason?

The law of unintended circumstances

Common sense said there would be these kinds of issues from America's mandated mitigation attempts. This is the law of unintended circumstances. Asian carp were introduced into the United States to control the weeds in canals and clean aquatic farms. But the Asian carp quickly made its way into the waterways and began pushing out native fish species by outbreeding and eating their food sources. Kudzu was introduced in the 1870s to protect from erosion. But you've seen this green, leafy plant overtake whole swaths of wildlife regions in the south. Kudzu can grow up to a foot per day each season, and grow the length of 50,000 baseball fields in one season.

These are examples of the law of unintended circumstances. Something that was meant for good - food, environment, virus mitigation - went horribly wrong. Now we are left to deal with the consequences.

It is distressing that speech therapists and psychologists didn't speak up sooner about what they were noticing in children they were treating. But even if they had spoken up, they likely would have been shouted down, canceled, and labeled as misinformation. Instead the narrative that was pushed was that kids are resilient and they need to sacrifice – just for a little while – in order to protect others. Parents who noticed what was happening to their children were asked to compromise their children's social and academic life in the name of public safety.

So what should parents have done? Whether they knew it in 2020 or learned the results in 2022, the results are the same. Putting masks on children was useless – but not without effect. The evidence is incontrovertible - putting masks on children was abusive, coercive, and harmful.

Should parents have gone along with what the local government, school board and society mandated was right and mask their children? Or should they have stood up for what they believed in and resisted the mandates of the government, the rules of their school board, and the norms of society?

Which action was more loving to their children?

A gift of human reasoning is to be able to conduct a risk-reward analysis and see beyond the moment. But with Covid-19, it seems that we were unable to see beyond the immediate fear of a virus to what the mitigation attempts of that virus would do to our children.

We seemed to have lost our ability to make moral judgments. We've abdicated that role to others. We're not using our vocations – as parents and citizens. Instead, we've been trained to automatically accept what any experts tell us – and even to accept someone's status as "expert" simply because they appear on a cable news show and are referred to as an "expert".

When people do their own research before purchasing a house or a car, they're considered a smart consumer. When they gather second or third opinions before receiving a medical procedure, they're considered a well-researched individual. But when those same people do their own research before allowing authorities in the government or employment to mandate wearing a piece of fabric on their face all day, then they are considered tinfoil hat-wearing conspiracy theorists. When they want to share this medical opinion, then they are canceled on social media.

We've found out that the difference between conspiracy theory and the truth is about 6 to 12 months. Or perhaps it's not a conspiracy theory ... but rather a spoiler alert. Or perhaps it is a conspiracy to not believe the mounting evidence before us.

See the truth for yourself

There is danger in believing everything is true, and similar danger in believing that everything is a conspiracy. We must use our Christian reasoning so we do not become naive, believing everyone is good and out to help us, but also do not become conspiracy theorists believing everyone is bad and out to get us.

In *The Matrix*, Neo is offered his choice of two pills.[84] The red pill represents an awakening, but one that will be difficult and painful. Neo's world will be rocked if he takes the red pill. But he will also be made uncomfortably aware of the truth of the world. The blue pill represents comfort and security. He will continue to live in blissful ignorance if he takes the blue pill. Is it time for us to take the red pill, despite the discomfort it may elicit? It is always the right time to exercise our human reason and be aware of those who are trying to influence us.

We understand that there is a narrative that is shared by the government, corporations, and the legacy media and social media. It's good to listen to that narrative ... but not necessarily believe that narrative. That's being naïve. Rather, listen to that narrative ... then do your own research. The truth is usually in the middle.

Like in the *Matrix*, sometimes you have to see the truth for yourself.

We've seen restaurants, businesses, big box stores, school classrooms, and other places install clear plastic barriers to protect against the virus. But scientists who study germs, air flow, and ventilation now admit that the barriers couldn't really stop an airborne virus. The barriers instead became a barrier to proper airflow and ventilation.

An August 2021 New York Times article stated, "Under normal conditions in stores, classrooms and offices, exhaled breath particles disperse, carried by air currents and, depending on the

---

84 Morpheus says to Neo, "You take the red pill, you stay in Wonderland, and I show you how deep the rabbit hole goes."

ventilation system, are replaced by fresh air roughly every 15 to 30 minutes. But erecting plastic barriers can change air flow in a room, disrupt normal ventilation and create 'dead zones,' where viral aerosol particles can build up and become highly concentrated."[85]

Attempts to contain the spread of a virus, as recommended by experts, simply concentrated the virus for easier spread among people.

We've seen people standing six feet apart with the new term "social distancing." Schools separated desks from each other in classrooms. Check-out lines put colored dots on the floor for customers to stand on while waiting in line. Churches taped off pews.

During a September 2021 appearance on CBS's "Face The Nation," Scott Gottlieb, the 23rd commissioner of the Food and Drug Administration discussed the CDC's guideline of six feet of separation. He said, "Nobody knows where it came from. Most people assume that the six feet of distance, the recommendation for keeping six feet apart, comes out of some old studies related to flu, where droplets don't travel more than six feet."[86]

Gottlieb went on to say that the CDC's initial social-distancing recommendation was ten feet. But most people couldn't imagine ten feet. Nor could stores, businesses, and schools be open with ten feet of separation between people. So the experts concocted six feet of separation. They also concocted a new term in the American lexicon of "social distancing," which has much broader implications than a term like "physical distancing."

The masks, plastic barriers, and social distancing may appear like people were at least attempting to do the right thing; as Christians, we want to put the best construction on everything. Yet the results are clear. The results of the masks, plastic barriers, social distancing, remote learning, lockdowns, and most everything else that was enforced by the experts had devastating

---

[85] Nytimes.com (8/19/2021)
[86] CBS News (9/19/2021)

results – especially upon our children. Especially upon the littlest and most vulnerable ones we are called to protect.

The results of mitigation attempts

To our great horror, we've witnessed depression and suicide rates among children and youth skyrocket since the beginning of Covid. Children and youth did not suffer from depression nor commit suicide because of Covid. These were the results of the government's and society's response to Covid - a response where parents were complicit in abdicating their parental authority over their children and exercising abusive policies against their children under the guise of "expert guidance."

In the spring of 2022, with midterm elections looming, suddenly most of the masks disappeared. The experts claimed they've learned things about Covid and masks. Yet what we knew about Covid we learned two months into the pandemic. The science didn't change. It was the political science that changed.

Government officials finally relented about enforcing masks because they realized citizens had reached their breaking point. They knew they would see the results of that breaking point at the ballot box. In April 2022, Dr. Fauci admitted about the virus, "It's not going to be eradicated and it's not going to be eliminated. And what's going to happen is we're going to see that each individual is going to have to make their calculation of the amount of risk they want to take. We're going to have to live with some kind of virus in the community." [87]

This is exactly the opposite of what he, the CDC, and other experts had been saying for over two years. But this is precisely what others who opposed all the mandatory restrictions had been saying since almost the beginning of the pandemic. Personal freedom. Bodily autonomy.

In the very beginning of the pandemic, infectious disease epidemiologists and public health scientists had grave concerns about the damaging physical and mental health impacts of the

---

[87] ABC'S *This Week* (4/10/2022)

prevailing COVID-19 policies. They created and signed *The Great Barrington Declaration*. As I write this, there are over 928,000 signatures of medical professionals who did not agree with a one-size-fits all approach to mitigating this virus. Here is a brief sampling of their advice. I encourage you to do your own research to learn more from the medical and health experts who were canceled by the legacy media and social media because they didn't fit the narrative of the government's experts.

> Those who are not vulnerable should immediately be allowed to resume life as normal. Simple hygiene measures, such as hand washing and staying home when sick should be practiced by everyone to reduce the herd immunity threshold. Schools and universities should be open for in-person teaching. Extracurricular activities, such as sports, should be resumed. Young low-risk adults should work normally, rather than from home. Restaurants and other businesses should open. Arts, music, sport and other cultural activities should resume. People who are more at risk may participate if they wish, while society as a whole enjoys the protection conferred upon the vulnerable by those who have built up herd immunity.[88]

A commonsense approach that most people had any time they were sick with the cold or the flu was stay home and avoid other people if they were sick. But the approach the past two years was to treat the healthy as if they were sick – even potential disease carriers.

Along with the masking and social distancing, many communities mandated lockdowns. In February 2022, Johns Hopkins University published a study asserting that "ill-founded" Covid lockdowns did more harm than good. They found that lockdowns in the U.S. and Europe had little or no impact in

[88] Gbdeclaration.org

reducing deaths from Covid-19. [89]

They found that the lockdowns during the early phase of the pandemic in 2020 reduced Covid-19 mortality by about 0.2% – a statistically insignificant margin well within a margin of error. "We find no evidence that lockdowns, school closures, border closures, and limiting gatherings have had a noticeable effect on COVID-19 mortality," the researchers wrote.

In the researchers' own bracing words: [S]tringency index studies find that lockdowns in Europe and the United States only reduced COVID-19 mortality by 0.2% on average. ... [but] they have imposed enormous economic and social costs where they have been adopted." In fact, Dr. Bhattacharya of Stanford University stated that the Covid-19 lockdowns are "the single worst public health mistake in the last 100 years." [90]

Anyone who owned a small business could have told you this in the first few weeks. Yet, they were forced to obey their governing authorities, risking ruin by closing or ruin through governmental fines and force.

In the beginning of Covid, governing authorities were placed in a difficult position. Nobody knew what our world was facing. "Fifteen days to slow the spread" seemed like a good idea. People did nothing except binge-watch Disney+ and felt they were doing their part to save the world.

In response to an unknown virus, authorities responded by shutting down the economy, curtailing air travel, teaching students virtually, closing down churches, and doing whatever experts thought would end a virus. Mandates trumped individual conscience and sound reasoning.

To be fair, in the beginning of the pandemic in early 2020 we didn't know what we were dealing with. But nothing has changed since two months into the virus to today. We can give people the benefit of the doubt in the beginning. But after that, if we continue giving people a pass, we lapse into moral relativism. That's saying

---

[89] Health.wusf.usf.edu (2/2/2022)

[90] Ibid.

that what they did was right because they thought it was right. As Christians, we do not and have never stood for moral relativism. We don't believe in an "ends justifies the means" mentality. We believe in objective moral realities, not subjective and emotion-bound arguments.

Many will try to convince themselves they were doing something good. But as we look back at the results from the past two years, would we say that any of this was good?

Oftentimes, authorities – governing or otherwise – feel the need to do something. Anything. Just to say, "Hey, we tried." But that doesn't mean that whatever they're doing and trying is the correct thing to do or try.

Growing up on a farm, I learned how to fix things with duct tape, baling twine, and metal wire. We fixed things, but that doesn't mean they were fixed properly. We did something. That doesn't mean we did the right thing. Doing something just to do something isn't good reasoning. Tape, twine, and wire weren't right for the job then. Masks, lockdowns, social distancing, and other mitigation attempts weren't right for this, either.

There were those who opposed Covid mitigation attempts from the very beginning. They used the gift of human reasoning and common sense. Reason is a good thing. The Lord says to his people, "Come let us reason together" (Isaiah 1:18).

The conscience

People also opposed wearing masks and all the other mitigation attempts on the basis of conscience. The conscience is our awareness of spiritual realities. "The intimate connection between faith and a good conscience is demonstrated in Paul's words to Timothy that he hold on to faith and a good conscience" (1 Timothy 1:19).[91] "It is the conscience of man which keeps him posted on the will of God. Conscience is a special function of the soul reacting continuously to the inward law and as such a sense-

---

[91] Peters, Paul. "The Natural Knowledge of God in the Light of the Law and the Gospel." *Our Great Heritage, vol. 2.* Milwaukee: Northwestern Publishing House, 1991. p. 100

organ for the precepts of his law."[92]

We read in the Lutheran Confessions about the purpose of our conscience:

> "Nor, indeed, do we deny liberty to the human will. The human will has liberty in the choice of works and things which reason comprehends by itself. It can to a certain extent render civil righteousness or the righteousness of works; it can speak of God, offer to God a certain service by an outward work, obey magistrates, parents; in the choice of an outward work it can restrain the hands from murder, from adultery, from theft. Since there is left in human nature, reason and judgment concerning objects subjected to the senses, choice between these things, and the liberty and power to render civil righteousness, are also left. For Scripture calls this the righteousness of the flesh which the carnal nature, i.e., reason, renders by itself, without the Holy Ghost."[93]

Former Wisconsin Lutheran Seminary professor Dr. Paul Peters writes about the conscience, "We may well remind ourselves of the fact that conscience does not only make accusations according to Romans 2:15, but at times it also makes defense and considers certain acts of man right and declares them right no matter what others may say to the contrary."[94] The conscience is a powerful motivator, and speaks to deeply and sincerely held beliefs.

"Conscience is like a judge within our soul. Its function is to declare us guilty or not guilty, or as Paul says in Romans 2, to either accuse or excuse us. The verdict which the conscience pronounces will differ greatly in different people, depending on the spiritual knowledge they possess, on the basis of which the verdict

---

[92] Raabe, John. "The Conscience." *Our Great Heritage, vol. 2.* Milwaukee: Northwestern Publishing House, 1991. p. 233

[93] Formula of Concord, Art. XVIII Of Free Will, par. 70, 71

[94] *Our Great Heritage Vol II*, p. 233

is reached."[95]

"Conscience is a precious gift of God. We note that human judges judge only after an act has been committed; our conscience works before, during, and after, and thus is a powerful factor in our lives."[96]

Our conscience is shaped by the will of God laid out in the Ten Commandments. It is also affected by God's will that is placed into the hearts of all people. The conscience of each person is individual and different. It is affected not only by the Word of God, but experience, emotions, relationships, upbringing, customs, and habits, among other influences.

In making ethical decisions, Christians will go to God's Word first, then use the gift of reason, then follow their conscience. Paul urges Christian citizens to obey the governing authorities not only out of fear of punishment, but also because of conscience (Romans 13:5). In his famous refusal to recant his writings, Martin Luther believed that what he had written about God's Word was accurate and true. He boldly confessed, "To go against conscience is neither right nor safe."

God has given each of us a conscience. But we have witnessed people being forced to capitulate to voices outside of their conscience. They are coerced into making their conscience captive to those voices. That is neither right nor safe.

When people believe that wearing a mask is useless or even harmful to themselves and the children in their care – but they are forced to wear a mask – that can be making them sin against their own conscience. When people are mandated to close their business when they know they need their business to remain open to provide for their family - that can be making them sin against their conscience. When people are pressured to remain silent about the damaging effects of these mitigation attempts when they know they need to be speaking out - that can be making them sin against their conscience.

---

[95] Ibid. p. 258
[96] Ibid. p. 258

The apostle Paul has some very strong words for causing people to sin against their conscience. "And when you sin in this way against your brothers and wound their weak conscience, you sin against Christ" (1 Corinthians 8:12).

Consider the message conveyed by such demands: Friend, your conscience must submit to another influence. Your deeply and sincerely held beliefs have no standing, in comparison with enforcement of an anti-conscience demand. Private belief and personal autonomy – generally respected and debated often in public case law – become subservient to an external mandate, without the recourse of discourse or debate.

I have had numerous people talk to me privately about the reasons why they cannot wear a mask. They may have already had Covid, received the vaccine, find it harmful to their own health, or other reasons. They may have done their own research and found that mask mandates are doing the opposite of what they're supposed to be doing. I'm always encouraging people to do their own research. And the research shows that the states that did not have mask mandates or enforce lockdowns fared better with Covid than the states that required masks and lockdowns.

I've had people tell me they've fallen down and became severely injured because the mask was blocking their view. Others have passed out in the store because they couldn't breathe properly. Others receive massive headaches or anxiety or other issues from masks. Still others have asthma and cannot wear a mask. While we might understand the desire for public policy during a time of pandemic, policies (by their very nature) do not accommodate individual needs – or individual consciences. There cannot be a "one-size fits all" decree when it comes to the human body. God's design of the intricacies and individualities of each person's body does not lend itself to "one size fits all" medical means.

People who force others to wear a mask have probably not studied and applied St. Paul's words: "And when you sin in this way against your brothers and wound their weak conscience, you sin against Christ" (1 Corinthians 8:12). We don't ever want to force others to sin against their own conscience.

If a Christian feels that he or she cannot wear a mask for one reason or another, St. Paul clearly says that the person forcing the Christian to go against his or her conscience is sinning against Christ. To make a law and call something a sin where God has not made a law or called it a sin is exactly what the Pharisees of Jesus' time were doing. To make a Christian go against conscience is exactly what the people in Corinth were doing, as quoted above.

If Christians are not wearing masks, we cannot assume they are sinning. They may feel that being forced to wear a mask would cause them to sin against their conscience. They may be using their American rights under the government God has established to peacefully protest or resist. To judge others and assume that they are sinning is going against Jesus' words in Matthew 7:1-5: "Stop judging, so that you will not be judged. For with whatever standard you judge, you will be judged, and with whatever measure you measure, it will be measured to you. Why do you focus on the speck that is in your brother's eye, but do not consider the beam that is in your own eye? How will you tell your brother, 'Let me remove the speck from your eye,' when, in fact, you have a beam in your own eye? Hypocrite! First remove the beam from your own eye, and then you will see clearly to remove the speck from your brother's eye."

Instead, it is best to put Luther's explanation of the 8th commandment into practice of "taking words and actions in the kindest possible way." I've had people tell me that they feel judged for not wearing a mask. I told them that I find that interesting since I've had others who wear a mask say they feel judged by those who don't wear a mask. My encouragement is always to follow the 8th commandment and take words and actions in the kindest possible way, which also means that we don't presume someone else's motives or judgments. I also tell them that if they feel strongly enough, the best policy is to follow Jesus' words in Matthew 18:15-18 to discuss it privately in person.

The weak and strong

In Romans 14, St. Paul talks about weak and strong Christians in light of those who eat unclean or clean foods. Paul does not want strong Christians to pass judgment on weak Christians. Nor does he want weak Christians to look down on strong Christians. Paul understands that the strong Christian is tempted to think that because the weak Christian doesn't see things clearly, his faith is in jeopardy. But Paul also knows that the weak Christian is tempted to think that because his fellow believer does things he himself thinks are sins, that means his fellow Christian is sinning.

That's why Paul begins the chapter advising, "Accept a person who is weak in faith, and do not pass judgment on things that are just a difference of opinion" (Romans 14:1).

We can apply Paul's counsel to the way people dealt with Covid. Some may have thought others were weak because they were wearing masks or staying home or getting a shot. But turn that around and some may have thought the others were sinning because they weren't taking the virus seriously by not wearing a mask or staying home or getting a shot and a booster. The key Paul says is that we shouldn't be passing judgment on each other. That's why Paul writes, "But you, why do you pass judgment on your brother? And you, why do you look down on your brother? For we will all stand before God's judgment seat" (Romans 14:10).

Instead of arguing and passing judgment on each other, God's goal is for both the weak and the strong Christian to live in peace (Romans 15:6) and to build each other up in the Christian faith. Too often, we saw people judging and tearing each other down. The devil loves the disunity he causes in Christian churches.

In Romans 14, Paul is writing to the Roman Christians specifically about eating meat, but we can apply this to anything that isn't commanded or forbidden by God. He concludes the chapter, "But the one who has doubts is condemned if he eats, because it does not proceed from faith. Everything that does not proceed from faith is sin" (Romans 14:23). It is a sin to act contrary to conscience. If a person incorrectly thinks God does not want him to do a particular thing, but he does it anyway, that person is sinning against the 1st Commandment. This means we need to be very careful when we are compelling someone to do something – or when we are compelled by someone to do something. This is also true of the government with its mandates and laws. Outward compliance can be compelled. Christian commitment cannot.

Loving your neighbor

Perhaps you've heard people on the subject of masks say "Jesus would have worn a mask;" "Jesus would have practiced social distancing;" "Love your neighbor and do these things." No, I'm pretty sure Jesus would not have worn a mask. He is the perfect Son of God. I'm pretty sure Jesus would not have practiced social distancing, either – since there was a rule for Jews to stay socially distanced from lepers. But Jesus broke that rule plenty of times. He not only closed the distance with the lepers, he talked with them. More than that, he touched them. When Jesus came into contact with disease, sickness, ceremonial uncleanness, or demon possession – he brought healing and wellness.

When people have been told, "Love your neighbor, wear a mask," are they really wearing the mask out of love or coercion?

We cannot demand how others show love to us. If a wife demands that her husband bring her flowers every week to show his love to her, is he bringing those flowers out of love or manipulation? If dad tells his children to go give grandma a hug, but they don't want to because she's old and smells funny ... when they finally give her a hug, is it because they are showing love to her or because they're afraid of being disciplined later? Kindness cannot be mandated.

Let's turn it around. Might people who are demanding (that others wear a mask, or receive a vaccine, or stay six feet away) be bullying? Can telling others they need to do this out of love actually be manipulating with guilt? Maybe you had a mother or grandmother who liked guilting you into doing something for her: "I raised you, I cared for you, I did so much for you. Surely you can do this one little thing!" Or you dated someone who tried to manipulate you: "If you really loved me you would ..."

Some people feel the personal choices of others are selfish and need to be regulated. What's especially selfish is expecting others to surrender their liberties so some may enjoy a false sense of security.

Demanding that others demonstrate love by wearing a mask, or getting a vaccine, staying 6 feet apart can be as manipulative as the Judaizers telling the Christians in Galatia, "Love your neighbor; be circumcised." St. Paul had some pretty strong words for the Galatians who gave in to the Judaizers and their unjust demands (Galatians 3:1-6).

As part of a group conversation I was in, one person mentioned that he had to wear a mask to two businesses as he made deliveries in their buildings. He asked, "Am I showing love by wearing a mask?" Someone answered, "You could be showing love. ... Or you could be perpetuating a lie." Is it loving to wear a mask because someone asks you to? Or is it loving to refuse to wear the mask? Are you helping a weak heart? Or are you enabling someone who has bought into a lie?

Consider how St. Paul refused to have Titus circumcised (Galatians 2:3-5). Circumcising Titus would have been tantamount to abandoning the gospel of justification among the Galatians who were demanding circumcision as part of Christianity. Yet, St. Paul circumcised Timothy to avoid offending the Jews (Acts 16:1).

Even though you feel very strongly about the uselessness or even harmfulness of masks, perhaps you wear a mask because someone asks you to. But then you refuse to wear a mask because someone else tells you to. It might seem like you are inconsistent. But you are actually being consistent with St. Paul. You wear a mask to not put a stumbling block in your relationship. You refuse to wear a mask with someone who has made the mask a stumbling block for you.

If you feel offended by someone not wearing a mask, it isn't that they don't love you. They may have medical, spiritual, or conscientious reasons. If you feel offended that someone is wearing a mask, it isn't that they are fearful or are lacking faith. They may have medical, spiritual, or conscientious reasons themselves.

And, from a human reason perspective: That person is not responsible for your feelings. That person's actions will only be distasteful if you assign some sort of blame, judgment, or guilt to their action. Taking their words and actions in the kindest possible way means recognizing such judgment within ourselves, and being okay with our own decision – even if someone else decided differently.

What was Jesus' answer to all this? One day, an expert in the law approached Jesus with a question, "Which commandment is the greatest of all" (Mark 12:28)? Jesus answered, ""The most important is: 'Hear, O Israel, the Lord, our God, the Lord is one. You shall love the Lord your God with all your heart, with all your soul, with all your mind, and with all your strength.' The second is this: 'You shall love your neighbor as yourself.' There is no other commandment greater than these" (Mark 12:29-31). Jesus did not get into the kind of debate the lawyer was used to. Instead, he saw beyond the man's question. The law is not about legalistic righteousness but about love. The lawyer didn't understand love, so he missed the heart of the commandments.

There has been a lot of discussion lately about love. People – even church officials – are telling others what to do out of love. Wear a mask, get a vaccine, stand apart from others, don't question, don't debate, the list goes on. But when you're told how to love, that's not love. That's obedience. Love is from the heart. You cannot make someone love you. They choose to do that. You cannot legislate love. Love is granted. It is given. It is a gift. Not a mandate. People – Christians – are just as confused about the nature of love as this Jewish lawyer was.

Churches must understand the boundary of personal choice and conscience. They must never bind someone's conscience. They must instead free the conscience with Christ's forgiveness. Churches are to concern themselves with Word and Sacrament ministry, rather than novel therapies and dubious facial coverings.

Christian freedom

I've discussed masks with the pastors in my ministry area on several occasions. Some suggested we should wear a mask because experts say it helps prevent the spread of the virus. I countered that then the mask is a medical device and people should have bodily autonomy over anything medically. Others then countered my counter by admitting the mask is nothing more than a piece of fabric. So I countered their counter by pointing out that if a mask is just mere fabric, it isn't going to do anything against an airborne virus. Then it is nothing more than a placebo.[97] I explained that you can't have it both ways.

When the city of Racine and state of Wisconsin where I live mandated wearing masks in indoor locations, our church did not enforce mask-wearing. We had always offered two worship services on Sunday mornings. In their Christian freedom, people used their reasoning and conscience to decide whether they would wear a mask to church or not. We then added a third Sunday worship service where we did mandate masks for those who felt more comfortable if everyone was wearing a mask.

At the beginning of the pandemic, as the city of Racine began issuing an indoor mask mandate, I called several of our city officials to get their opinion on how this affected churches. I was told by two different Racine representatives that "it is not the church's responsibility to enforce the government's mandates." That was from both an official in the mayor's office and a Racine alderman. That's good advice. The government should not be enforcing church rules, policies, or doctrines. The church should not be enforcing government rules, laws, or mandates. We each have our own separate roles to play in God's two kingdoms. We confuse the two kingdoms – earthly and spiritual kingdoms – when either authority encroaches into the other authority's

---

[97] In the M*A*S*H episode entitled "Major Topper," Hawkeye and B.J. convincingly swap sugar pills for morphine. Placebos can work. But they cannot replace real medicine. Plus, the medical professionals who are pushing the placebos are lying to their patients and the public.

domain.

We do have Christian freedom. We see things in different ways. We draw lines in different places. We can disagree. That's fine. That's good. That's healthy.

St. Peter gives us some great advice for how to live in Christian freedom: "Live as free men, but do not use your freedom as a cover-up for evil; live as servants of God. Show proper respect to everyone: Love the brotherhood of believers, fear God, honor the king" (1 Peter 2:16, 17).

One of the families at our Lutheran elementary school gave me permission to share their letter exempting their children from wearing masks in school. I like how the parent appealed to medical, religious, and legal concerns:

> Please acknowledge this notice written on behalf of my child. I, the parent, find concerns medically, religiously, and legally, of the current mask ordinance in place. Masks are ineffective for the purpose claimed by the mandate, cause physical harm when used as your mandate requires, and are only authorized for use by an EUA. We strive to do no harm to our own bodies and the bodies of others as our religion teaches, therefore we also find the mask mandate in violation of our deeply held religious beliefs and are requesting exemption for all current and future mask mandates as put forth by the city of Racine.

The next letter is from the administration at another Lutheran elementary school when the city of Milwaukee mandated masks. The administration left it up to the parents' judgment on whether or not their children would wear masks to school:

> In response to the rise of the Omicron variant of the COVID-19 virus, The City of Milwaukee Common Council, on January 18, passed an ordinance that "requires any person over 3 years old who enters a building open to the public to wear a face covering. The ordinance further

specifies that the indoor face covering requirement shall be in effect until Tuesday, March 1, 2022." Our acting mayor made effective with his signature this ordinance which applies to public settings. The final ordinance has been published and is now effective.

Throughout the COVID pandemic, our Lutheran School has honored our governing authorities by complying with their mandates and will do so with this most recent one.

However, you should be aware, the ordinance does allow for exceptions. First, it is not clear if this ordinance applies to our Lutheran School as it is a private institution and is not a building "open to the public." In addition, we invite our families, faculty, and staff to read for themselves the exceptions the Common Council has granted in the text of the ordinance which can be read here, see page six.

Our Lutheran School does not have the resources to track or collect proof that an exception has been met. Our Lutheran School also will continue to trust our families, faculty, and staff to use their judgment in determining whether an exemption is warranted. We will assume unmasked students come from families that have concluded an exemption is in order.

We thank you for your support. As always, we commend all of our Lutheran School families to God's loving care, and we encourage you to pray regularly for wisdom.

The Covid vaccine

Following the mandating of masks, social distancing, and lockdowns, was the mandating of the Covid-19 vaccine. Many in our nation viewed the vaccine as a path to get back to normal as soon as possible. But as more research and results came in, this

Covid vaccine turned out to be the *Star Wars Holiday Special*[98] of vaccines.

There were serious issues with the way people were bribed and bullied by their government and employers into receiving the vaccine. City and state governments bribed citizens into getting the vaccine by giving out free doughnuts or cream puffs, hamburgers and French fries, guns, pick-up trucks, and more. Colleges bribed students into getting the vaccine by entering them to win a scooter or scholarship. Grocery stores offered $10 gift cards.

But governments, universities, and institutions did more than bribe. They also bullied. Unvaccinated children were turned away from camps. Unvaccinated students were forced to take regular Covid tests and wear a mask while vaccinated students were back to normal. Unvaccinated adults were turned away from necessary surgeries. Unvaccinated firefighters, police officers, doctors, nurses, military personnel, and more were fired for not receiving the vaccination.

This was government-mandated segregation. It is unethical to make a citizen choose between their personal medical decisions and earning a living. It is immoral to force employees to receive a jab or lose their job. It is abhorrent to demand people get a shot they don't want for a virus they're not afraid of.

Children must first submit to parental authority

Some colleges and universities are advising their students to receive a vaccine because it is mandated by the government – or they are telling students to wear a mask on campus because that is the government mandate. They are advising Christian students to do this as submission to the government and out of obedience to the 4th commandment.

Yet, children are first under the submission of their parents. They are first to obey their parents under the 4th commandment. If the parents tell their students not to wear a mask for medical,

---

98 The Star Wars Holiday Special originally aired on CBS on November 17, 1978. It is rightfully mocked as a notoriously bad show. It does feature the introduction of Boba Fett, though.

emotional, or spiritual concerns, the parents are the primary authority over their children, not the government. If the parents advise their students not to receive a vaccine for health or religious freedoms, the parents are the primary authority over their children, not the government.

This is essential to reiterate: Children belong to their parents. God gave parents the primary authority and responsibility for the complete wellbeing of their child.

When employers, universities, schools - even churches - encourage, incentivize or castigate young people to undergo a medical procedure with wearing a mask, receiving a vaccine or anything else - simply because the government says so, they are placing the authority of the government above the authority of the parents. God gave parents the role of raising their children. The government is to assist parents in that role ... not subvert that role.

For employers, universities, and government entities to remove the medical decisions from the parents is nefarious. For employers and government entities compelling employees or citizens to transgress their human reasoning and conscience (such as their personal decision on wearing a mask or receiving a shot) is depraved.

Religiously, we know going against conscience, reasoning, and deeply held religious beliefs is wrong and indecent. Ethically, some of our governing authorities admitted this is an abuse of the federal government's power and the President's executive authority. Six U.S. Senators stated as much when they penned a letter opposing the President's mandated vaccine policy.

> "These COVID-19 vaccine mandates amount to a serious abuse of both federal power and executive authority. They also further strain the economic and social pressures our society currently faces, while completely ignoring existing evidence-based data on natural immunity from previous COVID-19 infection. Further, evidence-based research has conclusively shown that vaccination does not stop the spread of COVID-19. In any

> event, President Biden has no business forcing people to make a tragic choice between unemployment and an unwanted vaccination," the letter said. [99]

It is against the Nuremberg Code to use medical procedures on patients without their informed consent. When citizens or employees are coerced into receiving a vaccine, that is going against the Nuremberg Code – because in such cases, people are not given the information on risks, benefits, or side effects; they are not given the free choice to receive or reject a therapy. Informed consent requires all these elements. Consider the opening portion of the Code's first point:

> The voluntary consent of the human subject is absolutely essential. This means that the person involved should have legal capacity to give consent; should be so situated as to be able to exercise free power of choice, without the intervention of any element of force, fraud, deceit, duress, overreaching, or other ulterior form of constraint or coercion; and should have sufficient knowledge and comprehension of the elements of the subject matter involved as to enable him to make an understanding and enlightened decision..The Health Insurance Portability and Accountability Act (HIPPA) is a law that protects your privacy as a patient. It is against HIPPA laws for businesses, employers, and government authorities to demand to know your vaccine status to enter or work there – because they would be demanding private medical information as a condition of employment. [100]

Enforcement of the Covid vaccine

---

[99] Politico.com (2/14/2022)

[100]The Nuremburg Code is a set of ethical research principles for human experimentation created from the Nuremberg trials that were held after WWII.

I have a daughter in Army ROTC and National Guard. She opposes the mandatory vaccine policy. Does the military have the authority to force their soldiers to receive this shot? That's a good question. The President of the United States does have the constitutional authority as Commander in Chief to command the military. George Washington had all his soldiers vaccinated for smallpox. He couldn't win a war against the British if all his soldiers were sick. While there is precedent for requiring inoculation, the risk of Covid mortality for the young and fit is significantly less than the mortality risk for those in their 70s and 80s. Human reason would seem to urge caution on this experimental therapy for the military. This is why there are so many soldiers from various U.S. military branches that are suing the President because their religious exemptions to this shot were all denied.

The President has certain powers over the military by virtue of being the Commander in Chief. However, he does not have those same powers over American citizens. He cannot command American citizens to receive medical treatment. He is not the Physician in Chief, nor does he hold dictatorial powers over citizens.

The U.S. President is mandating businesses to compel this vaccine on its employees. But if the President's mandate is deemed illegal and unconstitutional, then the President is mandating businesses to do something that is both illegal and unconstitutional. Whether the mandate is found to be illegal and unconstitutional is really immaterial. Our bodies do not belong to the government. They don't belong to our employers. They don't even belong to us. They belong to God. Our bodies are temples of the Holy Spirit that come from God (1 Corinthians 6:19). Your body does not belong to your employer, your university, or your government. It is your body that belongs to God and given to you. You have bodily, personal autonomy. There is nothing Christian in an attitude that allows authorities to enslave employees and citizens' bodies.

Once you lose body sovereignty, you've lost possession of your own body.

In the past, we would always get a second opinion on a medical diagnosis from a doctor. We would get a second quote before having a repair done on our vehicle. We would get a second quote before a major home remodel. Yet, when it comes to the Covid-19 vaccine, the federal government, the media, and social media have shut down second opinions. An opinion that does not fit the prescribed narrative about the Covid vaccine is fact-checked on social media, denigrated by the legacy media, and deemed false, misleading, or missing context.

General Patton famously stated, "If everyone is thinking alike, then somebody isn't thinking." The ability to question, the ability to have dialogue, the ability to hypothesize – that's real science. Fully empowered and fully informed citizens are the greatest threat to tyranny. Making you look to the experts is conditioning you to become subservient to the state instead of living your freedom.

Notice how you are being hypnotized into believing you can't speak up because you're not an expert. That's like saying you can't grow vegetables because you're not a farmer, cannot fix a leaky toilet because you're not a plumber, cannot teach students because you're not a teacher, or cannot define a woman unless you're a biologist. When we lose our wits, we surrender to the mantra and motive – rather than resist with respect and resolve.

We used to be a country that celebrated the Renaissance man. Someone who knew a lot about a lot of subjects. Now we have established an elitism of experts.

These experts don't want questions. They just want authority, mindless obedience that applauds the Emperor's new clothing without a second thought that perhaps the Emperor is really naked. And even a child's simple question unravels the expert's authority.

When did we stop thinking for ourselves? Why are we so quick to run to an expert for comfort and guidance, or obey the doctor speaking at the news conference? Why are we so rash as to desert our God-given reason and take refuge in the experimental or farcical?

There are numerous stories of injuries after receiving the Covid-19 vaccine. Young healthy athletes are dropping to the floor with sudden heart conditions. People are experiencing dizziness immediately after receiving the shot. There are increasing reports of strokes, face paralysis, blood clots, and myocarditis – which is an inflammation of the heart muscle. There have been numerous cases of unexplained deaths. These are deaths of people who are in excellent physical condition – athletes, firefighters, actors, singers, and others. Miscarriages and stillbirths are on the rise. There has been an increase of neurological disease and cardiac arrests. Women are facing sudden and unexplained changes in their menstruation cycles. Post-menopausal women have started having a period after the shot. That's a red flag for cancer.

I encourage you to do your own research. Go to www.realnotrare.com to read horrifying, first person stories of vaccine-related injuries.

Also go to www.openvaers.com. According to that website, as of March 25, 2022 there have been 26,396 Covid vaccination reported deaths. There have been 145,781 total Covid vaccination proposed hospitalizations. There have been 1,205,753 Covid vaccination adverse event reports. There were more VAERS reports in 3 months of 2021 than the total reports made in the previous 360 months. According to VAERS data, there are more injuries from the Covid vaccine than all the other vaccines combined from 1990 to 2021. From the CDC's own VAERS data, there are over 1000 studies of people being injured from this vaccine.

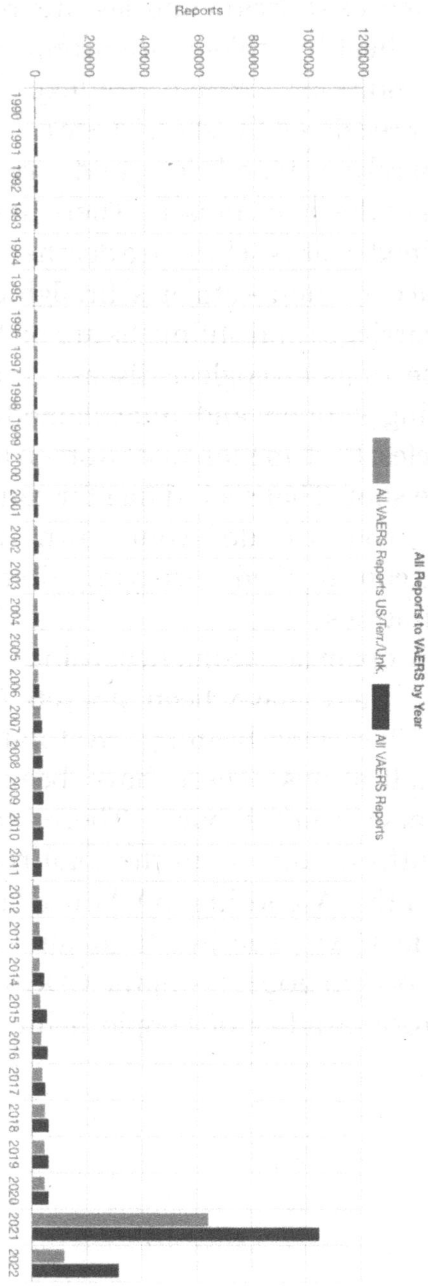
All Reports to VAERS by Year
All VAERS Reports US/Terr./Unk.
All VAERS Reports
Reports
0
200000
400000
600000
800000
1000000
1200000
Received Year
1990 1991 1992 1993 1994 1995 1996 1997 1998 1999 2000 2001 2002 2003 2004 2005 2006 2007 2008 2009 2010 2011 2012 2013 2014 2015 2016 2017 2018 2019 2020 2021 2022

You won't hear about these adverse reactions, hospitalizations, or deaths through the legacy media. You need to do your own research. Don't automatically believe the narrative. Find your own facts.

With this vaccine, all people want is to be treated like adults. Tell us the truth. The vaccine[101] failed to accomplish what the experts and authorities promised. When in the history of vaccines has there been a vaccine that needed 1, 2, 3, 4+ booster shots? Is that truly a vaccine? Or should it correctly be labeled as a "therapeutic"?

As one online discussion said: Why do the protected need to be protected from the unprotected by forcing the unprotected to get the protection that didn't protect the protected in the first place?

Religious exemptions for the Covid vaccine

Just like it is beneficial for you to read the exemption letters for masks, it is equally beneficial for you to read some examples of exemption letters for the Covid-19 vaccine. The first letter is a general letter that a fellow Lutheran pastor shared so that others could make use of it in their personal setting:

> I am requesting a religious exemption from (Name of Business) vaccination requirement. Receiving this vaccine directly contradicts my sincerely held beliefs. As a Christian I am guided by the authority of God's Word which warns of the danger of acting against one's conscience, "Everything that does not come from faith is sin" (Romans 14:23). As a pro-life Christian I am conscientiously opposed to vaccines that have either been produced or tested on cell lines derived from aborted

[101] According to Modern's SEC filing, the COVID mRNA "vaccine" does not fit a traditional vaccine. It is not a live virus vaccine, or a dead virus vaccine. It is a gene therapy. The CDC has changed their definition of "vaccine" to include the Covid shot in the same category as the MMR or polio vaccines, although these shots are categorically different.

fetuses. Since all three available COVID-19 vaccines in the United States have utilized fetal cell lines (Johnson & Johnson utilized the PER-C6 cell line in the production and testing phrase / both Pfizer and Moderna utilized the HEK-293 cell line in the testing phase)1 I am strongly opposed to receiving any of these vaccines. The Bible indicates that my body is a gift from God (Psalm 139:13-16) and a temple of the Holy Spirit (1 Corinthians 6:19-20). Therefore, the health and medical choices that I make provide an opportunity for me to worship God (1 Corinthians 10:31). I would ask that you not inhibit my ability to worship God according to the dictates of my conscience.

Thank you for honoring my conscientious objection.

As I'm sharing religious exemption letters, here is the letter I wrote for my daughter Miriam's religious exemption to refuse the Covid-19 vaccination for the Army ROTC. Her commanding officer told her it was the most comprehensive religious exemption letter he had ever received.

I am writing on behalf of my daughter and member of my congregation, Miriam Zarling. Miriam is seeking a religious exemption from the Covid-19 vaccine mandate. Miriam is a member of Water of Life Lutheran Church of Racine, Wisconsin. Water of Life is part of the Wisconsin Evangelical Lutheran Synod (WELS) which does not have an official position statement regarding vaccines. However, the WELS has steadfastly maintained a pro-life position that acknowledges that life begins at conception. Since all three vaccines that currently have Emergency Use Authorization in the United States have been tested and/or produced via fetal cell lines derived from aborted babies (PER-C6 and HEK-293 cell lines) our church honors the conscientious objections of those who are opposed to vaccines or therapeutics that utilize fetal cell lines. Our church is guided by the authority of God's Word which warns of the danger of acting against one's conscience, "Everything that does not come from faith is sin" (Romans 14:23).

Beyond the use of fetal cell lines, there are many reasons why Miriam and other members of our congregation and church body are conscientiously opposed to the Covid-19 vaccines. For one thing, we believe there is a grave danger in stimulating an adaptive immune response through the production of proteins rather than depending on the innate immune system fearfully and wonderfully designed by our Creator God. There are potential adverse long-term impacts to the immune system that we have not fully realized in addition to the clearly observed and identified short-term adverse reactions. As we learn of more and more cases of myocarditis, pericarditis, thrombocytopenia, miscarriages, Bell's palsy, anaphylaxis and even death in otherwise healthy individuals *(latest VAERS numbers from the CDC can be easily accessed at www.openvaers.com/covid-data)*, it begs the question why there is such pressure to get the vaccine especially for children and young adults who likely would not have any challenges in naturally overcoming Covid-19.

Miriam and other members of the WELS firmly believe that God designed our immune systems to handle most pathogens especially when properly supported by good nutrition, adequate sleep, sunshine, etc. Scripture makes it abundantly clear that our bodies are fearfully and wonderfully made (Psalm 139:13-17) and God the Holy Spirit dwells within our bodies as his temple (1 Corinthians 6:19-20). Therefore, we believe that as stewards of our God-given body and immune system a Christian can be conscientiously opposed to any artificial intervention that would interfere with the body's God-designed function.

The worldview of many leading scientists who are pushing this particular vaccine is a worldview that does not honor God's gift of life at conception, nor does it acknowledge a Creator God who is actively working through a person's God-given immune system. Their worldview believes that science must be the answer since this is part of the evolution of humanity. Our Christian worldview, however, cherishes God's gift of life from conception to natural death. Our Christian worldview is that God has blessed us with a breathtakingly beautiful and marvelously complex immune system complete with T-cells, B-cells, macrophages, antibodies, etc. that can target and attack foreign pathogens. Our Christian worldview is that God has blessed us with natural ways of supporting the immune system and he has also provided medical treatments that have been proven all around the world and demonstrated in peer reviewed studies to deal with Covid-19 when used prophylactically or early treatment methods. Therefore, Miriam is conscientiously opposed to any ideology that claims that there is only one way to deal with this pandemic, namely through a worldwide vaccination campaign.

Furthermore, our church supports the freedom of an individual Christian to make their own medical decisions based on their unique health history and conscientious beliefs in consultation with their doctor and pastor without coercion.

The Christian Church holds that a person may be required to refuse a medical intervention, including a vaccination, if his or her informed conscience comes to this sure judgment. While the Church generally encourages the use of safe and effective vaccines as a way of safeguarding personal and public health, vaccination is not morally obligatory in principle and so must be voluntary. As a Christian, Miriam is a citizen of Christ's Kingdom. She is also an American citizen. Based on the dual citizenship of these two kingdoms, Miriam is exercising her rights of personal, medical, and religious freedoms when it comes to the Covid-19 vaccine:

1. There is a general moral duty to refuse the use of medical products, including certain vaccines, that are produced using human cells lines derived from direct abortions.

2. A person's informed judgments about the proportionality of medical interventions are to be respected unless they contradict authoritative moral teachings.

3. A person is morally required to obey his/her sure conscience.

4. A person must do no harm to his/her body. There is mounting evidence of this particular vaccine doing great harm to people who have received it.

5. A Christian may judge it wrong to receive certain vaccines for a variety of reasons consistent with these teachings, and there is no authoritative Church teaching universally obliging Christians to receive any vaccine. A Christian might refuse a vaccine based on the Church's teachings concerning therapeutic proportionality. Therapeutic proportionality is an assessment of whether the benefits of a medical intervention outweigh the undesirable side-effects and burdens in light of the integral good of the person, including spiritual, psychological, and bodily goods.

Thank you for honoring the conscientious and religious objections of Miriam Anna Zarling.

At the beginning of this virus, I led a Bible study as we walked through Martin Luther's treatise: *How Should A Christian Act During a Deadly Epidemic?* In 1527 the epidemic named the Black Death raged through Germany, including the city of Wittenberg. Duke John ordered the professors and students of Wittenberg University to move to the city of Jena for safety. Professor Martin

Luther, who also served as a local pastor, resisted his governing authority and refused to leave and remained to comfort the sick. People wrote to Luther asking him whether a Christian could flee during the epidemic or should rather stay in his city even if it endangers his own health. After repeated appeals for his opinion, and after others began criticizing Luther's own actions, he wrote and published his letter to the people. I've included a few quotes. I encourage you to read the entire document online.

> If it be God's will that evil come upon us and destroy us, none of our precautions will help us. Everybody must take this to heart: first of all, if he feels bound to remain where death rages in order to serve his neighbor, let him put himself in God's hands and say, "Lord, I am in your hands; you have kept me here; your will be done. I am your humble creature. You can kill me or save me in this plague in the same way as if I were threatened by fire, water, drought, or any other danger." [102]

> Therefore, dear friends, let us not become so desperate as to desert our own people whom we are duty-bound to help and instead flee in such a cowardly way from the terror of the devil, or allow him the joy of mocking us and vexing and distressing God and all his angels. For the Christian who despises such great promises and commands of God and leaves his own people in need, is truly violating all of God's laws and is guilty of 10 the murder of his neighbor whom he abandons.[103]

> The devil is enjoying himself as he sees the terror and flight which he is causing among us.[104]

---

[102] *How Should A Christian Act During a Deadly Epidemic?* par. 15
[103] Ibid. par 24
[104] Ibid. par 31

I'm sure you've guessed where I stand on masks, lockdowns, social distancing, the Covid vaccine, and more. I'm sure members of my congregation have also been able to guess where I stand on these issues. But I don't speak about them publicly. If someone wants to ask me privately, I'll certainly do that. I let them know these are my own sincerely held religious beliefs. I don't speak for my church or church body. I only speak for myself. I won't try to convince them in any way. If they have questions, I encourage them to do the research and come to their own conclusions.

Sometimes my homebound members will want to talk about the vaccine. They'll ask if I'm vaccinated. I tell them, "Everything about this vaccine has become too political. I'm not comfortable talking about it. But if you want to talk about my colonoscopy, let's go." For some reason, that's the end of the conversation.

The Divine Physician

As pastors, we do not give advice on surgeries, procedures, medications, or therapies. We wisely remain silent on those medical procedures. As pastors, let us not wade into the quagmire recently created by Covid or the response to Covid. Everything having to do with this virus is also medically related. If pastors encourage people to receive the vaccine, that may turn off those who have strong feelings against the vaccine. If pastors discourage people not to receive the vaccine, they may turn off those who have strong feelings for the vaccine.

We work for the Divine Physician. That does not qualify us as physicians. Let the real physicians do their work on the body. We wouldn't want them doing our work. Instead, let us focus on being the physicians of the soul we were called to be. Our culture is already fixated on the treasures and pleasures, the threats and fears of this world. Let us as pastors give people what they really need.

What do they need? A real family to belong to in Holy Baptism. A unity unlike any other in the Sacrament of the Lord's Supper. A state of grace through confession and absolution. The peace that surpasses all understanding in God's never-changing Word for an ever-changing world. A Savior who loves us enough that no matter what we become infected with or die from – he has given us a home with him in heaven through faith in his atoning death and glorious resurrection.

We don't know the present. But we do know the future. We don't know what's going on. But we do know where we're going. We alone as Christians have been given the vision of faith to set the present into the context of the future. As pastors our calling is to announce to our members, our community, and our culture the coming of Christ in the flesh. Prepare the way of the Lord!

Many in our culture have lost hope. Let us give them hope for the present ... and for the future. A hope not built on anything in this world. But a hope built on everything in the world to come with our Savior Jesus (1 Thessalonians 4:13-14).

Fear

In *Star Wars: The Phantom Menace*,[105] Jedi Knight Qui-Gon Jinn finds young Anakin Skywalker on the desert planet of Tatooine. Anakin is strong in the Force, so Qui-Gon Jinn brings Anakin before Master Yoda and the rest of the Jedi Council. But Yoda can sense great fear within the boy. Yoda gives this sage advice on fear: "Fear is the path to the dark side. Fear leads to anger. Anger leads to hate. Hate leads to suffering."

Anakin spent 10 years fearing that he would lose his mother. After a dream of his mother being captured and tortured by the Tuskens, Anakin flew to his home planet of Tatooine, found his mother bound inside the Tusken' tent in the desert, freed her, and then released his anger by slaughtering all the males, females, and even children in the camp.

Later, Anakin had another dream of his wife Padme dying. He was looking for a way to prevent her death. It was this fear of abandonment that led him to feel betrayed by his master Obi Wan and the entire Jedi Council. He then turned to Emperor Palpatine for guidance and trusted a new master. In doing so, Anakin turned to the dark side of the Force.

Fear is a gift from God. It's fear that often keeps us safe. Not all fear is bad. A small child needs to have a proper fear of automobiles and traffic. Adults need fear so they don't plunge foolishly into stupid situations that most likely will result in an unhappy ending. A healthy fear stops people from saying and doing things that are harmful, hurtful, and downright dangerous. That's why King Solomon wisely teaches, "The fear of the Lord is the beginning of wisdom" (Proverbs 9:10).

But fear loses its godly purpose when it cripples us and rules us with an iron hand.

---

105 Despite popular opinion, I thought *Star Wars: The Phantom Menace* was a decent movie. Darth Maul was definitely cool. But JarJar Binks was just dumb. And don't get me started on Midichlorians!

Do not be afraid

Fear is a common, every-day emotion. Perhaps it is even the strongest of human emotions, often stemming from the unknown, unfamiliar, and indefinite. We could say that underlying all these fears is a common thread – the fear of being alone or of going it alone. Whether it is the fear of the little toddler standing desperately alone in the department store crying for his mommy, or the single mom or dad newly divorced and worried about the future, or the elderly person living alone in the house after 50 years of marriage – the greatest fear is being alone.

It's that fear of abandonment that led Anakin Skywalker to the dark side and becoming Darth Vader.

What are you afraid of? Are you afraid of the economy, of having your Medicare or Social Security cut or losing your job or your home? Are you afraid when your child is ill or cancer strikes or a loved one enters the hospital? Are you afraid of the monster under your bed or the bogeyman in your closet, or afraid of the dark or heights?

We fear because we falsely believe we are going it alone. We need to listen to the Lord remind us of his abiding presence. Before Abram made his big move to Canaan, as Joshua was trying to fill Moses' shoes as the next leader of Israel, or as Joseph and Mary were about to welcome the birth of the promised Messiah, God gave all of them the same message he gives you. "Do not be afraid." When the Israelites in Isaiah's day were facing deportation and captivity, God reassured his people with this promise: "Do not fear, for I am with you. Do not be overwhelmed, for I am your God. I will strengthen you. Yes, I will help you. I will uphold you with my righteous right hand" (Isaiah 41:10).

When my youngest daughter Belle was 5 years old, within the same week she learned how to swim without her floaties and ride her bike without her training wheels. Many people might discount a 31-pound, 41 inch tall, little girl swimming or riding her bike. But the whole time while she was learning, her dad was walking in front of her in the pool with arms outstretched or running behind her on the sidewalk with arms extended. Sure, she swallowed a little water and suffered a few scrapes, but that's how she learned, got better, and became more confident. She was then able to move on to even greater things.

To the devil and the world, you may appear to be frightened, weak, lonely, little boys and girls. But go ahead and let them dismiss you. They can't see whom you can see. When the Lord reminds you not to be afraid because he is with you, he really is with you. He is running behind you to catch you. He is walking beside you to rescue you. He is watching over you, keeping an eye on you, and always protecting you. Sure, you might get some scrapes and scratches, some bumps and bruises along the way. But that's only because your Heavenly Father is allowing you to learn, grow, get better, and become more confident. He is preparing you to do even greater things. He is preparing you with a faith that overcomes all fears.

Trusting this, we are still consumed with a myriad of fears. In 2020 and the two years following, it was easy to identify a single, predominant fear that gripped three billion people around the globe. The Covid-19 pandemic captured the attention of a worldwide audience.

There was the fear of the spread of the pandemic. Fear of those not wearing masks and gloves. Fear if you were wearing a mask your immune system would be compromised and children's speech development would be delayed. Fear of social isolation. Fear that there were no children's athletic events to attend, no sports to watch, no new entertainment to binge, no toilet paper or baby formula at the stores, no vacations or proms or graduations to enjoy.

In the dystopian novel *Brave New World* by Aldous Huxley, Soma was a free drug that provided all the pleasure of sex without the commitment. Soma kept the people completely pacified as they were manipulated and influenced by science and technology. The people allowed themselves to become slaves to instant gratification. Has government, science, and technology used the promise of replacing fear with instant gratification become this generation's Soma?

In the beginning, the fear of a world-wide novel virus was rational. But once we knew what we were facing, the media, the government, and experts induced within us an irrational fear. That's why millions of healthy people stayed indoors for over a year – even when it was proven that fresh air and vitamin D from the sun led to better outcomes. That irrational fear is why people wore masks while walking alone outdoors – even when it was proven there was no benefit in doing so. That's why parents did not allow their children to play with others – even though the mortality rate of healthy children from Covid was virtually zero percent.

Fear drove us to do irrational and unloving things all in the name of "safety." We allowed hospitals to not let us see our sick children or our dying parents – which caused even more depression and fear. We stayed away from nursing homes and subjected our children to "class" through a videoconference. We accepted the closure of our small businesses – which caused hardship and heartache on top of the stress of a virus.

The "cure" for Covid became worse than the disease.

Fear induced us into needlessly doing un-Christian things inside our churches. Christians are called upon to sing God's praises; we stopped singing. We are called to gather God's people for worship and fellowship; we limited the number of people inside the sanctuary and cut off fellowship. We are invited to celebrate the Sacrament as often as possible; we created weird ways of distributing the Sacrament for those in-person for worship and unintentionally treated the Sacrament as unimportant for those who worshiped online. [106]

Fear created a chasm between people in church. Those who wanted everyone to wear masks judged and cajoled those who

---

[106] Some churches in this country even attempted to provide Holy Communion via Youtube. Such a practice is not in line with the character of the Supper, and against the Biblical practice of closed communion. The Supper, by its very nature, is a fellowship meal where communicants gather together and receive the same Meal by mouth.

refused to wear masks. Those who refused to wear masks judged and belittled those who wore masks. So often we wavered between precaution and paranoia. There was virtue-signaling on both sides when it came to the virus.

All this over a virus that we knew – even early on – was survivable by virtually every single person who contracted it.

Testing God

As people wavered between precaution and paranoia, they verbally wondered if not wearing a mask – or not receiving a Covid vaccine – was sinful because we are "testing" God. In one of the temptations in the desert, the devil tempted Jesus by taking him to the pinnacle of the temple in Jerusalem. The devil told Jesus, "If you are the Son of God, throw yourself down. For it is written: He will command his angels concerning you. And they will lift you up in their hands, so that you will not strike your foot against a stone" (Matthew 4:6). Jesus quoted Deuteronomy 6:16 back to Satan saying, "Again, it is written: You shall not test the Lord your God" (Matthew 4:7).

The people of Israel sinfully tested God at Massah by expecting him to immediately provide them with a miracle of water that he had not promised (Exodus 17:1-7). We have no right to test God and expect that he will do miracles whenever we want. Believers should not test God by exposing themselves to needless danger while expecting God to protect them.

But in Malachi 3:10, God invited his people specifically to test him and see that he would provide for them. "Bring the complete tithe to the storehouse so that there may be food in my house. Just test me in this, says the Lord of Armies. See whether I do not open for you the windows of heaven and pour down blessing on you, until there is more than enough." Here the Lord wants his people to test him by bringing the tithes of their wealth to him and trust that God would take care of them with ten percent less income. In this case the "testing" of God was trusting him, not making demands on him.

So, who is truly testing God with masks and vaccines? Is it the ones who refuse to wear a mask and get the shot? Are they testing God by sinfully expecting him to keep them safe from Covid? Or are they simply putting their trust in God that he wonderfully designed the human body to cope with various viruses? They may be testing God in a godly way, trusting God will provide health and healing through the human body and the vitamins and other proven medicines he has given us.

Could the ones who feel it necessary to wear a mask on top of receiving the vaccine be the ones who are testing God? Perhaps they are not trusting their body's natural immune system and the vitamins and other medicines that God has given to humanity.

There are nuances to the application of Scripture. We should not be so quick to judge another person's actions or presume to know the motives of their hearts. We humbly repent of our own failings of sinfully testing God instead of trusting him (Matthew 4:7). We graciously thank God when we live as sanctified saints testing and trusting God to provide (Malachi 3:10).

The difference between the two kinds of testing mentioned in Matthew and Malachi is faith. The Israelites tested God at Massah (Exodus 17) because they lacked faith in him. The Israelites in Malachi's day were invited to test God because they had faith in him. Christ refrained from testing God because he knew – he had the faith – that God would send his angels for supernatural saving. Jesus didn't need his Father to PROVE such angelic deliverance. Faithless testing demands God to act in a certain way, without Scriptural warrant for such a belief.

Faith by its very definition takes risks. "Faith is being sure about what we hope for, being convinced about things we do not see" (Hebrews 11:1). Every day is a risk. I do a lot of bicycling. Every time I'm on the road with knucklehead drivers I'm at risk. Expressing your faith in a woke workplace is risky. Having a child enter the military is risky. Sending our children onto a bus with no seat belts, into a flu factory like a school building, and then onto an athletic field is always a risk. But we trust that the Lord (who, by the way, sends his angels to watch over his saints) is in control. When we trust God to take care of us, taking those measured risks is testing God in faith.

When we view God through doubt, and demand something of him as a way of determining whether he can be trusted, then we are sinfully testing God. That's no different than the time the Pharisees began to argue with Jesus. Mark reports, "To test him, they asked him for a sign from heaven. He sighed deeply in his spirit and said, 'Why does this generation seek a sign? Amen I tell you: No such sign will be given to this generation'" (Mark 8:11, 12).

Fear is the enemy of faith

President Franklin Delano Roosevelt famously said in his first inaugural speech in March of 1933: "So, first of all, let me assert my firm belief that the only thing we have to fear is ... fear itself — nameless, unreasoning, unjustified terror which paralyzes needed efforts to convert retreat into advance." FDR was speaking the truth. Fear is one of the great tools of the devil. Fear leads to instability, unhappiness, and a lack of contentment. It saps spiritual vitality, and it paralyzes the soul. Fear is the great enemy of faith.

We are being fed a constant diet of fear and anxiety so the government can provide us protection and safety – so that the government can promise something that only Christ can deliver. A fearful populace becomes a subjugated populace. All of us are guilty, to some extent, of looking to the government to fix our problems: education, the economy, energy, the climate, medical decisions, and more. We should be looking to each other as free citizens to create solutions to these issues. But we willingly hand more and more power over to the government. When we look to the government to protect us from poverty, protect us from disease, protect us from death, etc., by adhering to their policies, that is leading us into a pagan worship of the government. It is giving to Caesar what does not belong to Caesar, and taking from Christ what is rightfully his.

The beast out of the sea gets stronger and stronger.

The more freedoms we surrender in the name of safety, the fatter and lazier we become. We are quickly allowing the government to run every aspect of our lives. As long as we have our phone, Netflix, and Amazon, we're fine. But very soon we will end up looking like the passengers on the 700th anniversary of the five-year cruise of the Axiom in the Disney/Pixar movie *Wall-E*.

Instead of trusting in the government when we are fearful, we need to turn back to the Lord. St. Paul reminds us, "For God has not given us a spirit of fear, but of power and of love and of a sound mind" (2 Timothy 1:7). Fear sucks the life out of the soul. When fear shapes our lives, safety becomes our god. We worship the risk-free life. We willingly hand over risky decisions to others, sacrificing freedom at the altar of policy, and replacing Jesus with the expert du jour.

And that's just what we lose. What about our children? What sense of wellbeing is forsaken, what freedom is forgotten, what truth about our Almighty God is implicitly denied in the hearts, minds, and lives of our kids? They need the adults in their lives to demonstrate proper reactions to fear, and to live with Scriptural guidance that brings certainty and comfort.

Fears, warnings, and conspiracies aren't anything new. Here's what God spoke through Isaiah 2,700 years ago: "Do not call conspiracy everything this people calls a conspiracy; do not fear what they fear, and do not dread it. The LORD Almighty is the one you are to regard as holy, he is the one you are to fear, he is the one you are to dread" (Isaiah 8:12-13).

No wonder the Lord wages a war through his Scriptures against fear. It is our natural inclination to be afraid. That's why over six dozen times God's people heard their almighty Lord reminding them, "Do not be afraid." Abram, Hagar, Isaac, Jacob, Moses, Joshua, Elijah, David, Solomon, Hezekiah, Jehoshaphat, the Israelites, Zechariah, Joseph, Mary, the shepherds, the women at the tomb, the disciples after the resurrection, Paul, God's saints. They all heard the Lord announce to them, "Do not be afraid."

Fear, in itself, is not a sin. It is an emotion. Our emotions are gifts from God, and they function like a warning light on your car dashboard: An alert. The "check engine" light comes on, and alerts you to investigate. Emotions are simply alerts, and are not sinful in themselves. But fear can easily lead to sin.

For example, fear can lead to worry. Jesus teaches that unbelievers are the ones who worry:

"I tell you, do not worry about your life, what you will eat or drink, or about your body, what you will wear. Is not life more than food, and the body more than clothing? Look at the birds of the air. They do not sow or reap or gather into barns, and yet your heavenly Father feeds them. Are you not worth much more than they? Which of you can add a single moment to his lifespan by worrying? Why do you worry about clothing? Consider how the lilies of the field grow. They do not labor or spin, but I tell you that not even Solomon in all his glory was dressed like one of these. If that is how God clothes the grass of the field, which is alive today and tomorrow is thrown into the furnace, will he not clothe you even more, you of little faith? So do not worry, saying, 'What will we eat?' or 'What will we drink?' or 'What will we wear?' For the unbelievers chase after all these things. Certainly your heavenly Father knows that you need all these things. But seek first the kingdom of God and his righteousness, and all these things will be given to you as well. So do not worry about tomorrow, for tomorrow will care for itself. Each day has enough trouble of its own" (Matthew 6:25-34).

When Jesus speaks about worry it's really a discussion about worship. What we fear is what we worship. Whether that fear is of a virus, cancer, being laid off from work, the economy, the energy crisis, our dwindling bank account, or whatever keeps us up at night worrying. Follow the thread of that fear, and you will find the false god that you fear, love, or trust more than the true God. Fear detracts from the glory of God and the freedom he has won for us in Christ Jesus.

Fear that leads to worry would make sense if we had to deal with problems alone. However, the Lord reminds us that we are never alone. His abiding care is always with you. He reassures you that if he is always taking care of the birds of the air and the birds of the field, then he is also always taking care of you. Really, he values you more than he values the grass, flowers, and birds. He didn't sacrifice his Son to save your flower garden from sin. But he did sacrifice his Son for you. That's how much he values you. You are his special creation and that's why he answers your prayers for daily preservation in the words "give us this day our daily bread."

As Jesus is sending his disciples out into the mission field, he addresses several of their fears – the fear of persecution, the fear of death, and the fear of poverty. He taught, "Do not fear those who kill the body but cannot kill the soul. Rather, fear the one who is able to destroy both soul and body in hell. Are not two sparrows sold for a small coin? Yet not one of them will fall to the ground without the knowledge and consent of your Father. And even the hairs of your head are all numbered. So do not be afraid. You are worth more than many sparrows" (Matthew 10:28-31).

Jesus knows that fear can lead us to timidly pray where others can see us and too terrified to talk about Jesus publicly. We worry way too much about what other people say or think and far too little about what God says and what God thinks of us. We are afraid of rejection, afraid of failure, afraid of being made fun of, afraid of offending someone. All fears freeze us into inaction, into silence and into feeling all alone. Fear is one of the strongest of human emotions.

Fear comes from a lack of faith. Fear comes from worry and doubts. It is a failure to trust that God is in control. It is a failure to see that God has a plan. Basically, it is a failure to see that God is standing right beside you, walking with you through this worlds' dark valley of the shadow of death.

Stop being afraid

Three times in his instructions to his disciples, Jesus tells them to not be afraid. Do not be afraid to speak his Word. Do not be afraid to live his Word before those who can kill the body but cannot kill the soul. And do not be afraid, because as difficult as it may seem, your heavenly Father promises that you are not forgotten, but that you are very important to him. He values you even more than he values sparrows and hairs. He knows if a single sparrow falls. He knows how many hairs you have on your head (although some of you make it easier on him than others). If he knows and cares about those things, he cares and knows even more about the crown of creation whom he sent the King of creation to save.

"Stop being afraid" is the force of Jesus' verbs in the Greek. Stop being afraid – not just once, but always.

Why should we not be afraid of anyone or anything at any time? Is it because Jesus sells us life insurance to cover our losses? Is it because he gives us bullet-proof vests to protect us? Is it because he teaches us how to diffuse conflict?

Do not be afraid because as a student and servant of Christ you are like your Teacher and Master, Jesus Christ. Jesus has given you what you need to face the opposition of Beelzebub (Satan) and the members of his household (this world). He has given you his strength to support you, his promises to sustain you, and his Word which will not return to him empty. And this Jesus said: "Do not be afraid of anyone who can kill the body but cannot kill the soul" (Matthew 10:28).

John Chrysostom was the patriarch of Constantinople in the fourth century. Because Chrysostom was so outspoken in his witness for Christ, the Roman emperor had him arrested and charged with being a Christian. If Chrysostom did not renounce Christ, then the emperor would have this Christian leader banished from the kingdom. Chrysostom responded to the threat by saying that the emperor could not do so, "because the whole world is my Father's kingdom." "Then," replied the emperor, "I will take away your life." To which Chrysostom said, "You cannot, for my life is hid with Christ in God." The emperor next threatened with the loss of his treasure, to which this saint replied, "You cannot, for my treasure is in heaven where my heart is." The emperor made one last effort: "Then I will drive you away from here and you shall have no friend left." But again Chrysostom responded, "You cannot, for I have one Friend from whom you can never separate me. I defy you, for you can do me no harm."

We face opposition from the red dragon of Satan; the beast out of the sea of the government that persecutes Christians; and the beast out of the land of the apostate church that supports the beast out of the sea. These are terrifying creatures! Who could blame us if we renounce our faith, ignore our commitments, compromise our loyalties, shirk our responsibilities, and take the easy way out?

God could blame us. And he does blame us. "Whoever denies me before others, I will also deny before my Father who is in heaven" (Matthew 10:33). God knows these creatures and that the power they yield is terrifying. Yet he calmly reminds us, "Do not be afraid." Though standing up for Jesus, speaking out for Christ, and living the sanctified life of the Holy Spirit is not easy, it's worth it. Though the going is tough now, there is rest and joy awaiting us. The rewards that God gives us now and promises in paradise are rewards that Satan (and no amount of opposition here on earth) can take away from us. In the face of fear Jesus reminds us, "Whoever acknowledges me before men, I will also acknowledge him before my Father in heaven" (Matthew 10:32).

Behind our fear of a novel virus – and really, every other fear - is a very pale looking horse. St. John tells us of seeing the Lamb opening the fourth seal, "I looked, and there was a pale green horse. And its rider was named Death, and the Grave followed closely behind him. They were given power over a quarter of the earth, to kill people with the sword, with famine, with death, and by the wild animals of the earth" (Revelation 6:8). The Black Plague, the Spanish Flu, AIDS, SARS, Covid-19, Monkeypox, and any ailment, virus, or disease – they are all reminders that the pale rider of Death may look weak and sickly, but he is alive and well. He rides regularly to kill people with the sword or disease or natural disasters.

God spoke the curse of death upon Adam in Eden: "For you are dust, and to dust you shall return" (Genesis 3:19). That curse is acutely felt by each of the sons and daughters of Adam as we stare into the face of the pale rider of Death. Every death, every pandemic, every disaster is another time when our consciences remind us: You are sinful. You have earned death, and death will come. You cannot avoid it.

St. Cyprian

In 252 A.D., St. Cyprian of Carthage wrote treatises and preached sermons encouraging Christians who were enduring a plague. Understandably, many were afraid to suffer and die. Cyprian has some powerful words for Christians looking at Death riding towards them – and facing it without fear. St. Cyprian chastises that only non-Christians should be afraid to die:

"Doubtless, let him fear to die, and only him, who, unborn of water and of the Spirit, is the property of hell-fire; let him fear to die, who is without title in the Cross and passion of Christ ; let him fear to die, who is to pass from death here into the second death; let him fear to die, on whom at his going away from life, an eternal flame will lay pains that never cease; let him fear to die, on whom the longer delay confers this boon, that his tortures and groans will begin later." Unbelievers should be afraid to die for they have nothing to look forward to after death. Instead, they should fear death for they will then suffer the second death." [107]

He preaches that both the just and the unjust, the believer and the unbeliever will both die. But what is awaiting both of them is very different. "That without distinction between man and man, the just and the unjust die alike, think not, because of this, that the good and the wicked pass to the same end; the righteous are called to their refreshing, the unrighteous hurried into punishment; the faithful obtain a speedier deliverance, the unbelieving a speedier retribution." [108]

Cyprian addresses our love for this world. "Since the world hates a Christian, why do you love that which hates you and not rather follow Christ who has redeemed and loves you?" [109]

St. John in his epistle chastises Christians for loving this world more than loving their heavenly Father. "Do not love the world or the things in the world. If anyone loves the world, the love of the Father is not in him. For everything in the world—the lust of the

[107] The Plague of Cyprian, c. 252. Pressbooksbccampus.ca
[108] Ibid.
[109] Ibid.

flesh, the desire of the eyes, boasting about material possessions—is not from the Father but from the world. The world and its desires pass away, but the one who does the will of God remains forever" (1 John 2:15-17).

Are we loving the world more than loving the Lord if we do all we can to prolong this life? Certainly we want to be wise with our health. But being a Christian is risky business. Every day we put our lives on the line to give a Christian education to our children, to worship our Lord in his sanctuary, to carry out our vocations in our homes and workplaces, to share the message of Christ in a world that despises Christ. In every one of these ways we are putting our lives at risk. When we refrain from carrying out our Christian vocations in any way, we should ask ourselves the question if we are fearing this world more than fearing the Lord.

St. Cyprian preaches:

> "John in his Epistle cries out and says, warning us lest we be not made lovers of the world, while we indulge in carnal desires; Love not, says he, the world, neither the things that are in the world." He then quotes 1 John 2 and continues: "Rather, dearest brethren, in fulness of spirit, firm faith, and hearty courage, let us be prepared unto all the will of God; shutting out our dread of death, and thinking of the deathless-ness which comes beyond it. Herein let us manifest that we live as we believe; on the one hand, by not lamenting the departure of them we love; and on the other, when the day of our own summons comes, by going without delay and with a ready mind, unto the Lord who calls us." [110]

Cyprian is saying that as Christians we should never fear death. We should actually look forward to death.

Cyprian then compares the world to a collapsing building. Who would not want to escape it? He compares the world to a ship battered by a storm. Who would not want to find a safe harbor?

---

[110] The Plague of Cyprian, c. 252. Pressbooksbccampus.ca

We are strangers here. Heaven is our home. Rather than struggling to stay here, let us as Christians eagerly walk to the Promised Land of Paradise:

> We should consider, beloved brethren, and we should reflect constantly that we have renounced the world and as strangers and foreigners we sojourn here for a time. Let us embrace the day which assigns each of us to his dwelling, which on our being rescued from here and released from the snares of the world, restores us to paradise and the kingdom.
>
> What man, after having been abroad, would not hasten to return to his native land? Who, when hurrying to sail to his family, would not more eagerly long for a favorable wind that he might more quickly embrace his dear ones? We account paradise our country, we have already begun to look upon the patriarchs as our parents. Why do we not hasten and run, so that we can see our country, so that we can greet our parents? A great number of our dear ones there await us, parents, brothers, children; a dense and copious throng longs for us, already secure in their safety but still anxious for our salvation.
>
> How great a joy it is both for them and for us in common to come into their sight and embrace! What pleasure there in the heavenly kingdom without fear of death, and with an eternity of life the highest possible and everlasting happiness; there the glorious choir of apostles, there the throng of exultant prophets, there the innumerable multitude of martyrs wearing crowns on account of the glory and victory of their struggle and passion, triumphant virgins who have subdued the concupiscence of the flesh and body by the strength of their continency, the merciful enjoying their reward who have performed works of justice by giving food and alms to the poor, who in observing the precepts of the Lord have transferred their earthly patrimony to the treasuries

of heaven! To these, beloved brethren, let us hasten with eager longing! let us pray that it may befall us speedily to be with them, speedily to come to Christ. [111]

God did not create you to live in fear

A novel virus is not your enemy. Fear is. God will keep you safe until the day he has set from eternity for you to die. You will not die one moment sooner than that. God did not create you to live in fear. Fear that leads you away from faith in the Lord is one of the most beloved tools in Satan's toolbelt.

The only answer to fear is to learn that our entire lives rest in the hands of a Creator, who, even while calling the world to repentance, is still simultaneously proving himself patiently merciful with his fallen creatures. He longs for each of us to know that his saving love is far bigger and more powerful than anything that wants to make us afraid – viruses, illnesses, or even death itself.

Jesus promises, "Do not be afraid. I am the First and the Last—the Living One. I was dead and, see, I am alive forever and ever! I also hold the keys of death and hell" (Revelation 1:17, 18).

That's why our annual trip to the tomb with the women every Easter morning is so important for us as Christians. It is fitting that at the grave the angels tell the women: "Do not be afraid" (Matthew 28:5). It is fitting that the risen Jesus tells the women hurrying away from the tomb: "Do not be afraid" (Matthew 28:10). And it is fitting that Jesus reminds us repeatedly: "Do not be afraid."

There at that Easter tomb we hear a refrain that resounds almost 100 times in just the New Testament: "Do not be afraid." The women had come out to the grave of their (supposedly) dead Master with a mixture of fear, powerlessness, and hopelessness. But suddenly they learned that their dear Lord was no longer dead. Just as he had promised, death held no power over him. In his saving power, they no longer had any reason to live in

---

[111] Ibid.

hopelessness and fear.

As they left the tomb, already the Easter message allowed the fear in their hearts to begin to mix with a great dawning joy. Then, as if the angelic messenger's words had not been enough, Jesus suddenly stood before them. They heard their risen Lord's lips repeat the refrain: "Do not be afraid." His repetition displays the patient mercy of the Savior who knows how difficult it is to drive fear from the hearts even of his believers! His repetition reveals he will not abandon them to their clinging fears. He wants them to know that their lives – and their eternal lives – are in the hands of a crucified and risen Lord. There is nothing more to fear.

That same Easter message still resounds to this day: "Do not be afraid." Easter proclaims that there is nothing in ancient times, current times or future times that can rightfully make us afraid – not plagues or pandemics or World Wars or anything else that brings death.

The pandemic peeled away the proud and self-reliant façade people had created for themselves. Dust and ashes mortals like to hide their fears. Honestly acknowledge your own fears, but also rely upon the Easter hope that answers your fears. This Easter message, after all, had its first proclamation in a graveyard that suddenly became a place of hope rather than fear.

Our lives have never truly been in our own hands. Our lives rest in the nail-marked hands of the crucified and risen Christ. And even though fears still want to spook our hearts until heaven, yet here is where we go to silence them – our hope is not in ourselves. Our hope is not in mankind. Our hope is not in the media, medical experts, or government authorities. Our hope is in the God who wondrously created us and still more wondrously restored us to himself in the life, death, and resurrection of his Son. Our hope is in the fact of Christ's resurrection, communicated to us through an external Word given by God himself.

Even in a fallen world where Death rides its pale horse to haunt and hunt us down, Jesus still patiently reassures us: "Do not be afraid." Death's back is broken. Satan has been stomped. The gates of Hades have been ripped off their hinges. Christ rides victorious on his white horse (Revelation 6:2). He has conquered and he continues to conquer. "Death is the last enemy to be done away with" (1 Corinthians 15:26), If Death is done, nothing else can win. If Death has been destroyed, then there is nothing else to fear.

Death lies broken and defeated. And now you get to decide whether the rest of your troubles, the worst of your fears, and the greatest of your anxieties are worth your worries. Can the terrors of troubles outweigh trusting in the Almighty God? Can the wrath of war overshadow the Lord of Armies? Can the dread of demons live up to their demands? Can the panic of pandemics be greater than Christ walking victoriously out of his grave?

Fear of loss led Anakin to the dark side. Fear of a virus led a lot of people to do a lot of unreasonable and irrational things. Fear was used by Satan to create a wedge between Christians, and separate God's saints from his divine will. We must all admit that fear often leads us to the dark side – to the devil's side.

That's why we need to be reminded that we Christians alone have an answer to human fear. That answer is found in a graveyard. It is found at an empty tomb. It is found in a message that calms our fears while simultaneously making us messengers to the fearful hearts of others. "Do not be afraid," says the angel. "Do not be afraid," says the risen Lord. "Do not be afraid," say you and me.

"Death is swallowed up in victory. Death, where is your sting? Grave, where is your victory? The sting of death is sin, and the power of sin is the law. But thanks be to God, who gives us the victory through our Lord Jesus Christ" (1 Corinthians 15:54-57). Christ is risen! He is risen indeed! You have no reason to ever be afraid again.

Freedom

In one of the climactic scenes of the movie Braveheart, the mighty and numerous English army is lined up for battle on one side of the field. On the other side is the ragtag group of Scottish peasants.

William Wallace, who has been leading Scots in guerilla warfare against the English, rides his horse back and forth in front of the Scottish army. He addresses the men shouting, "Sons of Scotland, I am William Wallace."

A young soldier questions, "William Wallace is seven feet tall!"

Wallace confesses, "Yes, I've heard. Kills men by the hundreds. And if he were here, he'd consume the English with fireballs from his eyes and bolts of lightning from his arse." The army roars with laughter.

Wallace continues, "I am William Wallace, and I see a whole army of my countrymen, here, in defiance of Tyranny. You've come to fight as free men, and free men you are. What will you do without freedom? Will you fight?" There are murmurs and denials from the soldiers.

One soldier admits, "Fight? Against that? No!" Soldiers shout in agreement. "We will run! And we will live."

Wallace challenges, "Aye. Fight and you may die. Run, and you'll live ... at least a while. And dying in your beds, many years from now, would you be willing to trade all the days, from this day to that, for one chance – just one chance – to come back here and tell our enemies that they may take our lives - but they'll never take our freedom!"[112]

Giving up of freedoms

In response to Covid-19, we have seen American local, state, and federal governments use the pandemic as an excuse to extend their powers. We've witnessed countries like Canada, Germany, China, Australia, and France become blatantly tyrannical in the

[112] This is one of the great motivational speeches in cinema!

enforcement of their lockdowns.

What we experienced in America and all over the world in 2020 and into 2021 was the draconian suspension of civil liberties. Citizens were placed under house arrest. Only "essential" workers were allowed outside to do their jobs. Travel was limited to only what was vitally important. Many countries were one step away from declaring martial law.

Until 2020, would any of us have believed that hundreds of millions of freedom-loving people would willingly give up those freedoms? Citizens gave up their right to see their families, run their businesses, go to work, send their children to school, travel, engage in commerce, and even be with their dying loved ones. Whether we think any of those government-mandated restrictions were justified – would any of us have predicted that citizens across the world would have voluntarily given up those freedoms so quickly... and fighting months - even years later - to regain those freedoms?

Barbie gets it right in *Toy Story 3*. Towards the end of the movie, Barbie creates an awkward silence and a surprise moment by transitioning from her usual ditzy self to something politically charged. Amid confrontation, Barbie exclaims, "Authority should derive from the consent of the governed, not from threat of force!"[113]

The government is given by God to function as a protector of its citizens - not their custodian. The state is to defend the rights of people, not tell them where to live, what to eat, how to be educated, or to remove every hardship from their existence. They are to restrain evil and promote public good.

American citizens grant authority to the government. Governing authorities will gladly take what its citizens give it. As will be discussed in this chapter, citizens may need to resist and not comply so they can retain and even take back their rights and freedoms – rights and freedoms that citizens ceded to the government or that were taken by force by the government. These

---

[113] True words spoken with blonde, pony-tailed frankness!

rights and freedoms don't belong to the government. They belong to the citizens.

Governing and bureaucratic agencies have leveraged fears among the citizenry to gain more power for themselves. They have become ever more involved in the private lives of citizens by controlling their movements and whittling away autonomy over their own bodies.

In the beginning of everything with Covid, governing authorities created a plan to protect the populace. "Flatten the curve – two weeks is all it'll take." In good faith, most citizens trusted that plan. Some may not have agreed with the plan, but for the most part, they followed it. That is submitting to the governing authorities. That's trusting that the governing authorities have its citizens' best interests in mind.

But when more was learned about this virus and the plan from the governing authorities did not change ... or became even harsher and more dictatorial – then questions were raised among the citizens. And rightly so!

It was claimed early on in the pandemic that mandates, lockdowns, and suppression of freedoms was for the health and well-being of the public. We were told to stay home and stay away from others so that we wouldn't kill someone's grandma. C.S. Lewis correctly observed:

"Of all tyrannies, a tyranny sincerely exercised for the good of its victims may be the most oppressive. It would be better to live under robber barons than under omnipotent moral busybodies. The robber baron's cruelty may sometimes sleep, his cupidity may at some point be satiated; but those who torment us for our own good will torment us without end for they do so with the approval of their own conscience. They may be more likely to go to Heaven yet at the same time likelier to make a Hell of earth. This very kindness stings with intolerable insult. To be 'cured' against one's will and cured of states which we may not regard as disease is to be put on a level of those who have not yet reached the age of reason or those who never will; to be classed with infants, imbeciles, and domestic animals." [114]

No bad guy in history – except maybe in comic books – is evil for the sake of being evil. Evil flows out of mandating goodness. The most evil men in history felt the end justified the means. Even more than that, many depraved dictators felt that their diabolical cruelty was the correct, best, and honorable course of action!

It's like how Steven King used the friendly Bozo the clown to become Pennywise in *It*. Something created to be good becomes terrifying and terrorizing.

Those within the media, businesses, universities, and even churches did not seem to stop to ask whether the suspension of civil liberties was right, justified, or necessary. These are leaders who have abdicated their role as the moral compass of public opinion. Not only have they abdicated that role – in many cases they have sided with government and bureaucracy in promoting the invasion into private lives and the suspension of civil liberties.

Rahm Emanuel famously stated during the great recession of 2008, "You never let a serious crisis go to waste. And what I mean by that is it's an opportunity to do things you think you could not do before." [115] Governments have certainly put Emanuel's words into action as they've used the pandemic to claim more power for themselves.

Any government extension of power comes from a limiting of its citizens' freedoms. Thomas Jefferson stated succinctly, "The natural progress of things is for liberty to yield and government to gain ground."

Guarding freedoms

Should Christian citizens be willing to hand over their freedoms to their government? Or should Christian citizens zealously guard and defend their freedoms when they're threatened by their government? Our country is constituted such that the freedoms of citizens are preserved from government intrusion – and such that

---

[114] Lewis, C.S. *God in the Dock: Essays on Theology* (Making of Modern Theology)

[115] Spoken during a November, 2008 Wall Street Journal Forum.

citizens have the right and responsibility to actively and peaceably oppose government intrusion.

If your freedoms and rights come from the government, then the government can remove your rights and restrict your freedoms whenever they find it convenient. But our freedoms and rights in America are ours from our Creator. It is right there in the opening sentences of our nation's founding document: *"We hold these truths to be self-evident, that all men are created equal, that they are endowed by their Creator with certain unalienable Rights, that among these are Life, Liberty and the pursuit of Happiness."*

If the government can suspend its citizens' rights anytime it deems necessary, they aren't rights. They are permissions.

But the U.S. Constitution calls them "rights." Rights that are justly, permanently and non-negotiably handed down to us by the God of our Creation, and preserved from government intrusion. These rights do not belong to the government to extend or withhold; these rights belong to the citizens of America.

We return to what Jesus said to the Pharisees in response to their question, "Is it right to pay taxes to Caesar or not" (Luke 20:22)? Jesus answered, "Give to Caesar what is Caesar's and to God the things that are God's" (Luke 20:25). It is wrong for the government to take what belongs to God – its citizens' freedoms and rights. Those freedoms and rights were given by God to the citizens of America and announced in the U.S. Constitution. Those freedoms and rights do not belong to the government. They belong to "we the people."

American citizens give to the government what belongs to it – respect, honor, and submission. But they cannot give to the government what it doesn't deserve – their freedoms, rights, bodily autonomy, etc.

Our forefathers fought, bled, and died to win, protect, and extend our freedoms in this land. Those freedoms were then given to us. They are our inheritance. They are our possessions.

Additionally, our legal system (with concepts dating back to the English Common Law system) is predicated on a presumption of innocence with burden of proof resting with the prosecution. In other words, the government must present its case in court when it wants to restrict the free exercise of God-given rights. That's because rights cannot be suspended as though they were merely permissions; rights are individual possessions of citizens, which cannot be taken without due process and just cause.

We are called by the 7th commandment to protect our freedoms as our possessions. We are also called by the 10th commandment to protect the freedoms of those around us. To surrender our freedoms and those of our neighbors is to cheapen and despise those freedoms. If we don't protect them, speak up for them, exercise them, and defend them, they'll erode until they disappear. We'll have no inheritance from our forefathers to pass on to our children.

Ronald Reagan said it well, "Freedom is never more than one generation away from extinction. We didn't pass it to our children in the bloodstream. It must be fought for, protected, and handed on for them to do the same, or one day we will spend our sunset years telling our children and our children's children what it was once like in the United States where men were free."

It is freedom that allows us to have "food and drink, clothing and shoes, house and home, land and cattle, money and goods, etc." These are gifts God gives as part of our "daily bread." Freedom, then, is one of the greatest earthly possessions that our great God can bless us with here on earth.

As Christian citizens, we are called by God in his 7th, 9th, and 10th commandments to cherish, protect and prosper both our freedoms and the freedoms of our neighboring American citizens. No person, authority, or government has the right to steal, take, suspend, or remove our freedoms. These freedoms are our inheritance. In his commandments, God calls us to protect these freedoms so we may hand them down to our children and grandchildren as part of their inheritance. We owe it to current and future citizens - as part of our vocation as American citizens - to stand up to tyranny to protect and prosper our American freedoms.

We cannot take freedoms lightly

It was a sin for Esau to be careless with his birthright (Genesis 25:27-34). It is a sin for us to be careless with our unalienable rights as citizens. It's wrong to be frivolous with freedom.

William Faulkner wrote, "We must be free not because we claim freedom, but because we practice it." Vocation is the job God has placed before us. A vocation we have in common is we are citizens of the nation where God has placed us. In our vocation as citizens, we hold dear the inheritance of the rights and freedoms we have been given by God and won by our forefathers. In that vocation, we need to protect what has been given to us. If we don't protect our rights and freedoms, we will leave our children a world where they can't stand up ... because we never stood up before them.

President Ronald Regan said it well, "Government's first duty is to protect the people, not run their lives." It is part of our vocation to remind the government of what is and what is not their duty.

In *Star Wars Episode III: Revenge of the Sith*, as the Intergalactic Senate votes unlimited powers to Senator Palpatine to become Emperor Palpatine, Senator Padme Amidala utters in disbelief to Senator Organa, "So this is how liberty dies, with thunderous applause." [116] This turns out very poorly for the Star Wars Universe. But this statement is true in both the movie and in real life.

For those who are paying attention, we are living in the time where civil liberties are dying with thunderous applause. Citizens are afraid and so they are seeking security over freedom. Governing authorities are feeding the fear frenzy to secure more power for themselves, which always comes at the expense of citizens' liberties. As this happens, the very reason that our nation was created and unique is being destroyed.

We often live in fear. There is so much to be afraid of while living in a fallen world. Paranoia is crippling. Fear is the devil's greatest weapon to use against us. When the government behaves

[116] Spoiler alert! We learn that Palpatine has been the Sith Lord all along, manipulating everything for his nefarious plans.

like the beast out of the sea, it will then use fear to turn people away from security in God by providing that security itself.

In that fear we often look to the government for security. We are afraid of terrorists, so we take off our shoes and belts for a security check to fly on an airplane. We are afraid of bad teeth, so we allow fluoride to be put into our drinking water. We are afraid of bad neighbors, so we must get a permit to put up a fence in our yard. We are afraid of a virus, so we endure masks, mandates, and lockdowns. Every fear, every annoyance, every irritation that we complain to our government authorities about is followed by ordinances, restrictions, and regulations from the government. Every one of these ordinances, restrictions, and regulations will always be limiting citizens' freedoms. Some to our benefit. Others to our detriment.

As citizens, we have ceded so much over to the government. We have abdicated our leadership roles. God calls for us to educate our children, support the poor, care for the elderly and widows, take care of foreigners, and so on. These are the responsibilities of Christians within the church. They should also be the responsibilities of citizens of a nation.

But over the generations, we have given these responsibilities over to the government. Whether it is educating our children, caring for our elderly, providing for the poor, or taking care of foreigners, the government willingly takes those responsibilities from us.

Eventually we begin to look more and more to the government to meet our needs. When we look to the government to meet our needs, we are looking less to God to meet those needs. We begin trusting the government more than trusting God. Over time, this can lead to worshiping the beast out of the sea.

We see a problem – our neighbor built his fence two inches onto our property; the city sewer backed up into our basement; we struggle to find adequate insurance when we're elderly - and it is our knee-jerk reaction to look to the government to find a solution to that problem. If we think critically, can we recount situations where the government as a monolith entity better solved and handled a situation than the free market? Usually not. Yet, we go to the government again and again. When the government needs to create more bureaucracy to deal with issues, then more restrictions upon the citizens' freedoms ultimately follow.

Surrendering rights in exchange for security

America was founded as the grand experiment in world history that was not ruled by a monarch, dictator, or tyrant. Rather, America is a unique blend as a democratic republic. To James Madison and the other framers of the Constitution, there were important differences between a "democracy" and a "republic." A "democratic government" means majority rule. Adding "republic" means the democratic government has its powers limited by various widely divided voting blocs to protect the rights of as many people as possible. Our American founders were always protective of the rights of its citizens – especially protecting those rights from governing authorities.

America's founding fathers did not want a small group of people making the decisions for the many. That's why they didn't institute a monarchy. Our founders saw that throughout history, the majority of monarchies made their citizens into slaves and peons. The few would make the decisions for the many. Without a balance of power, citizens could very easily become slaves like the Israelites in Egypt. The first chapters of Exodus tell us what God feels about that.

As a democratic republic, we are a nation of people who are ruled by "the consent of the governed." That means if a government removes or infringes upon the freedoms of those they govern without their consent, they are acting unconstitutionally. It is actually the rights of the governed to be able to remove or infringe the powers of the government. That's the way the founders of America set up their unique form of government – to protect the governed from their own government.

We are a democratic republic. But we aren't that when our rights are taken away. Then we become something different - something tyrannical, something against our nation's rule of law.

Thomas Jefferson famously said, "When government fears the people, there is liberty. When the people fear the government, there is tyranny." Jefferson is defining two kinds of relationships between American citizens and the U.S. government. Either the citizens hold their governing authorities accountable to their oaths to uphold the Constitution, or the governing authorities become tyrannical ... because the citizens fail to fulfill their vocation of holding their authorities accountable.

We do not, dare not, should not ever relinquish the right to demand that consent be sought and ratified before we submit to a policy that affects us. That is both our right and our responsibility as citizens – and not subjects.

The American founders had this crazy idea that all individuals are created equal with certain inalienable rights, and that the government is created for the express purpose of protecting those rights. Jefferson also said, "Whenever any form of government becomes destructive of these ends [life, liberty, and the pursuit of happiness] it is the right of the people to alter or abolish it, and to institute new government ..." When the government becomes "destructive of these ends," the abuse of any individual liberties will be the death of all liberty.

When personal freedom is taken away – all that is left is to trust in either God or government. When citizens do not know God, all that's left is the government. Then the government becomes god. Then it operates as the dragon's beast.

So why have American citizens so willingly ceded their rights and freedoms to the government? Perhaps freedom has become so abundant that citizens can't be troubled with protecting and extending their freedoms. We have become like the heavyweight boxer who has gotten fat and lazy with his successes. Instead of putting the time in at the gym to train his body, he puts time in at the buffet table fattening his body. We have become fat and lazy with our freedoms and taken them for granted. We no longer honor or cherish the inheritance of freedoms handed down to us by our forefathers. So, like that fat boxer we end up taking defeat after defeat from opponent after opponent.

Forfeiting freedoms out of fear

Perhaps fear is another reason why we have forfeited our freedoms. After the Old Testament Israelites were freed from their Egyptian slavery, they began fearing their freedom. They didn't like the freedom of picking manna and finding other food in the desert to eat. They complained, "Who is going to give us meat to eat? We remember the fish we ate in Egypt free of charge, the cucumbers, the melons, the leeks, the onions, and the garlic. But now our lives are wasting away. We have nothing at all to look at except this manna" (Numbers 11:4-6). They grumbled against Moses and Aaron that they wanted to return to Egypt. "If only we had died in the land of Egypt! If only we had died in this wilderness! Why is the Lord bringing us to this land to fall by the sword? Our wives and our children will be taken as captives! Wouldn't it be better for us to return to Egypt?" So they said to one another, "Let's put someone in charge and return to Egypt" (Numbers 14:2-4).

All humans are the same. They can become terrified of their freedoms to make and live with their choices. They prefer the comfort and ease of being told what to do.

Freedom is hard. It takes responsibility. When we are free, when something goes wrong, we can only blame ourselves. But with an authoritarian government, when things go wrong, we can blame the authorities. For the Old Testament Israelites, freedom in the wilderness was difficult. It takes courage to want to be free.

In *Shawshank Redemption*, [117] Brooks Hatlen had been in prison since 1909. After spending so many decades in prison, Brooks grew so accustomed to living on the inside, that he didn't remember how the outside world worked. After being released on good behavior, Brooks had a very hard time readjusting to his new freedom. Brooks ended up writing a final letter to Andy and Red at the prison before committing suicide by hanging himself. The letter read in part: "I have trouble sleeping at night. I have bad

[117]After bombing at the box office, *Shawshank Redemption* is consistently ranked one of the best movies of all time.

dreams, like I'm falling. I wake up scared. Sometimes it takes me a while to remember where I am. Maybe I should get me a gun and rob the Food-Way, so they'd send me home. I could shoot the manager while I was at it, sort of like a bonus. I guess I'm too old for that sort of nonsense anymore. I don't like it here. I'm tired of being afraid all the time. I've decided not to stay. I doubt they'll kick up any fuss. Not for an old crook like me."

If we feel trapped as citizens in a prison run by tyrants, as American citizens, we need only to gather our fellow citizens/inmates and walk out boldly. Regrettably, others are guilting us into compliance and staying in the cage.

Frederick Douglass correctly observed, "The limits of tyrants are prescribed by the endurance of those whom they oppress."

The Freedom Convoy

A recent example of those who would no longer endure oppression was the Freedom Convoy in Canada. Over 50,000 truckers drove from Vancouver to Ottawa to protest the Canadian federal government's vaccine mandates. The truckers felt the need to protest what they believed to be government overreach. Their plan was to drive right into the heart of what they felt was a tyrannical government and politely ask them to please restore their freedoms. Politely – because they are Canadians, after all.

The Freedom Convoy was working to hold the Canadian government to its own laws. The Canadian Constitution has a charter of rights and freedoms that is analogous to the U.S. Bill of Rights. The protesters believed their constitutional rights had been violated numerous times on multiple counts. They protested to be able to use the freedoms they possessed and enjoyed as Canadian citizens. Their protest was telling the Canadian government to stop violating their constitutional freedoms.

The protesters were acting as a curb to their government – trying to hold the government accountable to their own laws.

The truckers parked in downtown Ottawa, clogging roads and stopping traffic. This was their peaceful protest. The truckers who were interviewed for news reports said they would leave if authorities removed the vaccine mandates, but those same truckers said they would stay "as long as it took." One trucker told a reporter, """It's just a matter of time until they realize that. We're used to being out on the road for weeks at a time, so it's not fazing us one bit, and with the amount of support they were getting from locals and people all around the world, we're just being encouraged more and more every day."

The truckers did receive a tremendous amount of support. Over $10 million was raised through an online site. Supporters set up tables in downtown Ottawa to provide food for the truckers. Truckers received donations for fuel for those staying in their trucks, and shuttle rides to and from their hotels. As one supporter told a reporter, "Well, we're just out here helping fuel up the trucks, keep the drivers happy, anything they need, we're trying to take care of them. They're fighting for our freedom, so we've got to fight for what they need."

The peaceful protest created its desired effect as Jason Kenney, Premier of Alberta, Canada, announced that several Covid-19 restrictions and mandates would end quickly. With how quickly the restrictions were lifted ... did the science change, or did the politics change?

Canadian Prime Minister Justin Trudeau did not back down so easily. First, he tried calling on two truck companies to come to Ottawa to tow away the semis. But the tow truck companies stood in solidarity with their trucker brethren and ignored the Prime Minister's plea for assistance.

During the stand-off with the truckers, the Canadian Prime Minister said, "Mandates are the way to avoid more restrictions." [118] That's like saying, "Restricting your freedoms is the way to avoid more restrictions of your freedoms." Using our gift of reason, that is a logical fallacy of circular reasoning. It simply doesn't make sense.

So, should the government be the arbiter of truth? Do we dare to accept everything governmental experts proclaim without

---

[118] Prime Minister Trudeau said this in a TV interview on 2/8/2022.

question? In response to any assertions by any experts, it's always beneficial to apply President Ronald Reagan's famous words about the Soviet Union, "Trust but verify." The Canadian truckers and their supporters had verified the Covid claims of their government and found them suspect. That's why they opposed the restrictions of their freedoms.

Ultimately, Trudeau invoked the Emergencies Act on February 14, 2022, in what he called a "last resort" to break the protesters. Under the Emergencies Act, federal authorities went after the bank accounts and other financial assets of the truckers, protesters, and anyone suspected of aiding the protests (even when such aid, including donations, had been given previous to the invocation of the Emergencies Act – when the donations had been made legally, for a legal, free speech cause). The government threatened that any vehicle involved in the protest could lose its insurance. The Emergencies Act gave the government the power to do this without a court order by police, or due process for the suspects. This act meant that the federal government was declaring war on its own people.

Hundreds of police officers then swarmed downtown Ottawa. For the weeks the Freedom Convoy had been in Ottawa, there had been no violence. It was more like a street party. But the police invaded the Ottawa streets equipped with riot gear and wielding tear gas. The videos are scary: peaceful protesters – some elderly and children – being pushed by police, run over by horses, or hit by officers with nightsticks.

St. Paul calls governing authorities God's servants (Romans 13:4). They are God's servants for the benefit of their citizens – benefitting citizens by service under, not power over. There is a big difference between treating citizens with respect and treating them with disrespect. Governing authorities are to treat people as citizens they serve ... not automatons who serve them.

Being a *Star Wars* fan, the Canadian government's reaction reminds me of a scene in *Return of the Jedi*. The Emperor is proudly standing on his Death Star with Luke Skywalker. The Emperor boldly tells Skywalker, "From here you will witness the final destruction of the Alliance and the end of your insignificant rebellion."

The Canadian government labeled the protesters as perpetrating "domestic terrorism." We need to understand that just because a politician or the media use a term to describe something, that doesn't make it true. If it's a lie, then it's a lie even when a governing authority tells it. When citizens allow lies to be declared without calling out those lies, they passively allow the government to slide closer to serving as the devil's beast. When citizens call out the lies, then they are actively working to pull the government closer to serving the Lord.

What about clergy?

For those reading this who are clergy, I have a specific question for you. When did pastors stop speaking to or calling out government leaders? Throughout the history of the Old and New Testaments, prophets and apostles called out their government leaders. Moses stood up to Pharaoh. Elijah stood up to King Ahab. Nathan spoke directly to King David. John the Baptist called King Herod to repentance.

Martin Luther and the Lutheran reformers opposed their princes and emperor when they were wrong. The history of the Lutheran Church is filled with spiritual leaders speaking out to political leaders. So why aren't most clergy today speaking out for truth and justice?

Would a pastor join a protest? Perhaps a better question is, why wouldn't he? If the protest is for life or liberty or justice or truth, why wouldn't a pastor be standing and marching for those godly issues? The truth is never political.

Some pastors have argued that there is a division of two kingdoms – earthly and spiritual. That's correct. But separating the two kingdoms so there is no influence from one side to the other is not Christian. Jesus told Pontius Pilate, "My kingdom is not of this world" (John 18:36). He doesn't mean that his kingdom has nothing to do with this world. Jesus is talking about origin ... not impact. Later in that same verse Jesus explains, "My kingdom is not from here." Jesus' kingdom is not from this world. But it certainly has an impact on this world. Jesus' spiritual kingdom surely influences and impacts the earthly kingdom.

If a government is harming its citizens, that's going against the 5th commandment. If a government is slandering its citizens, that's going against the 8th commandment. If a government is taking away the property of its citizens, that's going against the 10th commandment. Those are sins. Pastors don't have to call out the sins from the pulpit. They probably shouldn't. But they are still citizens, so in their vocation as a citizen, they can join with their fellow Christian citizens in calling their governmental leaders to repentance.

Where are the John the Baptists of today?

Standing up for those who cannot stand for themselves

Why did the truckers put their lives and livelihoods on the line over these government mandates? Why did so many people support the Freedom Convoy? Why did so many other similar convoys spring up around the world? Sometimes people need to be non-compliant for the sake of those who have no option but to be compliant.

A single mom of two children may not have the time, money, or energy to stand up to her employer. But perhaps other employees in the company with more seniority and clout can do it for her. A father trying to support his family may want to stand on principle against government overreach, but his first priority is providing for his family. So maybe the grandfather is the one who is in a better position to stand up to the government.

Truckers, by nature, are independent, driven, and not easily intimidated. They were the ones who chose to be non-compliant for all those who felt they had no recourse but to be compliant. But that's also why the truckers received so much support. Their supporters realized the truckers were standing up for them more than their own government was.

Freedom takes constant guarding by those who are free. America's founding fathers understood this. That's why the first two amendments were written to guard freedom. The first amendment states: "Congress shall make no law respecting an establishment of religion, or prohibiting the free exercise thereof; or abridging the freedom of speech, or of the press; or the right of the people peaceably to assemble, and to petition the Government for a redress of grievances." What is the reason for the first amendment? To protect citizens from an authoritarian regime that will limit citizens' speech, faith, associations, and more.

The second amendment states: "A well regulated Militia, being necessary to the security of a free State, the right of the people to keep and bear Arms, shall not be infringed." What is the reason for a second amendment? To protect citizens from a tyrannical government.

The first two amendments were written to protect the individual rights and freedoms of America's citizens from their own government. The first amendment guarantees citizens the right to civil disobedience. The second amendment protects citizens from the government when it uses force to suppress the first amendment. These first two amendments, legally and constitutionally, give American citizens the right to practice civil disobedience to protect their freedoms as guaranteed by the U.S. Constitution.

So many pastors consider it sinful and a refusal to submit to the government to practice civil disobedience. But how can it be sinful when citizens are submitting to their government's laws which promote civil disobedience?

Defending freedom

Citizens have a right to fight and defend their freedom. In the face of annihilation by aliens, President Whitmore called for the defense of freedom in *Independence Day*, "We will not go quietly into the night. We will not vanish without a fight. We're going to live on. We're going to survive. Today we celebrate our Independence Day!"

While England was being bombed by the Germans in World War II, the British were in the pubs enjoying beer and camaraderie. That says freedom no matter the looming threat. Patrick Henry famously said in 1775 in a Virginia convention convincing the convention to deliver troops for the Revolutionary War, "Give me freedom or give me death." That's how important freedom is.

Dr. Ian Malcom famously said in *Jurassic Park*, "Life finds a way." Freedom, too, finds a way. As Americans, we will always find a way around tyranny.

You cannot comply your way out of tyranny. We are one nation under God. Not one nation under government. Do or do not. There is no try ... when it comes to complying. [119]

If we want liberty, we must take responsibility for our individual actions. We teach personal responsibility for actions to our youth on the bus, in the classrooms in our Lutheran elementary schools, and in our pastor's Catechism classes. But when those children become adults, they are often being told to hand their liberties and responsibilities over to the government. No wonder our young people are so confused.

We teach our college students to resist their college professors when they are teaching the false theology of evolution in their classrooms. We train our members to speak up when their employers promote a fake ideology of critical race theory in the workplace. We encourage our athletes to challenge their head coach if they see him harassing or discriminating against a teammate. Yet, for some reason we ask citizens to be silent and compliant when their government is wrong, immoral, or illegal. That silence and compliance is a good recipe for those authorities who are not questioned to continue to misuse and abuse their power.

Resistance makes people stronger. We make ourselves stronger when we lift weights because there is resistance. We make our governing authorities stronger – healthier for all – when there is

---

[119] An application of Yoda's wisdom to Luke Skywalker when Luke thinks that lifting his X-Wing fighter out of the Dagobah swamp is too difficult. Yoda conveys that trying isn't going to solve anything. Doing will result in success. "Do or do not. There is no try."

resistance to poor, wrong, or harmful policies.

For the most part, those who practice civil disobedience are not resisting good policies. They're resisting the bad ones. It is the governing authorities who are resisting good policies and making good citizens into bad ones.

Laws can be just or unjust. If a law is unjust, the one who civilly disobeys the law is not wrong. Actually, the ones who are in the wrong are those who write and enforce unjust laws.

It has become common today for people to confuse being obedient with being a good person. But following rules that are unscientific or immoral, that are illogical and unfairly applied, that segregate and denigrate, is cowardly. Good people bravely stand up and resist unjust laws. Good people don't follow laws because they are compelled to. They follow laws because they are committed to what is good, right, and moral.

Jesus did not say that the greatest commandment was to submit to governing authorities. He said the greatest commandment was to love your neighbor. Perhaps loving your neighbor means to resist the government that is harming or hurting your neighbor – that is, removing freedoms, privileges, and rights from your neighbor.

A Christian individual may submit to the government as his personal liberties are infringed upon. But that same Christian individual may resist when the government infringes upon his spiritual, medical or mental liberties.

As Christians examine their reasoning for resisting, it cannot be just because something the government is proposing or imposing seems onerous or arduous. Rather, is God's will for his people being hindered? By resisting, are we protecting parental rights and responsibilities under the 4th commandment? Are we protecting life under the 5th commandment? Are we protecting the sanctity of marriage under the 6th commandment? Are we protecting our neighbor's property and means of income under the 7th, 9th, and 10th commandments? Are we protecting the reputation of ourselves and our neighbors under the 8th commandment?

When any government opposes God's moral law as clearly

stated in the 10 commandments; when they oppose Christians gathering for worship; or oppose speaking publicly in the name of Christ; they are uniting with the forces of the antichrist and the devil. A tyrannical government that attacks any proclamation of the gospel then becomes the beast out of the sea that thus sides with the great dragon of Satan. These allies of the devil may, can, and must be resisted. To do otherwise is to give free rein to the dragon that Jesus has told us he has chained and limited.

We not only need to promote freedom and do what is right. We also need to stand up to tyranny and oppose what is evil.

What are we to do?

In my church's Bible study on Romans, I read the first chapter of this book to the Bible study attendees. It was like story time at the library. When I finished reading, I asked if anyone had any questions. Someone commented, "You raised a lot of questions, but you didn't seem to give a lot of answers. So, what are we to do?" I answered and said, "This book isn't about giving answers. It's about creating a dialogue. Obviously, I have my position and reasoning. But I'm also willing to listen to someone else's position and reasoning. We may sway the other person. We may strongly disagree. The goal is to discuss, debate, and remain brothers and sisters in the faith. We're not going to win any battles fighting against each other. We are called to fight against the dragon and his two beasts. May the Lord give us the wisdom and strength to do that together – even when we may disagree on the best way to carry out that task."

Many equate civil disobedience with being lawbreakers. But they're judging the outward actions and not the motives. Two pictures of groups of people being arrested may look the same. One group is arrested for rioting. The other group is arrested because they were protecting property from the rioters. It is important that we take words and actions in the kindest possible way. We don't judge the actions without first understanding the motives behind the actions. That's what Jesus meant when he taught about judging (Matthew 7:1).

Rather than causing riot and revolt, those who are practicing civil disobedience may be protecting from true riots and revolt. The Freedom Convoy in Ottawa was blamed by Canada's Prime Minister for shutting down the economy for several weeks. But the Freedom Convoy was protesting how the Prime Minister had shut down the economy for months – and his policies were going to have long-term consequences. Demonstrators burning their vaccine passports in Italy, France, and Australia may seem extreme. But they are taking extreme action to protest how their governments are segregating and coercing the unvaccinated.

Some may consider resistance to governing authorities as being disrespectful and rebellious – while those who are resisting see their actions as preventing real riots and outright revolts. Civil disobedience can call urgent attention to societal ills that are being overlooked by a complacent society. Resistance that is done civilly and incrementally is more beneficial than the violence and revolution that can result when tyranny is left unchecked for too long. When grievances are unmet, they tend to inevitably produce riot and revolt. Too often Christians view resistance and rebellion as being different stages of the same thing. However, resistance and rebellion are actually opposing forces. Resistance is done to alleviate rebellion.

It is important for us to understand that something is not right just because it is legal. Nor is something wrong just because it is deemed illegal. There are plenty of examples of immorality being legalized. There are also a plethora of examples of moral behavior being categorized as illegal. Slavery in the United States was legal for generations. That did not make it moral. Abortion in the United States has been legal for generations. That does not make it less abhorrently evil.

In the past there were laws that maintained the segregation of races and prevented citizens from voting. Today there are laws that protect gay marriage, gender reassignment surgeries for children, and men competing in women's sports. In his *Letter from Birmingham Jail*, Martin Luther King Jr. put undiscriminating deference to law in proper perspective with this reminder, "We should never forget that everything Adolf Hitler did in Germany was legal."

Perhaps if German Christians would have had a little courage early on to resist the evil they were seeing in their government, the whole world would not have needed a lot of courage later on to fight that evil in a World War.

When citizens become complacent, laws that are immoral and unjust can be created. When they finally wake up, they must either remain quiet and live with those immoral laws – or speak up to challenge and change those laws.

Reliance

As we study civil disobedience, some will call it resistance. Perhaps it's better to look at it from the opposite angle and call it reliance. Upon whom are we relying? Are we relying on the government, or are we relying on ourselves? Are we going to simply trust everything the experts, officials, and authorities tell us? Or are we going to examine the data, consult other experts, and apply common sense and reason to a situation? Perhaps civil disobedience isn't so much resisting the government as it is reliance upon ourselves and our neighbors. That is the independent American spirit upon which our nation was built.

What is one of the reasons why Adam is blamed for the sin in the Garden? It was his moral cowardice to not step in and stop what was going on. He abandoned his role as a spiritual leader. He relied upon himself instead of relying on what God had told him to do. Even though it was Eve who was talking to the serpent, Adam is blamed for the sin. He was complicit in the evil.

How complicit are we when we see immorality and evil in our world ... but we don't step in? We see what is going on ... but we do nothing to stop it? We hear the devil's subtle whispering in our world ... but we don't speak up. We abandon our roles as spiritual men and women in our culture. We do not allow God's spiritual kingdom to have an influence on the earthly kingdom.

As spiritual men and women, we need to be willing to step in when we see the Ancient Serpent exerting his influence on those around us: Hollywood, public education, corporations, social media, and even governing authorities. We resist the evil by relying upon the good of our God.

Drawing the line

At some point, we do need to draw the line. For different people, that line can be at different places and at different times. That's fine. That's what this book is about. We can all arrive at the line from various places and at various times. We should be discussing, applying, debating, questioning, and challenging each other along the way – not getting upset with one another if we draw the line in different places. We use our gifts of wisdom, reasoning, and conscience to take personal responsibility seriously. Then we accept and trust our brothers and sisters in Christ, and take their words and actions of where they've drawn their line in the kindest possible way.

We all take our risk-tolerance into account. How much are we willing to suffer for standing up for what is right? We all need a little courage now to draw the line, to resist, to say no. Otherwise, we will all need a lot of courage later.

Perhaps we're so hesitant to resist on these big things because we should have been resisting all along on the smaller things. Perhaps we should have been resisting for generations as we saw immorality being codified into laws.

When we are resisting, we are announcing that we are not capitulating to evil. Rather, we are conquering evil with good. We are employing the same strategy for reacting to evil that God employed when he sent his Son (Luke 6:27-38).

God may use evil for justice. There are numerous examples of God using the evil of the Egyptians, the Babylonians, the Assyrians, etc., to carry out his ultimate will for the good of his people. That doesn't mean we support the evil or pray for its success. We pray and work to thwart that evil. "But I want you to continue to be wise about what is good, and innocent about what is evil" (Romans 16:19).

When we are standing strong with courage, it isn't just for us.

It's also for those who come after us. Do we not have a moral duty to the generations who are following us? Are they going to look at us and ask, "Why didn't they do more?" "Why didn't they do something?!"

When parents today don't resist, the next generation will grow up thinking this is normal and accept it without question.

As comedian J.P. Sears said, "We'll either be telling our children what freedom was or mandates were." Instead of allowing a government to deprive our children of freedoms, let's instead deprive our children of tyranny.

It takes strength to stand up, speak out, and fight. Especially when so many around us are calling for us to sit down, be silent, and surrender. Five Times August is the solo act of singer/songwriter Brad Skistimas. He states the position of resistance well in his song "I Will Not Be Leaving Quietly."

> You can hate me, try to break me Talk me down and denigrate me
> You can try to silence every word But I will not be leaving quietly, no
>
> I won't leave I won't leave
> I will not be leaving quietly
>
> And you can mock me, try to outsmart me You can shame me and try to blame me
> You can do your best to shut me up But I will not be leaving quietly, no
>
> I won't leave I won't leave
> I will not be leaving quietly
>
> I'm gonna stand here And I'll fight for every word
> I'm gonna shout the truth Until you know it's heard
>
> I'm gonna stand here And I'll fight for every word
> I'm gonna shout the truth Until you know it's heard

You can scold me, attempt to control me Ban me and
censor and label and troll me
You can push me and try to kick me out But I will not be
leaving quietly, no

I won't leave I won't leave
I will not be leaving quietly

And you can mute me, Strike and dispute me
Dumb down the rest, yea, but I'll keep refusin'
You can pretend like you've seen the last of me
But I will not be leaving quietly, no

I won't leave I won't leave

I will not be leaving quietly[120]

Here is a spoiler alert to *Braveheart*. At the very end of the movie, William Wallace has been captured. He has been taken to England outside the king's palace. He's in front of a crowd of people who have gathered for his execution. Wallace is being tortured as his executioner is doing something unspeakable to his nether regions. Wallace is urged to beg for mercy and bring his excruciating torture to an end with a quick death. But Wallace will not capitulate. He is defiant to the end. He shouts, "Freedom!" with his dying breath.

Robert the Bruce then surprises everyone by leading the Scots to freedom with victory in battle over England.

Here is a spoiler alert to end this chapter. When citizens stand up even though oppressors tell them to sit down; when citizens speak up even though tyrants tell them to shut up; when citizens don't leave even though bullies shove them along; when citizens refuse to be canceled even though intimidators coerce them; when citizens love their enemies even though the enemies hate them; no matter what, no matter when ... freedom wins!

---

[120] Written & Performed by Bradley James Skistimas. Copyright 2021 Seven Places Music (ASCAP). Quoted with permission by Skistimas.

Never give up.

In the Star Trek inspired sci-fi cult classic movie *Galaxy Quest*,[121] Commander Taggert and the stalwart crew of the NSEA Protector once enjoyed their intergalactic exploits as actors on the *Galaxy Quest* TV show. But now that the show has been off the air for decades, the heroic crew are washed-up actors, eking out a living attending a dreary cycle of fan conventions and promotional appearances. That's when the Thermians – real life aliens - arrive, begging Commander Taggert to help save them from the reptilian villain, Sarris, who threatens to destroy their home planet. Suddenly the crew find themselves aboard a real spaceship, facing actual peril.

The Thermians have no concept of fiction, so they believe the episodes of Galaxy Quest to be "historical documents." The Thermians have modeled every aspect of their society on the series, including a fully functional replica of the series' ship, the NSEA Protector.

Commander Taggert's famous tagline to his crew during the series, and that he repeats to Sarris whenever all seems lost, is, "Never give up. Never surrender."

"Never give up. Never surrender." It's good advice for us Christians. The seven-headed red dragon and his beasts out of the sea and out of the earth would love for us to surrender. They want us to look at all the evil they have fostered in our world and all the wickedness they have cultivated into our culture and give up.

How would you describe the culture we're experiencing in 21st century America? We are not so much living in an immoral culture as an amoral culture. They sound similar but there's a big difference:

In an immoral culture, people know right from wrong, but they choose to do what's wrong;

In an amoral culture, people don't know what is right or wrong,

---

[121] If you like Star Trek, you'll enjoy Galaxy Quest. It is a humorous spoof of the sci-fi tropes that still remains heart-warming.

so they gleefully choose what feels good based on their sinful nature.

People enjoy living in the darkness of their sin and unbelief. They welcome the darkness. More than that, they want us Christians to not only tolerate their amoral behavior, but we must accept and promote it. [122] When we don't accept and promote their damnable doctrines, then they will turn their sights on us for persecution. The voice of Scripture, the voice of Christians cannot be tolerated; it must be silenced.

Persecution

I have said for years in various Bible studies that what we need in America is a good old-fashioned persecution. We as American Christians have become lazy, lackadaisical, and apathetic in our Christianity. We are like the lukewarm Laodiceans (Revelation 3:16) that Jesus threatens to spit out of his mouth. We have wrapped ourselves so tightly in the soft cocoon of luxury with our homes, phones, vehicles, binge-watching, and social media that we live unaware of the terrible persecution our fellow Christians are already suffering at the hands of God's enemies.[123]

I think the persecution I've been asking for is now here. All you need to do is look around at the ways local, state, and federal governments have shut down churches these past few years. They were able to convince Christians that churches were "non-essential" and could be closed or have limited capacity for public safety. If churches decided to defy their local and state mandates, then those churches were fined and dragged before the courts. It seems as if Jesus predicted this kind of thing would happen

---

[122] Even in an amoral culture, the human conscience (the voice of God's law in the heart, part of the natural knowledge of God) still proclaims that sin is wrong. Silencing the voice of Christian witness is one shoddy attempt to assuage the guilt that speaks from within.

[123] When 40% of a congregation's total membership is regularly in worship any given Sunday, we think we're doing pretty well. If you doubt my assertion about our lackadaisical lukewarmity, compare attendance on Easter – or any other Sunday during the school year – with attendance on any Sunday in the summertime.

(Matthew 10:18).

Because of Covid mandates, Christians have been separated from one another and churches have been torn apart – all for the appearance of external unity. Christians have been constantly reminded about outward civic righteousness. Yet, the focus of true righteousness in Christ sadly has been forsaken.

Big Tech promotes progressive Christianity – which caters to the itching ears of the culture – but silences the sound doctrine of conservative Christianity (2 Timothy 4:3). Our culture cancels anyone who doesn't toe the line of whatever depravity they are promoting this week. There may not be blatant arrests of pastors and the boarding up of churches by government authorities like in other nations. At least – not yet. But we would be naïve to believe it's not coming.

In April 2021, Pastor Artur Pawlowski threw the police out of his Calgary church as they wanted to make sure the church was following their Covid mandates on worship. Because Pastor Pawlowski grew up under the boot of the Soviets in Poland, he had some rather strong words for them calling the police "Nazis" and "Gestapo."

When Pastor Pawlowski was interviewed by the *Daily Caller* the day after the intrusion by the police, he explained why he acted so strongly. "If they want to talk or inspect the building, they can call me and we can arrange that ... they preferred a method of storming." He said he was shocked to see armed, uniformed police officers enter during worship as if it was "their own home." "This is unacceptable. Even during the times of the Middle Ages, the knights were commanded to leave their swords outside the church, they were not allowed to enter the church. But these days, nothing is holy for those people. They just walk in like it's a restaurant."

"I grew up in Poland under the boot of the Soviets, behind the Iron Curtain. What I see right now, I see everything escalating and moving to the new level. They're acting just like the Communists were acting when I was growing up when the pastors and the priests were arrested, and some were murdered. Many were tortured. That's why I say what I say, because I see a repetition of history." [124] When someone who grew up behind the Iron Curtain tells us history is repeating, we would do well to pay attention.

Pastor Pawlowski spent 51 days in solitary confinement after he was arrested for allegedly inciting "mischief" while addressing a crowd gathered for the Freedom Convoy at the U.S.-Canada border in Alberta. [125]

In April 2021, Gracelife Church in Alberta had their pastor, James Coates, imprisoned for a month. Then their church building was raided and a fence was constructed around the building to keep members from worship during the Covid lockdowns. It was then guarded by dozens of officers. When a convoy of fellow Christians arrived to remove the fences, authorities sent over two hundred police officers to keep worshipers from meeting together inside the church for worship.

In June 2021, a police helicopter in Alberta, Canada discovered Pastor Jim Stephens and his congregation of Fairview Baptist Church meeting on a Sunday secretly in a different location since their church building had been closed due to the government's response to Covid. Police cruisers surrounded the church. The police didn't interrupt the worship services. Instead, they waited until Monday to arrest Pastor Stevens in front of his family.

Don't lull yourself into a false sense of security that this won't be happening soon in America. If it's not happening here, we Christians need to take a good look at ourselves asking why it isn't happening. Could it be that our culture can't tell that we are Christians? Is the government not trying to silence us because they can't hear us speaking? Have we become so soft and lazy that we'll succumb to the dragon and its beasts even before they have to go through the effort of persecuting us? [126]

---

[124] I encourage you to watch the video of Pastor Pawlowsi passionately defending his church and their freedoms to worship. Notthebee.com (4/6/2021)

[125] Faithwire.com (4/1/2022)

[126] Rod Dreher discusses this concept, which he terms "soft totalitarianism," at length in his book, *Live Not By Lies*. It is a truly terrifying book. It is terrifying as you see the totalitarianism of the

Persecution of Christians in America is coming. But we don't have to feel like ill-fated redshirts in a *Star Trek* episode. Don't be afraid of persecution. Welcome it. Jesus promises that the Holy Spirit will give us the right words to say. He promises that the gospel will be preached to all the nations before he comes. If the government or culture or Big Tech shut down one avenue of sharing the gospel, we just find another avenue. Jesus promises that his gospel cannot be stopped.

What do you think has happened in those Canadian churches where their pastors and parishioners have faced persecution and prosecution? The attendance at those churches has grown, even as the congregations meet secretly to avoid government persecution. Christians have become emboldened in the face of opposition. Their unbelieving neighbors witness their kind Christian believers being oppressed by government officials. They decide to check out Christianity. The Holy Spirit creates more converts.

It's like the early Christian Church as the two beasts – the Roman government and the Jewish Judaizers – persecuted the Christians, the Church grew. Christians stopped cowering. They proudly stood up to persecution. The pagans witnessed their neighbors being persecuted and felt the need to check out Christianity. The Holy Spirit then created more converts. The Church grew through persecution.

It's funny how tyrannical leaders never seem to understand: The more the Church is harassed, the more the Church grows.

As we see persecution coming upon our nation, we pray that God is using this coming persecution to wake us, move us, grow us, and revive the dying Christian Church in America.

Sheep among wolves

Jesus taught his disciples, "Look, I am sending you out as sheep among wolves. So be as shrewd as snakes and as innocent as doves. But be on your guard! People will hand you over to councils,

---

past in other countries being used with great effectiveness in present-day America.

and you will be beaten in synagogues. You will stand in the presence of rulers and kings for my sake as a witness to them. And the gospel must first be preached to all the nations. Whenever they arrest you and hand you over, do not worry beforehand what you should say. Say whatever is given to you in that hour, because you will not be the ones speaking; instead it will be the Holy Spirit. Brother will betray brother to death, and a father, his child. Children will rise up against their parents and put them to death. You will be hated by everyone because of my name, but the one who endures to the end will be saved" (Matthew 10:16-22).

We can no longer afford to be naïve that we will escape persecution. Persecution is the norm for God's people, not the exception (1 Corinthians 10:13; 1 Thessalonians 3:2-4; 2 Timothy 3:1). Jesus gives a realistic assessment for his followers of all ages of what to expect. The world may often seem cute, cuddly, and friendly. Satan often masquerades as an angel of light to appear innocent and harmless (2 Corinthians 11:14). But Satan will quickly take off the mask and appear as he really is – a roaring lion looking for someone to devour (1 Peter 5:8). The world is like ravenous wolves. You can hear the growling. The enemies of the Gospel can attack at any time.

The world has no love for the gospel, nor for those who confess the gospel. So, our dear Savior warns, "I am sending you out like sheep among wolves. Therefore be as shrewd as snakes and as innocent as doves" (Matthew 10:16). Snakes will usually quietly escape from danger, but they will stay and defend themselves if necessary. Doves are symbols of peace. We should not attack anyone and start trouble. But when trouble comes our way, people can be sure we didn't start it. That's what confessing Christ is all about. It's about trouble and danger. It's about standing firm against the assaults of Satan.

Jesus says that the work of reforming the world with the gospel is not going to be easy or pleasant for any of his disciples. People are naturally resistant to spiritual change because they are hostile to God by nature and do not want to hear what God has to say about their corrupt lives. We are not to expect popularity, but persecution. We will not receive unflagging adulation, but ardent flogging. We should not expect applause and gratitude, but should expect arrest and the grave.

In typical fashion, Jesus does not sugarcoat things for his disciples. If we are going to follow him, we need to know what we're getting ourselves into. Jesus tells us just how seriously he takes suffering in his name. "If anyone wants to follow me, let him deny himself, take up his cross, and follow me. In fact whoever wants to save his life will lose it, and whoever loses his life for my sake will find it" (Matthew 16:24, 25). Taking up a cross doesn't just mean suffering ... it means dying. We should expect hatred, suffering, persecution, and even death as faithful followers of Christ.

When we shrink from the suffering, remain quiet and keep our heads down, are we truly carrying the cross in Christ's name?

The possibility of having a Christian elementary school lose its voucher money or a church being fined for opposing gay marriage is definitely a cross that may be imposed on us. The risk of churches losing their tax-privilege status is a risk that continues to grow. The cross may come, but it is definitely a cross worth bearing.

This needs to be the confession of the Christian: "You can take away my home, my stuff, my family, my freedom, my health ... but you can't take away my faith." Once you make that clear to yourself and to those who are persecuting you, you and they know you are truly free. Nothing they do to you can really harm you. Like the apostle Paul, if you live, you live to the Lord, but if you die, you die to the Lord. Either way, you'll be with the Lord.

Christians must remember that we will suffer for our faith in this world (John 16:33; Luke 6:21, 25). We are like sheep being led to the slaughter. God promises godly eternal joys and blessings (1 Corinthians 2; Isaiah 63). God promises the godless with eternal condemnations and wailings (Matthew 8:12; 13:42).

Christ testified to Pilate, "My Kingdom is not of this world" (John 18:36). That means our kingdom is not of this world, either. We are not called to be Christians in order to have good days in this life – for as Christians we are but strangers here. We are guests who are citizens of the Kingdom to come. We patiently suffer in this world waiting for the world to come.

The Reformer Martin Luther expected hatred from people – particularly when it became clear that he and the Roman Catholic Church were not only on a different page but in a different book. He expected to die a martyr's death because he had taken on the church and its false teachers. That's why he resisted getting married for so long. He didn't want his wife to be made a widow or future children to be fatherless. But even though Luther knew he might die at any moment after being branded a heretic by the pope and an outlaw by the emperor, he would not remain silent. In fact, on one occasion, Luther received a note from a man who urged him not to go to a meeting in Augsburg to which Luther's enemies had invited him. What was Luther's response? "Even in Augsburg, in the middle of his enemies, Christ reigns." Luther expected hatred from the enemies of the gospel; even more than that, he expected help from his gracious Lord.

Moses and the prophets, the apostles and early Christians, Luther and his fellow reformers, knew that Jesus' words would come true, "All men will hate you because of me" (Luke 21:17). We as twenty-first century Christians and modern-age reformers certainly do not go looking for trouble – enough trouble will find us. It has been said that where Christ builds a church, the devil builds a chapel. Wherever the gospel is proclaimed, Satan must attack. Wherever we soldiers of Christ lift high the cross, Satan's minions inflict pain and pressure. Wherever Christ reigns as King, this world's prince still scowls.

We may not fear beheading, loss of property, imprisonment, or death, like other Christians in centuries past or Christians suffering presently around the world. We don't fear a den of lions or a fiery furnace, but persecution abounds when we're faithful to the Word. We lose relationships because of a Biblical belief that honors the sanctity of marriage. We lose promotions because of worship priorities. We lose friendships because we won't join in sinful talking or walking.

We are called old-fashioned for our insistence on a six-day creation and marriage being a lifetime commitment of love between one man and one woman. We are ridiculed as backward for our persistence that the Bible is the inspired, inerrant Word of God which is our rule and norm for life, and criticized for our demand that salvation is in Christ alone. Whether it is in the college classroom or the business boardroom, the high school hallways or network news, we know we will face criticism, corruption, ridicule, and resistance. We know this because Jesus has insisted on sending us out as sheep among wolves. We know there is enmity between those who follow Satan and those who follow the Savior. We know that our love for our heavenly Father and our brotherly Savior may conflict with our earthly relationships with our parents, siblings, spouse or children. "Brother will betray brother to death, and a father his child; children will rebel against their parents and have them put to death" (Matthew 10:21).

Satan will use these emotional attachments to silence our confessions. He slows the spread of the gospel as we cower in fear. Our sinful nature doesn't want ridicule but craves acceptance. Instead of expecting resistance, we expect results and instant change – and we soon become frustrated. We imagine the world is filled with cute kitties and darling dogs, whereas, in reality, they are really ravenous wolves, red dragons, and terrifying beasts.

So, we cower, give up, and give in. We join the crowd. We don't stand up and stand out, but sit down and blend in. We shut our mouths, keep our money in our homes instead of using it to expand God's kingdom, and focus on ourselves instead of doing God's mission work.

Fellow sheep, don't be fooled into faintheartedness. Don't be coerced into cowardice. Don't be intimidated into silence. Don't let the world lead you astray. Don't let the devil tempt you and his demons trick you. Jesus says very clearly who you are up against – wolves, lions and enemies of the Gospel. Expect the wolves to attack. As you allow the Holy Spirit to reform your former sinful way of life, expect derision and insults. As you work with God's

Word to reform the world, expect hatred and persecution.

Also expect help from your gracious Lord, the Shepherd of helpless and hapless sheep. Even as we stand on trial for our beliefs, we are witnesses to our enemies. Even as we are arrested and persecuted, the Holy Spirit is giving us the boldness to speak clearly. Luther concludes his Battle Hymn of the Reformation: "And do what they will – hate, steal, hurt or kill – though all may be gone, our victory is won; the kingdom's ours forever!"[127] Even as we face the hatred of men, we are comforted and encouraged with the knowledge that a life free from all suffering and pain awaits us.

Besides, what's the worst that can be done to us? Imprisonment? Jesus is there. Suffering? We suffer in Jesus' name. Hatred? We need only the love of God. Loss of property? Our treasures are in heaven. Death? We die in Christ and are with Christ for eternity! God shut the lions' mouths to show his Church of all ages that God is able to guard and keep his own. What a comfort it is when Jesus promises, "All men will hate you because of me, but he who stands firm to the end will be saved."

We are encouraged to say what we couldn't or didn't say before. We are reassured that even when our friends and family fail us, the Lord will never fail. "It is better to take refuge in the Lord than to trust in human benefactors" (Psalm 118:8).

We have the confidence of St. Paul, "I am not ashamed of the gospel, because it is the power of God for the salvation of everyone who believes" (Romans 1:16).

Devil-proof

The apostle Paul wrote numerous warnings and encouragements in his epistles to those who were suffering persecution. Paul knew from experience what it was like to suffer persecution. Paul was hated for his preaching of the gospel message. He was chased out of town, beaten, stoned, arrested, put on trial and more for the sake of the gospel.

I want you to imagine you are part of the mob that really hates

---

[127] A Mighty Fortress Is Our God

the apostle Paul. Your mob preaches circumcision, blood sacrifices and eating clean foods. Paul preaches Christ crucified. Your mob preaches the Jews are God's chosen children. Paul preaches that people from all nations are God's children through faith in Jesus. Your mob preaches salvation by works. Paul preaches salvation by grace alone.

You and the mob really hate this guy! He preaches everything exactly the opposite from you.

The mob wonders, "What should we do with Paul?" You suggest, "Let's make him suffer!" Everyone chants, "Make him suffer!" People call out, "Let's chase him from city to city!" "Let's cause riots while he preaches!" "Let's get him arrested!" "And beaten!" "And whipped!"

Everyone agrees.

Then one guy stands up and says, "I think all that's a good idea, but I just read in Paul's letter to the Christians in Rome that he rejoices in suffering, because suffering produces endurance, and endurance produces character, and character produces hope. If we make Paul suffer ... we'll only make Paul happier!"

You suggest, "Let's kill him!" Everyone chants, "Let's kill him!" People call out, "Let's hunt him down and stone him!" "Let's encourage Caesar to throw him to the lions!" "Or cut off his head!"

Everyone agrees.

Then one guy stands up and says, "Normally I would think that's a great idea, but I just read in Paul's letter to his friends in Philippi, 'For me to live is Christ and to die is gain' and 'I desire to depart and be with Christ, which is better by far.' Paul is looking forward to dying!"

Now nobody knows what to do. You can't make Paul suffer - he rejoices in suffering. You can't kill him – he's looking forward to death.

What to do?

Then you suggest, "Let's let him live! That's the worst thing we can do to Paul!" Everyone agrees. They change, "Let him live! Let him live!"

Imagine the frustration of the devil. He wants to make Paul

suffer, but Paul rejoices in suffering in Christ's name. He wants to persecute Paul, but Paul considers it an honor to carry Christ's cross in persecution. He wants Paul dead to end the hated missionary's life, but Paul is looking forward to death.

You give Paul suffering, he praises God. You give him good, he praises God. You give him evil, he praises God. You give him the certainty of death, he praises God. Because, unknowingly, all these enemies are leading Paul to the joys of life eternal.

Do you see what happened to Paul? He became "devil-proof."

Jesus teaches us to pray in the seventh petition of the Lord's Prayer, "Deliver us from evil." As we pray this petition, we want to become "devil-proof" like St. Paul. By "devil-proof," I mean that all the devil's rage and evil only provides opportunity to draw closer to Jesus, his Word, his grace, his refuge, and his salvation. Allow the Holy Spirit to devil-proof you as everything you do is done to God's glory, as you remember your Baptism daily, as you receive the Lord's Supper often, as you pray continually, as you meditate on God's Word regularly, and as you gather for worship and fellowship with your church family consistently. Then when the Evil One – the devil – tries to admonish or arrest, hurt or harm, eliminate or eradicate you, it won't work.

Paul was devil-proof because he was content suffering in Christ's name. He explained to the Christians in Corinth, "That is why I delight in weaknesses, in insults, in hardships, in persecutions, in difficulties, for the sake of Christ. For whenever I am weak, then am I strong" (2 Corinthians 12:10). We might think Paul had lost his mind after being hit in the head too many times with stones. Who in his right mind delights in weaknesses, insults, hardships, persecutions and difficulties? It is when we are weak by having our freedoms removed, we find our strength in Christ. When we are insulted for being a Christian, we remember they are insulting Christ first. When we face hardships because of our connection to Christ, we find our comfort and ease in Christ. When we are persecuted, we rejoice that we are counted worthy of persecution like the apostles. When we face difficulties, we remember we never learn anything by doing the easy thing.

Paul encouraged the Corinthians to weigh their earthly troubles against their heavenly glories. "Yes, our momentary, light trouble produces for us an eternal weight of glory that is far beyond any comparison. We are not focusing on what is seen, but on what is not seen. For the things that are seen are temporary, but the things that are not seen are eternal" (2 Corinthians 4:17, 18). Trouble from persecution does not seem light, but when compared to eternity in heaven, the trouble believers face in this life is really momentary and light. Our current troubles seem weighty and long ... but they are light and short compared with eternity. Stop focusing on what is seen, and focus on what is unseen.

In his epistle to the Christians in Thessalonica, Paul speaks about the fierce persecution by the Jews and about the Thessalonians' faithfulness. He writes that the Thessalonian Christians were models to be imitated as Christian role models. "You also became imitators of us and of the Lord, when you welcomed the word during a time of great affliction with the joy from the Holy Spirit, so that you became a model for all the believers in Macedonia and Achaia" (1 Thessalonians 1:6, 7).

How were the Thessalonian Christians models? They bore their persecution joyfully. Thessalonica was a crossroads of the empire, so other Christians saw what they were going through. They left Thessalonica committed to a similar response.

Popular culture hates it when we say that Jesus is the only way. Any TV show or movie automatically portrays a pastor or a priest as close-minded, as a buffoon or a bigot. They portray fathers as being idiots and mothers capable of doing it all without the dad. They portray gay or straight people living together as right and exciting, but straight married couples have all the issues. Very few Americans have been arrested or brutalized or killed for their faith. But that could always change. Jesus said that we will face persecution because the world hates us. We may not be physically injured for standing up for God's will and Word. But we could be canceled, fired, bullied on social media, and so on. But God only allows things into our lives that work for our good. We pray that others see us, as Paul saw the Thessalonians, and they are encouraged and emboldened by us.

The Lord wants others to watch you as you welcome God's Word while you are being persecuted. Others will notice your Christian attitudes and actions. Lord willing, they will follow your lead. It might be the elderly saint who takes in her grandchildren when she learns her daughter is an unfit mother, raising her grandchildren as if they were her own children. Perhaps the quiet father and husband who puts in 60 hours a week at work, then cooks meals for his family on the weekend in between his kids' games, then gets to church early to shovel snow, turn on lights and usher for the worship service. Maybe the mother who tucks her children into bed each evening and prays for and with her children. Other people see these quiet Christians modeling their Christian faith and – we pray – thank God for these faithful saints.

Christians who suffer for their faith are often asked why they suffer so calmly. Times of suffering – be it persecution, illness, family issues, financial problems, or whatever – give us a chance to put our faith on display.

What is the natural, sinful human reaction when we face persecution? The natural thing is for us to give up our faith and cave in. The natural thing is to turn on one another, perhaps turning one another in to the authorities.

Patient endurance

St. Paul explains that the exact opposite was happening in Thessalonica. "So we ourselves boast about you in God's churches in regard to your patient endurance and faith in all your persecutions and in the trials that you are enduring. This is evidence of God's righteous verdict that resulted in your being counted worthy of God's kingdom, for which you also suffer" (2 Thessalonians 1:4, 5).

Paul was boasting about the Thessalonians as he traveled on his missionary journeys. He bragged that their faith was growing more and more. In fact, Paul says that every one of the members of this congregation was growing in love for every other member. God was working through the gospel to support and nurture their faith, even in this very difficult situation. False doctrine from the inside causes Christians to separate from each other and weaken. Persecution from the outside causes Christians to band together and become stronger as the body of Christ. As we begin to face persecution as Christians here in America, we cannot let it pull us apart. Rather, we stand strong and march forward united in the faith as the soldiers of the cross.

After commending the Thessalonians for the way they've been enduring persecution, he reminds them about Christ's return. When Christ Jesus comes in judgment, the tables will be turned. Then the persecutors will be the troubled ones, but the persecuted will have relief because they will be glorified. This would encourage the Thessalonians even more in their trials.

"Certainly, it is right for God to repay trouble to those who trouble you, and to give relief to you, who are troubled along with us. When the Lord Jesus is revealed from heaven with his powerful angels, he will exercise vengeance in flaming fire on those who do not know God and on those who do not obey the gospel of our Lord Jesus. Such people will receive a just penalty: eternal destruction away from the presence of the Lord and from his glorious strength, on that day when he comes to be glorified among his saints, and to be marveled at among all those who have believed, because our testimony to you was believed" (2 Thessalonians 1:6-10).

Two things will happen on the Lord's Judgment Day. God will judge his saints as worthy of eternal life because they held to Christ by faith, and God will punish the enemies of the gospel for all that they have done to his saints throughout the history of the world. God will undo all the pain that sin inflicts on his precious saints, including the pain of persecution.

This is important for Christians to remember as we suffer at the hands of governments, religious institutions, unbelievers, social media bullies, etc. We don't take revenge. We leave room for God's vengeance. Until then, we turn the other cheek, forgive seventy multiplied by seven times, pray for those who persecute us, and live as lights in the darkness. God will bring trouble on those who trouble us.

The Lord's judgment cannot be stopped. It's coming whether people are prepared or not, whether people try stopping it or are welcoming it. God's judgment will be terrifying to his enemies. His judgment will be welcomed and comforting to God's saints.

The apostle Paul made Pastor Timothy aware that he was going to be persecuted. "Indeed, everyone who wants to live a godly life in Christ Jesus will be persecuted, while evil people and impostors will go from bad to worse, deceiving and being deceived" (2 Timothy 3:12,13). The Old Testament prophets, John the Baptist, Jesus, and the apostles all faced persecution. Timothy could expect persecution, and so can we. Jesus told us to expect this persecution. "Remember the saying I told you: 'A servant is not greater than his master.' If they persecuted me, they will persecute you too. If they held onto my word, they will hold on to yours as well" (John 15:20).

What will happen to everyone who, because of faith in Christ, leads a godly life? They will be persecuted. Scripture points out that Christians will be persecuted by two groups – the government and the apostate church. The beast out of the sea and the beast out of the earth.

How does St. Paul encourage Timothy to respond to this persecution? "Preach the word. Be ready whether it is convenient or not. Correct, rebuke, and encourage, with all patience and teaching. For there will come a time when people will not put up with sound doctrine. Instead, because they have itching ears, they will accumulate for themselves teachers in line with their own desires. They will also turn their ears away from the truth and will turn aside to myths" (2 Timothy 4:2-4).

Whether it seems like a good time or not, publicly, and clearly proclaim God's Word – both to friends and foes. Proclaim these truths even when they are not popular or acceptable in our culture. I love the opening line in Martin Franzmann's hymn: "Preach you the Word and plant it home to those who like or like it not ..."

Personally, I think we are dealing with a lot of issues today because pastors and people have stopped preaching to our culture. They may preach about it, but not actually deal with it. They may preach a sermon that discusses doctrine, but is severely lacking in application of those Scriptural truths to the everyday challenges of life in our amoral culture. We're afraid. But every moment we remain silent, the devil keeps talking. He keeps gaining ground, while we keep losing ground.

As Professor Dumbledore so wisely put it, "It takes a great deal of bravery to stand up to your enemies, but a great deal more to stand up to your friends." [128]

Christianity is unsafe

We are often afraid that if we speak up we'll lose our social media, job, house, family, or life. But safety cannot be the only thing. Otherwise, we would never do anything. Christianity by its essence is unsafe.

St. Peter wrote his epistles as encouragement for Christians who would be suffering persecution in the name of Christ. The early Christians of Peter's day and following were accused of being anti-government. A faithful Christian confession may bring that same anti-government accusation. But, "... dear friends, do not be surprised by the fiery trial that is happening among you to test you, as if something strange were happening to you. Instead rejoice whenever you are sharing in the sufferings of Christ, so that you may rejoice and be glad when his glory is revealed. ... But if you suffer for being a Christian, do not be ashamed, but praise God in connection with this name. ... So let those who suffer according to the will of God entrust their souls to their faithful Creator while doing what is good" (1 Peter 4:12, 13, 16, 19).

The Christian Church seems one day to be strong and secure – and the next, about to perish. In fact, in every age of her history, the Church has seemed to be on the brink of complete destruction. Persecution from the outside has threatened the Church's ruin when violent governments raised the sword against her. At other times, the godless philosophy of the world wedded to simple personal fulfillment and the pleasure of the moment has

---

[128] Rowling, J.K. *Harry Potter and the Sorcerer's Stone.*

threatened to seduce entire generations away from her doors. At still other times, the moral or doctrinal corruption within her own walls has become so pervasive that any thought of the Church's survival has seemed naïve at best.

The world was filled with wickedness and unbelief, so God preserved the Church with a worldwide flood while keeping Noah and his family safe on the ark. The Pharaoh was trying to slowly kill the Israelites by drowning their baby boys and working the parents to death; so God drowned Pharaoh and his army in the Red Sea and preserved Israel in the Promised Land. The early Christian Church was prosecuted and persecuted by Roman emperors, yet God allowed the persecution to strengthen and spread his Church throughout the world. Russia, China, India, and Africa had once driven Christianity to near extinction in their countries, but now Christianity is growing and expanding in those places at miraculous rates.

It is at such times, times of suffering – whether for the individual Christian or the Church as a whole – that the promise of God is most comforting and reassuring. St. Peter reminds us that when we suffer in the name of Christ, this isn't something new or strange. This persecution has been happening to Christians since the time of Christ. In fact, it was happening to God's prophets and people as the prophesied and promised the coming Christ. So, don't be ashamed that you're suffering for resisting a government opposed to Christ. You are suffering according to God's will, whose Word promised this suffering at the hands of governments would happen. Don't be afraid when you're suffering for not complying with the false religions of the age. You are suffering while entrusting your soul to the true Lord of all ages.

St. Paul encourages, "Do not owe anyone anything except to love one another, for the one who loves another has fulfilled the law" (Romans 13:8). We might demonstrate love by submitting to unjust laws of the government out of respect for the government as we trust in God's providence. We might also demonstrate love by resisting unjust laws out of protection of our neighbors, as we also trust in God's providence to use us for carrying out his divine will.

Consider what we pray in the first three petitions of the Lord's Prayer. We pray for God's name to be hallowed – be kept holy – because on every side, in the world and in the Church, in our life and in our flesh, God's name is always under attack. Judged by outward appearance, it always seems like God's name, his revelation of himself in his Word, is being thrown aside and under the bus in favor of unbelief, doubt, and indifference. Yet God's name continues to be hallowed in worship and Bible studies in our churches, in the classrooms of our Lutheran elementary schools, high schools, and colleges, and in our various vocations. Christ is sitting on his Father's throne and he makes sure that kingdoms will fall and governments will crumble before God's name ever stops being hallowed.

We pray for God's Kingdom to come. It appears that God's Kingdom – Christ's ruling activity in our hearts and lives by his Word – is always on the brink of being overtaken by the devil, the world, and our sinful flesh. But Jesus Christ could not be overtaken by the ruler of hell, or defeated by the Caesar of his government, or stopped by the sinful flesh of his enemies. Jesus appeared defeated, crushed, and a man of sorrows while dying on the cross. But it is through that suffering and death that Jesus crushed Satan's head, defeated death, and forgave sinful flesh. He rose from the grave and is seated at his Father's right hand, with all authority to move governments according to his will and topple kingdoms when they get in his way.

We pray for God's will to be done. It appears the will of evil men and of the evil that lurks within the shrine of our own hearts will win the victory. But even when we, others, and whole nations live and act opposed to God's will, he still turns that opposition into accomplishing his will. That's what St. Paul means when he writes: "All things work for the good of those who love him" (Romans 8:28).

That's why day and night we pray, "Hallowed be thy name, thy kingdom come, thy will be done!" There are promises in those petitions. Promises of victory. Promises of forgiveness. Promises of faith. Promises that even when we bring suffering upon ourselves because of our sinfulness, or we suffer evil at the hands of others in the name of Christ, we can endure. We can survive. We can thrive. Victory, forgiveness, faith, and salvation are ours in Christ.

The beast will be beaten

Knowing there is a promise at the end of suffering makes all the difference. Our present can be calm because our future is set. St. Paul assures us, "For I am convinced that neither death nor life, neither angels nor rulers, neither things present nor things to come, nor powerful forces, neither height nor depth, nor anything else in creation, will be able to separate us from the love of God in Christ Jesus our Lord" (Romans 8:38,39).

This is reassuring because the kind of persecution the beast out of the sea – the persecuting government – will bring upon Christians will be truly terrible. It will be a war, just as the beast has always waged warfare against God's people. Jesus Christ instructs St. John to write down this revelation as a warning and encouragement to his persecuted saints throughout the ages.

"The beast opened his mouth to speak blasphemies against God: to blaspheme his name, his dwelling, and those who dwell in heaven. He was also given permission to wage war against the saints and to overcome them, as well as authority over every tribe and people and language and nation. All those who make their home on the earth will worship the beast—those whose names have not been written from the beginning of the world in the Book of Life, which belongs to the Lamb that was slain. If anyone has an ear, let him hear: If anyone is to be imprisoned, he is going to be imprisoned. If anyone is to be killed with a sword, he is going to be killed with a sword. Here patient endurance and confidence are needed by the saints" (Revelation 13:6-10).

Christians do not simply resign themselves to their fate. We do not engage in fatalistic resignation or hopeless despair. Rather, we endure what comes because we refuse to worship the beast – and instead choose to remain faithful to the Lord. Ours is true endurance borne of faithfulness. We are kept from bowing to the beast because, by God's grace, our names have been written in the

Book of Life.

As we look at our world, we see it belonging to the devil. He won the world after the fall into sin at the tree in the Garden. He has released his terrifying beasts to persecute Christians with the full force of kings and councils, governments and tyrannies, and to influence the apostate church with its lies and pagan doctrines.

Yet Jesus won the world back through his atoning death on the tree on Golgotha and victorious resurrection from the garden tomb. With the eyes of faith through the Word, we see Jesus in ultimate control. After all, he is the King of Glory. The psalmist reminds us of this: "Lift up your heads, you gates. Lift yourselves up, you ancient doors, and the King of Glory will come in. Who is this King of Glory? The Lord strong and mighty, the Lord mighty in battle. Lift up your heads, you gates. Lift up, you ancient doors, and the King of Glory will come in. Who is he, this King of Glory? The Lord of Armies -he is the King of Glory" (Psalm 24:7-10).

Jesus is the Lord of Armies. He will lead his angelic Armies for the last and greatest battle. It will be against the kings of the earth (Revelation 12:16-21). On that last and great day, justice will be served. The enemies of Christ will be cast down once and for all. The saints will be gathered for a royal welcome around Christ's throne.

That means we have nothing to be afraid of. We have no reason to cower. There is no reason to hide or be silent or keep the King's glory a secret.

Christian soldiers living in enemy territory

Yes, right now it seems like the devil and his demonic forces are in control of our culture. But he isn't. Not really. You and I are Christ's operatives in this world, Christ's people and members of Christ's kingdom even as we live under the external reign of the devil, the ruler of the kingdom of the air.

But we're not secret agents. At least, I hope not! There shouldn't be anything secret about what we're doing. We should be out in the open. Speaking. Teaching. Recruiting operatives for the King of Glory.

We should be boldly teaching the reality and importance of two distinct sexes – men and women. Anything else is a lie from the lips of the devil.

We should be teaching that any sexual lifestyle outside of a man and a woman in marriage is an abomination of God's created order. Anything else is demonic deceit.

We should be teaching that all life is precious – in the womb, special needs, the sick, injured, and elderly. Anything else is Satanic slander.

It is scary stuff that we are Christian soldiers living in enemy territory...but it isn't scary for us! It should be scary for the devil and his allies, because we are on the winning side! We're on the side of the Lord of Armies! We're on the side of the humble Savior laid in a manger and laid upon a cross who is also the King of glory seated on his golden throne!

Now we need to speak up where we are. We need to encourage our families to find a school that aligns with God's biological truths about sexuality. We need to encourage each other to use Christ's eternal truths to evaluate every government and university, conversation and influence in our culture.

Like the disciples, we go out in the world with a message. It is a message that makes demons flee and the devil shudder (James 2:19). No one can intimidate us. No one can frighten us. We will not yield to them. For what can they do to us? They may take our possessions. They may take our freedoms. They may take our lives. But they cannot take away God's kingdom. That is ours forever (Matthew 5:10). It is at the Last Judgment when God blesses us for carrying forth the cross and confession.

Jesus went into the grave. Not to become like the dead but to rescue the dead. We engage the culture. But in doing so, we cannot become the culture. We cannot become like those we are fighting. Then the dragon would have won. Then we have unwittingly become his allies. We go into the depths to rescue people from the depths with the gospel of Jesus Christ.

The gates of Hades

One time Jesus was with his disciples at Caesarea Philippi in the northeastern area of Israel. It was a city dominated by immoral activities and pagan worship. In that area the people first worshiped the fertility gods of the Canaanites like Baal and then later switched to worshiping the fertility gods of the Greeks like Pan.

When Jesus brought his disciples to the area, they must have been shocked. Caesarea Philippi was like a red-light district in their world and devout Jews would have avoided any contact with the despicable acts committed there. It was a city of people eagerly knocking on the doors of hell.

Standing in the shadow of the pagan temples of Caesarea Philippi, Jesus asked his disciples, "Who do you say that I am?" Peter boldly replied, "You are the Christ, the Son of the living God" (Matthew 16:13, 16). The disciples were probably stirred by the contrast between Jesus, the true and living God, and the false hopes of the pagans who trusted in "dead" gods.

Jesus continued, "I tell you that you are Peter, and on this rock I will build my church, and the gates of Hades will not overcome it" (Matthew 16:18).

I have to admit that I often got this picture wrong. I remember being taught that this is a defensive text where the Christian Church will stand strong against the forces of Satan attacking us as Christians. It wasn't until I was on a trip to the Holy Land and I stood at the mouth of that exact cave in Caesarea Philippi that I finally got it!

How wrong I was! The gates of the Christian Church are not being attacked. The Church is attacking the gates of hell! Christian soldiers are advancing against the forces of Satan. We are given keys as our weapons: "I will give you the keys of the kingdom of heaven; whatever you bind on earth will be bound in heaven, and whatever you loose on earth will be loosed in heaven" (Matthew 16:19). We can either call people to repentance by binding their sins to them or we can free captives from their sins by forgiving them.

Gates were defensive structures in the ancient world. By saying that the gates of Hades would not overcome his Church, Jesus suggested that those very gates of Hades were going to be attacked!

The image here is not of God's city being attacked and repelling the attackers, but the city of the devil being attacked by the warriors of God. The city is this world, claimed by the prince of this world – the devil – after the Fall. The devil flaunted his claim on this world before the Lord with Job and in the wilderness (Job 1:7; Matthew 4:8-9). The prince of this world even had the audacity to try to defeat the King of creation with desert temptations. But Jesus would not be overcome.

Rather, the King attacks the fortress of the devil. He comes into the very domain of death and the devil. He enters the battle by taking on human flesh and blood. The devil snickers and the demons roar as Jesus is nailed to the cross. But it is with blood and wood that Jesus defeats the devil. He removes the power of sin by taking sin's sting upon himself. He releases the devil's foothold on this earth by being struck by the serpent's fangs in his divinely human feet. He frees souls from death by his own glorious resurrection from the grave.

The Church of Christ is the mighty host of the Lord that does not wait inside a fortress repelling attacks. We are those who march forward against the gates of hell with the good news of the cross. The cross is a battering ram against sin, death, and the devil. It is the light for those captive to darkness. It is freedom for a world marked and claimed by the enemy but retaken by God in Christ. Nothing can harm us – not the sea, the land, the wind, the devil – for we have received the seal of baptism on our foreheads. We have been marked and claimed by Christ (Revelation 7:1-2).

The Christian Church is not weak and vulnerable, just waiting to be attacked on all sides. Instead, Christ's words transform fearful and reluctant disciples into stormtroopers for the Master.

Jesus presented a clear challenge with his words at Caesarea Philippi: He didn't want his followers hiding from evil. He wanted them to storm the gates of hell.

There is plenty of evidence that the seven-headed red dragon is using his two beasts to attack Christians. So, how are you doing with your attacks against evil? Are you on the offensive or the defensive? Jesus' followers cannot successfully confront evil when we are embarrassed about our faith.

After Jesus spoke to his disciples about storming the gates of hell, he also gave them a word of caution: "If anyone is ashamed of me and my words, the Son of Man will be ashamed of him when he comes in his glory" (Luke 9:26). Jesus knew that his followers would face ridicule and anger as they tried to confront evil. And his words come as a sharp challenge – no matter how fierce the resistance, his followers should never hide their faith in God.

Unfortunately, many of us have cowered under the confusing and mixed-up message that society portrays. We don't want to be judged in the court of public opinion. We don't want to be vilified on social media. We don't want to offend anyone, so we accept the sin that is all around us, even within our own homes, rather than confronting it. We are afraid to go on the offensive.

Or we just try to avoid the sinful culture altogether. We hide in our churches, schools, and homes, and shut the door on the evil that influences our culture. We are hunkered down on the defensive.[129] But Jesus challenged his followers to go on the offense — to proclaim the truth without shame.

Our schools and churches should become staging areas rather than fortresses – places that equip God's people to confront a sinful world instead of hiding from it. Jesus knows that the pagan world will resist, but he challenges us to go there anyway, and to build his Church in those very places that are most morally decayed.

By looking at the world, it may seem like Satan is in charge. But as Christians, listening to the Word, we know that Jesus is really in charge. St. Paul promises the ultimate victory, "The God of peace will soon crush Satan under your feet" (Romans 16:20). The

---

[129]This basic approach was discussed by Rod Dreher in his 2017 book *The Benedict Option*.

mighty fortress of Christianity will stand. The gates of Hades will not.

Jesus tells us today that we are to go on the offensive. Church memberships may shrink and churches may close their doors, but the Christian Church will never die out. It can never be defeated. The Scriptures promise that the Church will stand forever. Nothing can keep our Redeemer from upholding his promised salvation. Neither false expectations nor the gates of hell, neither an Egyptian army nor a flowing river, not even the great tribulation of the end times will keep our God from preserving his Church.

So go on the offensive. Take back the ground we've lost. Claim more territory for Christ's Kingdom. Win more souls for Christ.

One of the great lines in the movie *The Princess Bride* is when Miracle Max says to Inigo and Fezzik, "Have fun storming the castle!" Storming Satan's castle may not seem like much fun – not with all the mistreatments, persecutions, imprisonments, and deaths. But winning is always fun. And Christ has already assured us of the victory. The two beasts have been beaten. The red dragon is defeated. Death is dead. Sin has been struck down. The gates of Hades will not overcome.

Never give up. Never surrender. Go on the offensive. Have fun storming the gates of Hades.

Conclusion

Resisting the Dragon's Beast: What Happens When God's Servant of the Government Behaves Like Satan's Servant is about study, discussion, and application. It is understanding that at times governing authorities are serving as God's servants because they are following God's will and benefiting God's people. They are bringing peace and prosperity upon God's people. That's Romans 13. But there are other times governing authorities may be serving as the dragon's beast because they are opposing God's will and persecuting and harming God's people. They are agents of chaos, bringing fear and anger upon God's people. That's Revelation 13.

There may be times when we witness governing authorities behaving as God's servants. Then we are praying the petition in the Lord's Prayer, "your will be done." But there may be times when those very same authorities are behaving as Satan's servants. Then we are praying the petition, "deliver us from evil." No matter what the government is doing or how they are acting, we Christians keep praying the same Lord's Prayer. We praise God for his governing authorities when they are opposing evil and acting as his servants. We pray to God to oppose the evil of the governing authorities when they are acting as Satan's servants. We have to admit that navigating through this path of submission or resistance can definitely feel like every day is the Kobayashi Maru and you're not James T. Kirk. [130]

We trust God is always in control in all things and all times. There will be kings, officials, and rulers who will join with all creation in praising the Lord. We also know that the kings and rulers of the world join together against the Lord. The kings of the earth, the nobles, the military leaders, the rich and powerful who

---

[130] The Kobayashi Maru is a training exercise in the Star Trek universe designed to test the character of Starfleet Academy cadets in a no-win scenario. As a cadet, James T. Kirk defeated the Kobayashi Maru by reprogramming the test because he didn't believe in no-win scenarios. (I understand this reference was truly geeky. But I wanted everyone to know that I don't only know and understand Star Wars.)

have opposed Christ will hide from him on the Last Day. St. John assures us that these kings, rulers, and governing authorities "will wage war against the Lamb, but the Lamb will overcome them, because he is Lord of Lords and King of Kings" (Revelation 17:14).

Governing authorities can bring peace and prosperity upon God's people. They can also be agents of chaos, bringing fear and anger upon God's people. No matter what governing authorities do – serve the Lord or serve Satan – we Christians are studying, discussing, and applying God's Word and will to every decision we make. When we do that, God receives the glory!

Bibliography

Colvin, Matthew, trans. *The Magdeburg Confession: 13th of April 1550 AD*. Createspace: North Charleston, S.C., 2012.

Deutschlander, Daniel W. *The Narrow Lutheran Middle: Following the Scriptural Road*. Milwaukee: Northwestern Publishing House, 2011.

Gurgle, Stephen Scott. *The War to End All Germans: Wisconsin Synod Lutherans and the First World War*. Milwaukee: University of Wisconsin-Milwaukee Press, 2012.

Pelikan, J. J., H. C. Oswald, & H. T. Lehmann, eds. "Dr. Martin Luther's Warning to His Dear German People." *Luther's Works*, vol. 47, American Edition. Philadelphia: Fortress Press, 1971, pp. 3–55.

------------. "How Should A Christian Act During a Deadly Epidemic?" *Luther's Works*, vol. 43, American Edition. Philadelphia: Fortress Press, 1999, pp. 119-138.

The Magdeburg Confession: Thirteenth of April 1550 AD. Matthew Colvin, trans. North Charleston, SC: CreateSpace, 2012.

Peters, Paul. "The Natural Knowledge of God in the Light of the Law and the Gospel." *Our Great Heritage, vol. 2*. Milwaukee: Northwestern Publishing House, 1991, pp. 222-255.

Raabe, John. "The Conscience." *Our Great Heritage, vol. 2*. Milwaukee: Northwestern Publishing House, 1991, pp. 256-260.

Whitford, David Mark. *Tyranny and Resistance: The Magdeburg Confession and the Lutheran Tradition*. St. Louis: Concordia Publishing House, 2001.

CPSIA information can be obtained
at www.ICGtesting.com
Printed in the USA
JSHW032107030423
39807JS00005B/17

9 781645 942108